P9-CAN-574

STRIKE IT RICH!

Also by Peggy Hardigree
Working Outside: A Career and Self-Employment Handbook

STRIKE IT RICH!
Treasure Hunting with Metal Detectors

PEGGY HARDIGREE

HARMONY BOOKS/New York

To the memory of Ray and Nannie Hardigree

ACKNOWLEDGMENTS

The author wishes to gratefully acknowledge the help given by Charles Garrett of Garrett Electronics; Pam Doan of White's Electronics; Mike Patton of Fisher Research Laboratory Division of Cohu Industries; and the research staff of Relco Industries.

Copyright © 1980 by Peggy Hardigree
All rights reserved. No part of this book may be reproduced or utilized in any form or by any means, electronic or mechanical, including photocopying, recording, or by any information storage and retrieval system, without permission in writing from the publisher.
Inquiries should be addressed to
HARMONY BOOKS
a division of Crown Publishers, Inc.
One Park Avenue, New York, New York 10016

Printed in the United States of America

Published simultaneously in Canada by General Publishing Company Limited

Book design by Wendy Volin-Cohen

Library of Congress Cataloging in Publication Data

Hardigree, Peggy Ann, 1945–
    Strike it rich.

    1. Treasure-trove.   2. Metal detectors.
I. Title.
G525.H27   1980   622'.19   80-12094
ISBN 0-517-542161 (cloth)
        0-517-541602 (paper)

10   9   8   7   6   5   4   3   2   1
First Edition

Contents

Introduction

On the day I began writing this book, Kent and Jim Pepper, two Florida brothers, accidentally unearthed a hoard of gold nuggets weighing 2 pounds and worth at least $10,000. Their discovery was broadcast on the front pages of newspapers across the country, surprising the many who mistakenly believe that the treasure trove of this country is exhausted.

But to a million amateur treasure hunters this news was not at all surprising. It was simply further confirmation of what they had known all along: that buried treasure in this country *does* exist, to the tune of billions of dollars, and the possibility of finding some part of it is stronger now than ever before.

The greatest treasure hunt in the history of the world is now on— the search for the vast wealth that lies hidden across America. Treasure hunters unearth an estimated $25 million worth of treasure each year and this represents only a tiny part of the treasure that is known, beyond a shadow of a doubt, to exist in our land.

According to the most conservative estimates, at least $4 billion worth of lost treasure is scattered throughout the country, and about $22 billion more lies in the relatively shallow waters just off our coastlines. The inland treasure consists of misers' hoards, pirates' loot, and much, much more. Probably half of it was hidden away following the bank failures of the Great Depression, and more is being stashed away each day. The offshore treasure consists of the gold, silver, precious jewels, and valuable artifacts taken down with the hundreds of ships that have been lost near the American shores. Much of it may be beyond the reach of amateurs, but scuba divers recover vast amounts each year; small fortunes have been amassed by treasure hunters who collect gold and silver coins washed ashore from these wrecks.

The monetary value of lost treasure is constantly on the rise. Coins stashed away by the bank robber of a century ago may have been worth only a few hundred dollars to him—but today each coin might be worth hundreds, even thousands, of dollars.

The 1851 gold dollar provides one example of how the worth of such treasure increases. Just three decades ago this coin was fetching a top price of about $7. By 1974, dealers were paying as much as $250 for the same coin; by 1979, the top price for a good specimen had risen to more than $400. Certain other coins are increasing in value at an even faster rate.

Yesterday's junk can be today's treasure. The bottle in which the miser of yesteryear stashed away a few coins may be worth far more than the coins to the modern collector. The button from the jacket of a soldier of the American Revolution may be worth as much as any coin he carried in his pocket. The barbed wire a Western rancher used to fence his land may be worth more than anything buried on the land itself. As more people collect, the value of collectibles increases.

Estimates of the worth of American treasure seldom include the value of the great *natural* treasure that is within reach of most Americans—a treasure that is almost certainly worth far more than all the gold, silver, and precious jewels hidden by marauding pirates, fleeing bandits, and bank-fearing misers.

About fifteen minerals are classed as gemstones. Contrary to popular belief, each and every one has been found in America, and more are found each year. Diamonds, emeralds, rubies, sapphires—all of these and other gems of comparable value offer instant wealth to their lucky finders and are within reach of the amateur. Contrary to popular belief, our gold- and silver-bearing regions are not limited to the Western part of the country, and they are far from being exhausted. Both these precious metals are found in dozens of widely scattered parts of the country, and as with the gems, they hold out the very real prospect of instant riches.

America has always been a land of treasure hunters. Most of us grew up knowing that the Spaniards came to plunder the great wealth of the Aztecs and Incas—to hunt for their "cities of gold." We learned that John Smith, a founder of the colony at Jamestown, sought a fabulous city with streets of gold along the shores of Chesapeake Bay. Because of the great strike made there, Sutter's Mill is well known to almost every American.

We grew up hearing of the great lost treasures. Who has not heard of the Lost Dutchman? Or Oak Island? Or the treasure hidden by the armies of Montezuma as they fled the Spaniards? Such tales fueled our childhood dreams. These tales remained just dreams until certain events occurred that made treasure hunting a sport the average person could participate in.

The most important development was a device used in warfare—

the mine detector. Soldiers returning from the battlefields of World War II, where they had used these or seen them in use, recalled the childhood tales of lost treasure and began to see new possibilities for these implements. The very nature of the tales about treasure began to change. Before the tales had always been shadowy and told of treasure that was lost or hidden; now the newspapers and other media began to carry factual accounts of treasure being *found*. Among this new breed of treasure hunter, many were professionals. But as reports of their success spread, they were joined by a small but steadily growing number of amateurs.

Military mine detectors were bulky, crude, heavy, and often inaccurate devices, and the early metal detectors were not much better. As interest in treasure hunting grew and the market for metal detectors expanded, a new industry sprang into life and better products were created. About twenty companies now offer at least two hundred models priced to fit every pocketbook. Even the least expensive model is superior to the crude devices of three decades ago. The sophisticated metal detectors of today are not only light enough to be carried by anyone, highly sensitive and relatively easy to operate, but they can be used underwater. They can distinguish between worthwhile metals and unwanted junk such as bottle caps and pull-tabs from aluminum cans. Comparing one of these to a military minesweeper of thirty-five years ago is like comparing an Apollo spacecraft to the plane flown by the Wright brothers at Kitty Hawk in 1903.

Not all the early users of metal detectors were seeking treasure, at least not in a narrow definition of the term. Coin collectors, realizing that Americans carry in their pockets coins with millions of dollars in numismatic value and that any coin stands a fair chance of being lost, were quick to see the possibilities of these electronic tools. They began to appear with their metal detectors wherever people had passed and coins changed hands—at parks and on beaches, around parking meters, and outside vending machines. Shooting coins, they called it, and it may be the best way ever found to build a coin collection or a tidy bank account.

Other collectors joined in. Not only were users of metal detectors turning up coins, but they were finding metal tools and utensils, jewelry and tableware, relics and antiques—and the interest in all of these was growing as Americans became more affluent and their leisure time increased.

Collecting had been only a hobby for most people. Inflation made it an investment technique and in some cases, a business. The demand for collectibles grew at a dizzying rate, and with it grew the value of the rarities being sought. Some of those who had built large and quality collections—the collections could be of almost anything of wide interest—found themselves wealthy. This, in turn, created more demand, and subsequently higher prices, for collectibles of all sorts. Prices are still going up.

At the time of the great California gold rush of the last century, gold fetched only $16 an ounce, and the cost of living in the goldfields of the last century was so high that the prospector had to pan two ounces of the yellow metal a day to buy just the barest essentials. Few regions will yield two ounces of gold daily to a modern Argonaut, but at today's prices, an ounce or two each *week* will provide a decent living—and there are hundreds, if not thousands, of spots in America with the potential for producing that much gold.

The new gold rush is nationwide. Most of the activity is in the great mother lode country of California, where as many as 100,000 part-time Argonauts take to the hills each weekend and where some of the better-equipped prospectors are earning as much as $150 a day. But prospectors in other regions are quietly cashing in on the bonanza created by the fantastic prices for gold. As I write this, I have before me reports of individuals who are successfully working claims in Alabama, Washington, Georgia, Vermont, Montana, Pennsylvania, and Tennessee. Gold, as the old saying goes, is where you find it—and people are finding it across the width and breadth of America.

Not every person who leaves home with a metal detector, pick, or gold pan is going to strike it rich, of course. But a surprising number have done exactly that. Consider:

George Banks, an electrician from Lewiston, Idaho, was using his metal detector to search the area around an abandoned racetrack near an old ghost town in Washington. He had barely started when it led him to a privately minted gold coin dated 1855—one of only three in existence. The coin is valued at $300,000.

In Wisconsin, a novice treasure hunter using his metal detector just a few miles from his own home, turned up an ancient bronze coin that had been struck in Greece. How the coin came to this country is a mystery, but its worth has been estimated at $100,000.

By walking the beaches of Florida—one of the great treasure hunting areas in America—one resident of that state has garnered a tidy fortune of more than $500,000 in coins and jewelry over a period of fifteen years.

If these accounts do not excite you, the jade deposit recently uncovered near Jeffrey City, Wyoming, may. It holds hundreds of tons of the dark green mineral worth an estimated $65 million—the largest such deposit in the world. Discovery of the same mineral—a single huge chunk of it—recently put $180,000 in the pockets of two amateur scuba divers.

One young married couple, camping for three months along a tributary of the Feather River in California and panning gold as a team, finally broke camp and headed home with $32,000 worth of dust and nuggets.

A San Francisco salesman, working in the same region, panned out a single nugget weighing 26.4 ounces. As a collector's item it is worth at least a dozen times what it would bring on the gold market.

Few, if any, single nuggets, however, can compare in value to the discovery made by a treasure hunter in Utah. After doing the proper research, he located a lost gold mine and obtained the rights to it. These rights he sold to a large firm for $150,000, plus a share in the annual profits. The initial figure is about what he expects to earn each year for years to come.

There are many ways of striking it rich—there is richness to be found in family participation, in learning about history and local customs through research, search, and discovery, and in following a sport that one enjoys. And treasure hunting may be the most exciting sport of all. Always, always, there is the slim but very real chance that the next "bleep" of the metal detector will reveal a long-buried treasure worth millions. The next swish of the gold pan may turn up pay dirt. The next swing of the pick may make you wealthy—the thrill of the possible never dims.

Treasure hunting can add pleasure to many of the hobbies and activities you already enjoy, even if wealth is not your goal. The portable and relatively inexpensive metal detectors can go where you go—in the camper or car, to the beach, the back country, or on your fishing trips, to be brought out and used as you wish. You may find your share of the billions waiting to be claimed.

Good hunting!

1

Treasure Hunting Equipment

The basic piece of equipment used in modern treasure hunting—the metal detector—is the direct descendant of an invention that came about almost as an afterthought.

Dr. Gerhardt Fisher, a research scientist under contract with the Navy, was working at an air base near Sunnyvale, California, in the late 1920s. He was trying to develop a radio direction finder that would use a loop antenna that could be rotated. After extended effort, he had developed a unit that worked to perfection—except when it was aimed toward the nearby town of Redwood City.

It soon became evident that the problem was interference from the metal tank, mounted atop a high tower, which held the city's water supply; long after his contract with the Navy had ended, Dr. Fisher continued to work at understanding the phenomenon of the electronic signals bouncing off that metal tower. His research led to the development of the first device for the detection of buried metal.

Those first detectors were cumbersome, difficult to operate, and not as accurate as they might have been. Modern detectors weigh as little as 2 pounds and are extremely sensitive. Most children can learn to operate one. But there are certain things you should know before setting out to buy a detector.

Most modern metal detectors have the same appearance. A control box at the end held by the operator contains the batteries and the machine's electronic circuitry. On the upper surface of this box are located the unit's control knobs and usually a meter that announces the intensity of the signals being received. The case also holds a speaker that emits audio signals to alert the operator. This case is linked by a telescoping metal rod to a circular search head, made of metal or extremely tough plastic, which the operator moves over the area being searched.

Despite their similarity in appearance, the different models available are designed for different purposes and for use in different environments. Among the less expensive models, a metal detector that is suitable for hunting coins or other objects buried close to the surface may be totally useless in hunting for relics and other objects that are more deeply buried. The model made for the purpose of locating metal deep under the surface may be worthless in hunting coins. Yet another model may be needed when exploring for gold. If you intend to buy one of the less expensive models—one costing much less than $250—you should know in advance the type of treasure hunting you intend to do and select a metal detector specifically designed for that purpose.

The higher-priced detectors—those ranging from $250 upward—are touted by the manufacturers as multipurpose machines, and indeed some of them are. They can be tuned for deep searches, set to pick up objects near the surface, and are waterproof up to the control box so they may be used in hunting gold or searching in shallow water.

But not all metal detectors function effectively everywhere. Some are almost useless along saltwater shores or where the soil has an extremely high mineral content, while other models operate quite well under these conditions. By talking to local treasure hunters and asking about the equipment they use, you can easily learn which types are effective in your area. Most treasure hunters scouring a beach or other public area will gladly tell you about their equipment and its effectiveness. You can also get advice by contacting one of the treasure hunting clubs listed in the appendix to this book.

You may not want to start with one of the higher-priced models. The features they offer are usually worth the money only to those who are avidly devoted to the sport. Most experts suggest starting with a detector in the $150 to $250 price range, and then later, if the urge is still there, moving up to a more costly model.

For searching out coins and other metal objects that lie on or very close to the surface of the ground, you might be able to get by with a machine costing $100 or even less. But you should show extreme caution when considering one of these. Most detectors in this price range are little better than toys—they are barely able to detect an oncoming freight train at a distance of more than 2 inches.

If you need to hold down your initial costs, buying a used or reconditioned metal detector of higher quality is a far better course. Used or reconditioned detectors, as well as demonstrators, are frequently offered by retail detector outlets and may also be ordered from some of the manufacturers listed later in the chapter.

When you feel ready to start looking at detectors, try to choose one that is ruggedly built and capable of taking a lot of abuse. Treasure hunting is more physical than most beginners expect, and you want a device that is going to last many years, not one that is going to fall apart the first time it is dropped.

Look also for a machine that feels comfortable when you try it out—this has mainly to do with how the machine is balanced. With a few, the handle is placed at the very end of the shaft, a design that causes your wrist and forearm to bear the full weight of the entire detector. Such a design, even when the detector is relatively light in weight, will quickly tire you out.

A better design is when the handle is placed so that it causes the control box to counterbalance the weight of the search coils at the other end. With the handle positioned at the point of equilibrium, or close to it, you will find the machine far easier to carry over long periods of time.

Now you are ready to start shopping for a detector.

TR, BFO, or VLF-TR?

Until quite recently, the treasure hunter was offered two basic types of metal detectors: the transmitter receiver or TR type, which has a direct relationship to the developmental work done by Dr. Fisher, and the beat frequency oscillator or BFO, which is a descendant of the detectors used by the military during World War II to locate buried explosives encased in metal. Manufacturers have now added a third type, the very low frequency transmitter receiver or VLF-TR. By understanding the differences between the first two types—which still account for a large percentage of the market and which you are most likely to encounter if you decide to buy a used or reconditioned detector—you will understand the features and operation of the third type, the very low frequency transmitter receiver.

The basic TR detector has long been the most popular type; it is less expensive and easier to operate. It is a fixed audio, noise change detector. When the machine is put into operation it emits a sound that is barely audible. The degree of amplitude is changed when an object interferes with the signal being transmitted. If the source of the interference happens to be metal like a coin, you have "detected" it and can add it to your collection. A carefully designed and quality-built TR can be used for a wide range of general treasure hunting.

These TR metal detectors will operate quite well in coin, relic, and buried-treasure hunting. They perform in searching the innards of old buildings, in beachcombing, or where the goal is to detect metal of any type. Their greatest drawback is that their coils do not allow for the positive identification of ores and minerals. Some TRs also cannot accommodate the extra large coils needed for deep penetration of the ground.

The TR has generally been the type of detector suggested for beginners because of the ease with which it may be tuned, as well as the quickness and simplicity of its response. If this type appeals to you, ease of tuning is the one feature you should absolutely insist upon; because of the great variation in mineral content in the ground—which affects all these detectors—the TR requires frequent tuning, which can be a real nuisance if that tuning is difficult.

Mineralization of the ground is a problem that has always plagued users of TR detectors. With some of the older models, the operator working over mineralized ground had to turn a control knob that lowered the electronic gain of the detector (it normally operates at about 100,000 cycles per second). But reducing the gain of the detector also lowered the device's response or sensitivity to metal.

Some of the newer and better TRs offer an alternative to this way of coping with mineralization. With these TRs, the search coil transmits two signals, one of them produced when the search coil passes over ground containing iron or other minerals. This produces a signal the operator can tune out without greatly reducing the gain of the detector or lowering its efficiency in any way.

The TR detectors have certain other disadvantages. If you wish to detect metal objects at greater depths, larger and far heavier search coils must be used, which can be awkward. Many of the TR detectors—because the coils lack proper shielding, especially in the lower-priced models—operate erratically over wet grass and weeds. Some are prone to interference from power lines, fluorescent and neon lights, and other influences. But their greatest flaw is their inability to discriminate.

Without the ability of the machine to discriminate, many treasure hunters become quickly discouraged. The TR machine cannot do this effectively because it is very much like an electric light bulb—it is either on or off—you either get a loud and clear signal or you get no signal at all. If you simply want to locate an old dump and dig down on the chance that it holds something worthwhile, or if you are just searching for lost coins on or near the surface, this lack of discrimination is generally no problem. When the machine gives out its signal, you dig.

But because the machine sends out pretty much the same signal when the detected metal is a rusty nail as when it is a coin of gold, the inability to discriminate can cause a lot of wasted digging. Some authors, treasure hunters, and manufacturers of transmitter receiver detectors suggest that the failure to distinguish between types of metal can be overcome with experience. They claim the operator can learn to discriminate based on the strength of the signal—but they never mention the frustration you must endure while gaining that experience. Discrimination is a feature that can save you countless hours of wasted digging. Many treasure hunters have usually chosen a beat frequency oscillator, or as they are known to those who build, sell, and use them, a BFO detector.

A beat frequency oscillator, when operating, emits through its speaker a sound that is of constant volume when the device is tuned to its metal-detecting mode. The sound is generally a series of "bleeps" that speeds up when metal is encountered and slows down when minerals are present. The beats also increase in frequency in proportion to the amount of metal within range, continuing to do so until the machine has reached its limit.

Advanced and professional treasure hunters have always considered a carefully designed and well-constructed BFO detector with a full complement of search coils an essential tool. With such an outfit one can successfully participate in all types of treasure hunting, including prospecting. Gold nuggets and placer deposits will give a different signal from those produced by the black magnetic sand in which placer gold is commonly found. Coin shooting, beachcombing, relic hunting, and deeper searches for hidden caches and old dumps—all are possible with a BFO detector.

The ability of the BFO detector to discriminate between types and amounts of metals is somewhat offset by the fact that the machines are far more difficult to learn to operate. But their ability to discriminate is not their only advantage over the standard TR detectors.

Open search coils (search coils are described more fully later in this chapter) are standard equipment on most BFOs. This allows the operator to see the ground through the opening in the center of the coil, a feature which can save a lot of time and one that is seldom available on the TR detectors.

In addition to the audible signal, most BFO detectors come equipped with a visual meter. It is easier to pinpoint the exact location

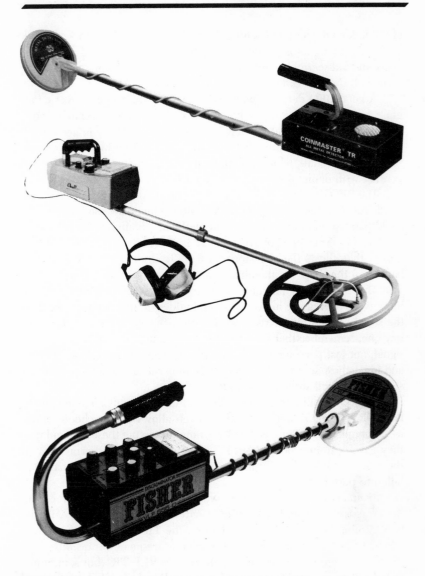

Top: Transmitter Receiver (TR) detector. COURTESY OF WHITE'S ELECTRONICS, INC. *Middle: Beat Frequency Oscillator (BFO). This detector, the Challenger, has dual search coils—a large one for deep searches and a small coil for shallow detection.* COURTESY OF RELCO INDUSTRIES, INC. *Bottom: Very Low Frequency Transmitter Receiver (VLF-TR). This is becoming the most popular detector.* COURTESY OF FISHER RESEARCH LABORATORY, INC.

of the hidden object by watching the meter; it helps confirm very weak signals by giving a discernible reading when the audible signal may be weak and indiscernible, and a reading can still be had when the audio is turned all the way down.

A good BFO detector will also operate quite properly over damp grass and weeds—as long as its search coils are 100 percent electrostatically shielded, a feature that you should demand if you are considering this type of detector. If the search coils are unshielded, you will receive false signals, which cannot be ignored, whenever the coils are in contact with damp grass—a real source of irritation.

The BFO detector responds a bit slower than the TR type. This is a disadvantage when hunting for coins, where a fast response is needed to avoid passing them over, but it is actually an advantage when looking for certain other types of treasure. It is this slower response, for instance, that allows the operator of a BFO to discern the size, and perhaps even the shape, of the object causing the signal.

The BFO metal detector is far more versatile and designed for more types of treasure hunting, under a wider range of conditions, than the standard transmitter receiver detector. But before you rush out to buy one, remember that with the BFO you must learn to interpret the signal, not just perceive it. For ease of operation in searching for coins and for shallow searches in areas where mineralization is no problem, a standard TR will serve just as well.

Several manufacturers also offer combination units. These contain both TR and BFO circuitry, and a switch allows you to choose either mode of operation. But a word of warning: in testing these, I found that they gave optimum performance in one mode, but acted erratically in the other. It was generally in the transmitter receiver mode that they failed to perform.

As you have seen, the biggest weakness in the transmitter receiver detectors is their inability to discriminate. Until quite recently, it had been assumed that, by their very nature, the TRs could never be given this feature—then along came the very low frequency transmitter receivers with ground exclusion base. Known as VLF-TRs (but sometimes called GEBs as an abbreviation for ground exclusion balance), these modified transmitter receivers combine the best features of the TR and BFO detectors. But, of course, they too have their shortcomings.

With their ground exclusion balance feature, the operator can tune out bothersome mineralization and all other false signals that might be received from the ground itself. They have the fast response of all other

TRs and are easy to tune and operate. They have a *limited* ability to discriminate.

The problem with the VLF-TRs is that they discriminate by exclusion. For example, when checking a beach for coins, you would probably tune the VLF-TR to discriminate against foil and pull-tabs, which it will do very nicely. But in excluding these bothersome items, you will also tune out many rings and other small pieces of jewelry. In like fashion, if the VLF-TR is tuned to discriminate against nails, it will fail to give off a signal when other small bits of iron—including perhaps some small iron relics—are encountered.

The discrimination feature of these new detectors makes them vastly better than the older TRs—but they really perform best when you have a fairly good idea of what you are looking for. Of course, you can always sweep an area several times, searching it once for coins, again for relics, and so on, and in this way it does as well as any detector on the market.

Search Coils

Choosing the right search coils, or loops, as they are sometimes known, is just as important as selecting a detector that is suited to your treasure hunting needs. As with the detector, the coil must be the proper one for the type of searching you intend to do.

In selecting a coil, there are two important facts: the smaller coils—3 to 8 inches in diameter—are designed to detect objects of every size at shallow depths; the larger coils—8 to 24 inches across their face—search out larger objects deeper in the ground. The coils must also be of a type matched to the detector. TR or VLF-TR coils are not interchangeable and will not work on a BFO detector, nor will a BFO coil work on a transmitter receiver.

When buying a metal detector you will receive at least one search coil with the machine; generally, this will be a coil matched to the most common use of that particular detector, or a so-called all-purpose coil. But as you expand your activities and begin a variety of treasure huntings, you will probably want to add some coils that are individually designed to meet your specific needs.

Since a coil of 4 or 6 inches in diameter will detect coins and other small metal objects near the surface far more readily than can be done with a 10- or 12-inch coil, beachcombers and other coin shooters prefer the smaller loops. But when these coin shooters go looking for relics, artifacts, and other large objects buried deeper in the ground, they will switch to a loop 10, 12, or 14 inches in diameter (or larger). There are also coils designed for use in gold prospecting, searching under water, and other specialized types of treasure hunting.

In the early days of the great modern treasure hunt, switching coils was a job that almost demanded a degree in engineering. But the modern detector and its coils are designed so that the job can be accomplished in about thirty seconds.

If you prefer not to change the coils at all but still want the versatility, you might consider buying a detector that will accept one of the true dual purpose coils. Patented about twenty years ago, this system offers a small coil set inside the loop of a larger one. In a typical model, the inner coil has a diameter of 5 inches, the outer coil, 12 inches. With a flick of a switch you can direct energy to the coil you want to use, thus searching shallow one minute and delving deeper the next.

Such dual coil systems are common in the BFO detectors, but the coils sometimes fail to operate independently of one another. You can check for such independent operation by turning the machine on and moving a piece of metal past the coils, directing energy to first one coil and then the other. A strong response should come from the coil that is energized, while the nonenergized coil should emit only a very weak signal.

You should also check to see that the coils are electrostatically shielded. If you can visit the dealer on a damp day, the coils can be tested for shielding by holding them very close to damp grass; if this is not possible, try aiming the search coil at a neon sign or an overhead fluorescent light. If in either case it emits random crackling sounds, the search coil may lack proper shielding and you should shop around for another.

Search coils offered for use with the TR and VLF-TR detectors vary widely in efficiency. These coils do their work by producing an electromagnetic field, and two coils of equal size do not always produce electromagnetic fields of the same size and configuration.

TR and VLF-TR search coils are covered by a casing, usually of plastic. Inside the casing are two coils. One coil acts as the transmitter that sends out the signal. This signal bounces back from any detected object and is received by the second, or receiver, coil. Very often, this receiver coil is far smaller in size than the coil that transmits the signal, so the actual response area may be much smaller than you would assume by looking at the plastic casing. This smaller response area can not only slow you down in your searching, but may also cause you to miss items that might otherwise be detected. It is a problem that can be avoided by choosing coils with total response.

In a search coil with true total response, the two coils are of the same size and are mounted close together within the housing. The entire lower surface of the loop will thus receive any signal that bounces back, which means you can cover a much greater area with each sweep of the detector.

To check a search coil for total response, just tune the detector until it will respond to a coin or other small piece of metal. Lay the unit flat on a table, making sure it is not aimed at any large metal object that will cause a false reading. Starting at the top of the search coil, move the coin back and forth across the loop, working your way toward the bottom. The detector should give off a continuous signal no matter where the coin is held; any silent areas reveal that the search coil does not have true total response.

Not all coils are completely waterproof, though most are protected to a certain extent from damage by water. Since some of the very best coin shooting, as well as other types of treasure hunting, occurs in shallow water, you will almost certainly want at least one search coil that is truly submersible. These, like the standard search coils, come in many sizes.

Most coils are designed to allow them to swivel on the shaft of the detector. This feature permits you to adjust the angle of the coil, which can often be a real advantage and can sometimes greatly reduce the strain on your back.

Cost? Coils range in price from about $25 upwards, with the very largest costing around $180. A full selection can add substantially to your treasure hunting investment, but they may also greatly increase the dividends that investment pays.

Detector Accessories

The simplest and least expensive of the metal detectors may have but one switch that turns it on and off like a light bulb, and it may not accept a single accessory. Some other detectors have so many knobs and switches that the control box looks as if it belongs in the cockpit of a

747, and the device can be fitted out with a bewildering array of accessories. Several manufacturers allowed me not only to test their detectors but also to try out the accessories they offer. The following is intended to help you understand what these options are all about:

Tuning Control • You will certainly want a metal detector that allows a fine tuning of the sound you get from the speaker as well as the reading from the visual meter. Without the feature of fine tuning you will never really be able to do sophisticated searching, and the success or failure of your treasure hunting ventures will hinge mainly on your luck.

Metal or Mineral Mode Selection • With this option you are able to select the type of material that will cause the search coil to respond. When looking for coins, the detector would be turned to the metal mode, for example. When in this metal mode, the detector would also respond to certain metallic ores, as well; and there are a few minerals, such as calcite, which will cause no response when the detector is in the mineral mode of operation. But for all its imperfections, this mode selection is a very desirable feature, and sooner or later you will probably want a detector that has it.

Discriminator Mode • The ability to discriminate has already been discussed, but its usefulness in treasure hunting cannot be stressed enough. Metal detectors discriminate in various ways and with varying degrees of accuracy, and it is in this area that the greatest amount of research is being done. By the time this book is in your hands, probably every manufacturer will offer at least one machine with this ability, and they may offer new ways of doing it.

You can get by quite well without the discrimination feature if you intend to limit your searches to old dumps, abandoned buildings, and other areas where anything you find may have some value, but this feature is nearly essential if you intend to search beaches, parks, and similar areas.

Battery Check • This is another feature that is certainly worthwhile. With it, you are able to get an instant reading of the condition of the batteries that power the detector; without it, you are likely to find yourself miles from home with an inoperable metal detector. Just by flicking a switch on the control box, you can activate a meter that will indicate the strength of the batteries.

The number of batteries needed, and the life of those batteries, depends on many factors. Both are closely related to the number and type of accessories the detector has, as well as the detector itself. Some detectors use single-battery systems. Most are powered by clusters of penlight batteries, the small "AA" size, and they require a dozen or more. These are fairly expensive, but when they become too weak for use in the detector, they will still power flashlights, portable radios, tape players, and other appliances that do not require so much electricity.

Some metal detector manufacturers claim that their machines can be operated for as long as 200 hours on a set of batteries, but this is, at best, dubious. Even without a full line of optional equipment, I exhausted set after set of batteries in a variety of detectors in less than 100 hours.

A word of warning about these batteries: remove your rings and any other jewelry when handling them. It takes a lot of electricity to power a good metal detector, and if the battery terminals come into contact with metal, dangerous arcing can result.

Battery Charger and Rechargeable Batteries • To avoid being caught in the field without power, carry a spare set of batteries. However, a set of batteries can easily cost as much as $10, depending on the metal detector, and this can become a major expense for the treasure hunter. The battery charger is an option that quickly pays for itself. At present, this option is offered only by White's Electronics, and only with their top-of-the-line detectors. It is such a worthwhile accessory that I'm certain it will soon become commonly available. A battery charger costs about as much as three sets of batteries, yet during its lifetime it could easily save you hundreds of dollars.

Another word of warning: you must use special rechargeable batteries with these chargers—if you attempt to recharge standard batteries, they may explode.

View Meter • Sometimes known as sensitivity meters or intensity meters and standard equipment on most BFOs, these are more sensitive than the audio signal and are therefore worthwhile. Most treasure hunters use them only to check on audio signals that are weak, but I have found they help me pinpoint the exact location of buried objects with greater accuracy than I can otherwise achieve. Be sure the meter is located so your hand or arm will not make it difficult to see.

Earphones • These are essential if you are going to be hunting for treasure along beaches when the surf is high and pounding, on extremely windy days, around roads with heavy traffic, or in other situations that make it difficult for you to hear the speaker signal. Many experienced treasure hunters swear by them, insisting they make it possible to discern the slightest change in the speaker signal. Not all detectors will accept earphones.

Hip Mount • This option allows you to remove the control box and carry it in a special sling over your shoulder, or attached to your belt. It greatly reduces the amount of weight that must be held in your hand. In searching shallow swimming areas, for example, some coin shooters mount the control box—which must be kept dry—on an inflated inner tube; this gives them the freedom of movement they need to locate coins with the search coil held in one hand, while scooping them out with some device held in the other.

Telescoping Shaft • A feature you should look for because without this, the detector may also be awkward to transport and store. If you are unable to adjust the length of the shaft to fit your height, you are going to be constantly uncomfortable and will tire quickly.

Indicator Light • Detectors with this feature make it possible to hunt treasure after dark. They signal with a light that flickers on when metal is detected. They are especially useful for treasure hunting on beaches and in parks where you must wait until the crowds leave and then begin your search as darkness is falling. Garrett and Compass are two companies that offer detectors with this feature.

Coil Covers • These covers come in sizes to accommodate the various coils and are snapped into place to protect the costly coils from damage when being used over sand, gravel, or rough terrain. They cost $4 and up, depending on size, and are one of the better investments you can make—especially if you do your treasure hunting in rugged country.

Dealers and Manufacturers

Depending on where you live, there may be one or several detector dealers in your area, each representing one or more of the companies that manufacture such equipment. In the *Yellow Pages* of your telephone book they will be listed under "Metal Locating Equipment." If by some remote chance there is no dealer in your town, the addresses of the nearest ones may be obtained by writing to the companies listed below.

There are some advantages to buying from a dealer. It gives you a chance to look over, try out, and get the "feel" of a variety of models, and you may be able to get faster service when repairs are needed. Dealers who accept trade-ins may also have used models for sale.

If you are seeking used equipment, however, your best hope of finding it lies in writing to the Used Equipment Department of White's Electronics (at the address listed below) and asking about the detectors their salespeople have used as demonstrator models. Other manufacturers may offer used equipment from time to time, but White's appears to be the only one that does so on a regular basis.

It is possible, but not likely, to save money by buying directly from the manufacturer. Most manufacturers do not undersell their dealers, but a few dealers do overprice their detectors. In doing some comparison shopping, I found one local dealer charging nearly 15 percent above the price suggested in the manufacturer's catalog. So, even if you decide to buy from a dealer, it might be a good idea to obtain the manufacturer's catalog and compare prices before making the purchase.

Whether you buy from a dealer or directly from the manufacturer, protect your investment by demanding a guarantee. The standard warranty covers a twenty-four-month period during which the seller agrees to replace all defective parts, with no charge for labor.

Listed here are most of the firms that manufacture and sell metal detectors. Those marked with an asterisk are the largest and have nationwide dealer networks. All will gladly send a catalog and the addresses of local dealers.

C and G Technology
2515 West Holly
Phoenix, AZ 85009

° Compass Electronics Corp.
3700 Twenty-fourth Avenue
Forest Grove, OR 97166

° Detectron
Division of Tinker & Rasor
417 Agostino Road
San Gabriel, CA 91778

D-Tex Electronics
614 Easy Street
Garland, TX 75040

Excelsior Electronics
7448 Deering Avenue
Canoga Park, CA 91303

° Fisher Research Laboratory
1005 I Street
Los Banos CA 93635

J. W. Fisher
Anthony Street
Taunton, MA 02780

Gardiner Electronics
4729 North Seventh Avenue
Phoenix, AZ 85013

° Garrett Electronics
2814 National Drive
Garland, TX 75041

General Electronic Detection Co.
16238 Lakewood Boulevard
Bellflower, CA 90706

J. K. Gilbert Company
Highway 80
Leesville, TX 78112

The Goldak Co., Inc.
1101-A Air Way
Glendale, CA 91201

Jetco Electronic Industries
1133 Barranca Drive
El Paso, TX 79935

Metrotech Underground Explorations
P.O. Box 793
Menlo Park, CA 94025

Ray Jefferson
Main and Cotton Streets
Philadelphia, PA 19127

Relco Industries
P.O. Box 10839
Houston, TX 77018

3-D Electronics
88 Hansard Street
Lebanon, OR 97355

Treasure Electronics
Route 1 Box 56
Benton, LA 71006

° White's Electronics Inc.
1011 Pleasant Valley Road
Sweet Home, OR 97386

2

Getting Started in Treasure Hunting

No matter which type of metal detector you have, you will quickly learn that operating it correctly is something of an art. If you buy it from a dealer, he will probably take you through each step of its operation, allowing you to test it both inside and outside his store. He may also refer you to local treasure hunters or treasure hunting clubs who will help you become acquainted with the use of your equipment. All of this is going to leave you with a feeling of supreme confidence—until you get the device home and, looking at it, realize you can't recall a single thing you've been told.

No two metal detectors are exactly alike. Some of the cheaper, simpler, and less sensitive ones are ready to go with the flick of a switch. Others require as many as twenty separate steps to prepare them for operation. Generally speaking, the better the machine, the more complicated it will appear to be.

Start out by reading the instruction book carefully. This is the only way to begin to know the machine you have bought. Go over the booklet until you understand the purpose of each part of the control system.

When you have an understanding of the control system, don't rush right out and start digging up your yard each time you have a signal. This is one of the worst mistakes made by beginners. Not only are you likely to be wasting your time, but you could end up looking pretty foolish in front of your neighbors. It's not very probable you will find much until you have mastered the art of tuning the machine, and the best place to practice this is in the privacy of your own home.

Tuning the Detector

This is the most important part of operating a metal detector, and to do it correctly you must touch the control knob delicately, as if you expect it to sting. In the case of the TR and VLF-TRs, you start by putting the device in the metal mode of operation, then rotate the control knob until no sound comes from the speaker and the meter needle (if the detector is so equipped) rests on zero. Next, turn the knob until the faintest sound is heard and the needle begins to climb. This is what is known as the threshold.

With the detector on this setting, try sweeping the search coil over a coin placed on a table. You should get a clearly audible signal from the speaker, and the needle should leap across the face of the meter. If not, the machine is probably tuned higher than its threshold level, and you should very lightly turn the control knob so the sound level is reduced and the meter needle swings back nearer to zero. Repeat the coin test. When the machine is properly tuned and passed over the coin, the change in tone will be so clear that you will have no doubt at all about the signal you are getting.

If your detector has the mineral mode of operation on it, a mineral sample will come with the machine. Repeat the tuning process, using the sample instead of a coin. Return to the metal mode of operation.

Now try passing the detector over some other metal objects—bits of foil, pull-tabs, bottle caps, etc.—and try to acquaint yourself with the strength of the signals they give off. It takes a great deal of time to learn, but old hands can almost always identify such common objects by the strength of the signals.

As you repeat these experiments, try varying the distance between the metal object and the search coil. You will notice that the signal also changes in relation to this distance. Experienced treasure hunters use this to tell how deep an object is buried.

There are times when you may want to operate the detector without sound, but when tuned to this threshold level it will not be at its most effective. When operated with no sound at all, there will be times when the machine will fail to detect; when the sound is tuned too high—beyond its threshold level—your ear will not be able to perceive all the variations in sound.

The subtle differences in signal strength are easier to see than to hear, but you should not rely entirely on the meter: in searching, there is a natural tendency to keep the eye on the search coil, which could cause you to miss a signal from the meter.

After you have learned to tune the detector to this threshold level and recognize the signal changes, try out its discrimination feature (if it is a VLF-TR and is so equipped). This means turning the discriminator knob to one of its various settings—to reject foil, bottle caps, pull-tabs, or nails. In passing the search coil over an object of the type being rejected, you should not get a signal.

Unlike the TR and VLF-TR metal detectors, the BFO does not offer the option of silent operation. It must be operated with continuous sound. The tuning knob should be adjusted until the speaker emits a fast and steady series of beeps. Then pass the search coil over the coin and note how the frequency of the beeps changes, not abruptly but gradually building and dying. Try testing it on other metal objects, and see if you can tell the difference in the way the signals change.

With either type of machine, once you have it properly tuned, you are ready to try some experiments. But remember that they are only experiments, and don't start tearing away at your walls—which is precisely what more than one excited beginner did—the first time you receive a signal.

Try tracing the wiring in your house or apartment. Start at an electrical outlet and follow the conduits to the fusebox. Run the detector over your carpet, noting the signals you get each time you are over one of the nails holding it in place.

Next spread newspapers or magazines over the floor. Leave the room while another member of the family hides several coins under these. Then come back and hunt these out. Then mix in some nails, bottle caps, and so on, and see if you can learn to tell which is treasure and which is junk. Now you are ready to take your metal detector outside.

Putting the Detector into Use

Remember: to work at their most sensitive level, all metal detectors must be given a few minutes in which to warm up. This is an essential requirement when you are taking the machine from an indoor to an outdoor environment and thus subjecting its circuitry to a sudden change in temperature. The accuracy of its signals can be adversely affected if you fail to wait; so while you are allowing the machine to warm up, you can make good use of the time by making your own proving grounds.

In some unused corner of your backyard, bury a few metal objects at various depths. Then, after the metal detector has been given a few minutes to warm up, see if you can get a signal from these objects. Prior to each treasure hunting trip you make, the detector should be tested at this spot, to assure you that the device is in good working order, the batteries are strong, and the signals are all they should be.

Be aware, as you begin, that weather conditions can affect the operation of the machine. Signals are stronger on wet or rainy days, or when the humidity is extremely high, than on other days. After some practice, you will be able to anticipate such weather-caused variations.

With the machine tuned to the threshold level, turn the speaker volume to the level of sound you desire. These two settings should not be confused. The control knob determines how sensitive the machine will be; the speaker setting determines the loudness of the signal.

Adjust the shaft of the metal detector until the device feels comfortable in your hand when held with the search coil just above and parallel to the ground. When you grasp the handle, you should be able to touch the search coil to the ground without bending or stooping. An erect stance is far less tiring.

With the detector in one hand and your digging instrument (described later in this chapter) in the other, select a strip of ground and search it by walking straight ahead, moving the search coil from side to side in the widest arc possible. Search as far left and right as you comfortably can. The distance between each arc should be no wider than the search coil you are using. With a 10-inch loop, for example, the arcs should be spaced no more than 10 inches apart. This is best accomplished by taking small steps that match the diameter of the search coil.

Keep the search coil exactly the same distance above the ground at all times. Failure to do this is probably the most common error made by beginners. If you fail to maintain the same distance, you will get varying signals—these signal variations will make it impossible for you to learn to recognize the different signals given off as you encounter metals and minerals of different kinds.

When using coils of less than 8 inches in diameter (probably the size that will come with the detector), keep the lower face of the coil flush against the ground, lifting it only to avoid rocks and other objects that might damage it. When searching with a coil of this size, you must keep the face an inch or less above the surface of the ground.

Coils larger than 8 inches in diameter are held somewhat higher—usually 3 or 4 inches above the surface. This not only helps keep the coil free of ground mineralization, but also makes it possible to perceive metal objects buried deeper in the ground.

Make your search slow and deliberate. If you move the search coil too quickly over a strip of soil, you will almost certainly fail to detect what is buried there. Worst of all, the items you are most likely to miss are those which are most deeply buried, and with coins especially, these are the ones that have been there longest and are likely to have the greatest value.

With even the smallest piece of turf, it is best to divide it into sections, perhaps marking these off with stones at the corners, so the sections can be carefully scanned one at a time. And don't switch abruptly from one spot to another. Be thorough and relentless. Where a novice has skipped from spot to spot, a tenacious treasure hunter can often come away smiling.

At the slightest response from the detector, you are ready to pinpoint exactly where the object is going to be found. Move the search coil back and forth over the spot causing the response. A series of zigzag patterns will give you a better idea of the exact location. Then, when you think you have it fairly well located, moving the detector over that spot in two tiny sweeps forming an X will pinpoint it exactly.

Tools for Digging

Since at least half of your time on any reasonably successful expedition is going to be spent digging, it makes sense to start out with the right tools. Remember that the hole you dig in order to retrieve a coin should not be much larger than the coin itself. Most coin shooters carry a probe of some sort—a long thin screwdriver or a sturdy knife with a narrow blade. Where the soil is reasonably loose, it is often possible to pry the coin out, leaving only the tiniest disruption to tell anyone you were there.

A common garden trowel is also useful. By forcing it down into the soil and carefully moving it in a circle, you can cut out a cone-shaped divot that can be easily replaced without damage to a lawn.

Where the soil is harder and contains a lot of clay, you will need a sturdier implement. Many metal detector dealers offer special digging tools; usually these have a sharpened edge that can be used for hacking away roots. They are also offered through the mail by some of the metal detector manufacturers, usually at a cost of less than $10.

An Army trenching shovel, which can be obtained at most surplus stores and has a blade that folds back against the handle, can be useful for deeper digging. When exploring old dumps, or any other areas where valuable glassware is likely to be encountered, you will want to have with you a longer probe. A steel rod, at least 15 inches long and sharpened on one end, makes a good one; you can force it into the soil and locate bottles before they have a chance to be broken by your digging tools.

Where the soil is very loose and sandy, as it is on dry beaches and dunes, some sort of sifting device can be handy. Wire mesh baskets, such as those used in the kitchen for deep-frying, are as good as any. Sifters are often sold as children's toys. These can really speed up your work in sandy areas.

A pouch in which to carry your find is also a good idea. It need be no fancier than a drawstring bag you can sling over your shoulder, or a sack you can attach to your belt. Without something like this in which to place your find (considering all the bending, stooping, and kneeling you must do as you dig), you are likely to lose items from your pockets almost as fast as you are digging them from the ground.

Later, as you try some of the specialized types of treasure hunting described in this book, you may need and want specialized equipment. But these implements will serve you quite well in most situations close to home—and that is where I suggest you first put them to use, not only because you should practice, but also because vast amounts of treasure lie hidden in backyards all across America. Don't forget to repair any land you happen to damage.

Treasure in Your Own Backyard

When first you begin experimenting with your metal detector, you are going to notice your neighbors looking at you with curious eyes, whispering something like, "Well! I always suspected old so-and-so was just a little bit funny! Now I know it!" And you are going to feel that everyone around is watching you—probably you are going to be right. Then a curious thing may happen.

Your detector is going to lead you to something. It may be only a penny, a nickel, a dime, or a quarter—but it will at least be *something*. There are not many areas where people live that do not hold at least a coin or two.

Unless you start digging craters on your front lawn, or have already established yourself as the neighborhood ogre, you are almost certainly going to find at least one or two of your neighbors dropping over. They will ask about that curious machine you are using: what you are looking for, what you are finding.

If you'll take just a few seconds to show your neighbors your intriguing device and give them a brief explanation of how it works (don't gloat too much as you show them what you have found), you'll find at least one of your neighbors inviting you over to sweep his yard. Then his neighbor, and his neighbor's neighbor. . . .

Once people see what you are about and understand that your hobby can be followed without needless destruction of property, they are surprisingly good about tipping you off to treasure hunting spots. They will tell you about friends who own old farms or abandoned buildings. They will offer to introduce you and they will ask about accompanying you on a treasure hunting trip to some spot they know about. Nothing except winning the lottery will lead to more new friendships than ownership of one of these intriguing devices.

According to Charles Garrett, owner of Garrett Electronics and one of the most successful treasure hunters ever, about 90 percent of all treasure hunters practice their hobby in their own hometowns—often within walking distance of their homes. Usually it is a family hobby, with the youngest and the oldest participating, and there can be little doubt that this makes for improved family relations. Remember that these backyard treasure hunters account for the greatest part of the $25 million or so in treasure that is found each year. The literature put out by the metal detector companies, the pages of the treasure hunting magazines, and even the local and national newspapers carry a surprising number of documented accounts of treasure hunters who have struck it rich without dashing off across the country to look for the long-sought Lost Dutchman Gold Mine or other treasures that may exist only in fanciful imaginations.

Virtually every manufacturer can refer you to real people who have recovered the cost of their metal detector in just a few days. Garrett recounts the story of a retired engineer in St. Louis who, on the first day out with his metal detector, found nearly 40 coins, added almost 70 more the next day, then found 267 on his next day out—all within a block of his own home. Within a year, the man had amassed a staggering total of more than 31,000 coins—many of them rare—and had collected a double handful of jewelry, including a diamond wristwatch that he gave to his wife for her birthday. All of this he found in his own neighborhood, in local parks, schoolyards, and under the lawns belonging to his friends and neighbors.

An Atlanta treasure hunter was even quicker in recovering his investment. While tuning and testing the detector behind his house, he began to pick up signals. By the time he had searched his own lawn and the lawn of a neighbor, he had recovered more than 335 coins, most of them with numismatic value. Top prize was an 1834 silver half dollar worth several thousand dollars!

Out Texas way, another new treasure hunter picked up a signal in his backyard that led him to a Mason jar filled with old coins worth several times what he had paid for the detector, and a group in Pennsylvania, working right in their own neighborhood, dug out an old chest from behind an abandoned house and found it brimming with jewelry worth thousands of dollars.

In working your own street or neighborhood, there are certain spots that are more likely to be profitable than others and certain techniques you can follow that will improve your chances for success. The best general advice is to start out by going after the small treasures—let the big ones take care of themselves. Those pennies, nickels, and dimes, occasional watches and rings, may not individually seem worth your time, but they very quickly add up. When enough items are found, the odds are good that among them will be some with collector's value. One thing is obvious about treasure hunting: its most successful practitioners are those who slowly but surely build their fortunes.

In checking over the lawns of friends and neighbors, be especially thorough around and under shade trees, even more so if the house is an old one. In the years before television changed our lives, many a family congregated on the lawn under such trees, and the loose change that fell from their pockets over the years causes such areas to be among the most profitable you can search.

In searching around these older homes, the area just outside the back door is another one that pays off. In the days before inside plumbing became common, housewives often tossed the dishwater out the back door. Now and then they accidentally pitched out a spoon, fork, or knife right along with the water, and today, with any piece of silverware bringing a minimum of about $8, these can be well worth finding.

If the house once had an outside toilet, you should also check out the sites where the facility would logically have stood. Use a larger search coil over these areas for deeper detection, and don't be hesitant about digging into them, for the waste will have long since been assimilated by the soil. Odd as it sounds, these sites are so extremely profitable that a few treasure hunters specialize in searching them out. They seek them for the old coins that were lost through the holes or the cracks in the flooring, for the bottles or junk that were sometimes tossed down them, and for the rubbish that was used to help fill the hole when the facility had to be moved to a new site.

If the house is old and surrounded by a few acres or so, you should certainly try to locate old dumpsites. Trash collection is a relatively modern innovation, and what was discarded as the trash of yesteryear is often tremendously valuable today. In urban areas, most of these old dumpsites have been covered over by new construction, but in many rural areas they remain accessible. They may be located behind the house and sometimes cause a recognizable depression in the ground.

In rural areas, too, where the mail is placed in a box on a post at the roadside, be sure to carefully search around the base of each post. In the days before the Postal Service stopped providing service, any postage due on a letter was left in these mailboxes for the postman to collect. While reaching from his car to retrieve the coins, the mailman frequently dropped one or all of them—and there most of them remain, often rare and valuable. One treasure hunter in Minnesota has amassed a coin collection worth well over $75,000 by concentrating his efforts almost entirely on the ground around mailboxes along country roads.

Whether the house is old or new, rural or in the city, be sure to search carefully around the edges of any porches it may have. Very often a dropped coin bounces over the edge of the porch and the unfortunate loser never attempts to find it. The ground under old wooden porches with cracks between their boards will almost always yield some coins, as will the ground beneath open outside staircases on apartment buildings.

As you search these areas and begin making a few finds, another general rule applies: when you get a signal and find a coin or any other object, dig it out and then check and recheck the spot until you are absolutely certain it holds nothing else. For some odd reason, things seem to be lost or thrown away in clusters—more than one beginner has walked away from a spot holding a single coin in his hand, then watched in dismay as some more thorough companion laughingly retrieved more coins from the exact spot.

Once you have thoroughly searched each and every inch of the property owned by you and your neighbors, you are just starting to tap the treasure hunting opportunities that exist right in your own neighborhood. Start expanding your search by looking for places where people congregate, or where they once did, and concentrate especially on the spots where money has changed hands. Grassy areas around bus stops may be the most overlooked, yet profitable, treasure hunting spots in America. If you dropped a dime or a quarter as you were preparing to board a bus, would you stop to look for it and risk missing the bus? Since money is constantly being lost there, some treasure hunters set up a regular route of these spots and visit them almost as frequently as the bus.

The same is true of the grassy areas around parking meters. Since the posts make the grass pretty hard to mow, a dropped coin can be difficult to find in these areas—unless you happen to be using a metal detector. As an example of how hot these grassy areas can be, one Minnesota man who concentrates on them has—in a period of just a few years—filled two whiskey barrels with dimes and nickels and several gallon jugs with pennies . . . after setting aside the coins with high collector's value.

Since the coins and other lost items around these spots are being replenished on a more-or-less regular basis, it is useless to worry about whether the spot has already been searched by another treasure hunter. In any case, running a preliminary check would take just as long as searching the spot for coins, since each individual area is likely to be so small. But as you start exploring larger areas, especially those places where you feel you might be competing with other treasure hunters, you *may* save yourself some time by checking it out first.

Many experts suggest this simple test: pick out two or three of the most likely looking spots (the ground around the picnic tables at a public park, for example), and sweep them without using the discriminator mode of the metal detector. The complete, or even near, absence of foil, bottle caps, pull-tabs, or other junk, according to this theory, suggests that the area has been searched only recently and you will do better by concentrating on another spot.

Others strongly disagree with this thinking. They point out that the absence of junk could just as well mean only that the area has been searched by a detector without the ability to discriminate, or by someone unable to properly read the detector's signal. Most good spots are almost never totally exhausted.

The second school of thought is, I believe, the correct one. No two metal detectors are exactly alike; even two of the same model, in the hands of two different operators, are not likely to be tuned to exactly the same setting. Signals may be affected by the weather, as well as by how the search coil is held in relation to the ground. And even if all these things were not valid, to cover each and every inch of a large plot of ground and extract from it every bit of metal would be—to say the least—a monumental task.

As one local treasure hunter I met at a park in the center of Dayton, Ohio, told me, after displaying a sizable handful of coins he had found that afternoon, "I specialize in going over the places that are 'hunted out.' When my friends come to me and tell me about some new spot they've found and how they've worked it for all it's worth, I make a mental note to get there as soon as I can. I've got a long list of those 'played out' places, and I just keep going back again and again."

No matter which school of thought seems right to you, there are certain types of places, you will find, that are always more rewarding to your efforts.

Schoolyards are always excellent spots, especially the older ones. In days past, schools were relatively small and were surrounded by bare dirt yards, where the children played, roughhoused and, in many instances, hid things that are now valuable. If you are a longtime resident of your town and know it well, you may know the location of a former schoolhouse, perhaps even the one you attended.

If you are not that familiar with your area, old topographical maps will show you their locations, or you may also look them up in old directories at the local library; the latter is preferable because such directories may contain photographs that will make your work much easier. Pay dirt is most likely to be found around swings or slides, the schoolhouse gate and door, the outhouse, and old trees.

Baseball diamonds and football fields are also very fertile. Like all places where large numbers of people gather, coins and other times are continually being lost at these spots—especially around the concession stands and under the bleachers. One law student is reported to have paid his way through school by concentrating almost entirely on these areas.

Recreational areas such as picnic grounds, fairgrounds, carnival sites, fishing camps, drive-in theaters, and amusement parks are prime hunting places. Your chances of finding large numbers of coins and relics are even greater when the site has been used for a very long time, and, of course, the older the site, the greater the chance that the items will be old, rare, and valuable. And don't search only for those spots still in operation; some of the very best spots are those no longer in business.

The old Georgetown Racetrack, just outside the Delaware town of that name, has been closed for many years now, its bleachers and paddocks fallen into decay and partially destroyed by fire. But it has long been one of the very best treasure hunting spots in its area, yielding a small but steady flow of coins and relics to the treasure hunters who continue to visit.

From around the turn of the century until the period following World War II nearly every major city in the country had an amusement park, sometimes two. Many of these are gone now—closed for economic or safety reasons. But they are absolutely terrific hunting grounds, if you can get permission to go over them. Just try to imagine, if you will, the number of coins that changed hands at Coney Island during its heyday, and you will begin to see the potential of these spots.

The old Luna Amusement Park of Seattle shows how profitable these amusement parks can be. Destroyed by fire in 1931, the grounds of the former park attract literally hundreds of treasure hunters on any summer weekend—yet they have been yielding old gold pieces and other valuable coins for years. The Lakeside Amusement Park in Dayton, Ohio, is by no means as large nor as old as those mentioned above. Closed because of tax problems in the 1950s, its rides and most of its buildings are gone now. But it is a good example of how profitable such places can be: in a single afternoon recently, I collected nearly 200 coins from just a few square yards in the area where the roller coaster once stood. None of these was extremely valuable, but I have no doubt that rare coins are to be found there, so I'll be going back . . . again and again.

If your local park has a bridle path, you should almost certainly check it out. The entrance to many bridges may also provide you with surprising finds. Usually this is where fishermen park and leave their cars when they go down to the river to practice their own form of recreation. If there is a level, shady spot here, it is likely to be used for family picnics. While these are not as rich as some of the areas just mentioned, many treasure hunters report successes in working them.

By doing the simplest research at the library, you may also be able to locate the site where a military camp once stood. During mobilization for both World Wars, dozens and dozens of temporary camps were set up around the country. As any veteran can tell you, the flooring in those barracks frequently had gaps wider than the boards, just right for letting the wind in, while letting coins and other small objects fall through. Most of those old camps are gone now, torn down and replaced, but if you can locate the site of one, where thousands once congregated, you will probably have a trove you can work for years. Members of a treasure hunting club in Houston, Texas, located such a site, took thousands and thousands of coins, buttons, rings, bottles, and watches from it in a single weekend—and are still working the site today.

If you live in the South or Midwest, you should keep an eye on the section of your newspaper that reports the church and religious news. In these sections of the country and especially during the summer months, traveling evangelists often set up large tents and hold old-style revivals, some lasting a week or two. By appearing with your detector after the evangelist has left with his tent, you should be able to pocket quite a few coins that missed the collection plate.

Such camp meetings have been held for at least a century. If you can locate the site where one was held in the distant past (the chapter on research will give you more tips on doing this), by going over old newspapers, you will probably be in even better shape. In the second half of the last century and throughout the early decades of this one, camp meetings drew thousands of people, many of whom traveled long distances and surrounded the main tent with temporary living quarters of their own. As often as not, a carnival atmosphere prevailed, with a great deal of visiting about, buying, selling, and bartering. In a few instances, the preachers were followed around by saloonkeepers and madams, who also set up their tents and offered their wares to those who were missing the message. These spots are so rich in treasure that looking for them is the biggest specialty in some regions. St. Louis treasure hunter Harry Seybold recently unearthed a copper pot holding several hundred gold coins dating back to the 1870s on just such a site. One South Kent, Connecticut, couple enriched themselves to the tune of 10,000 coins in less than five years of concentrated effort on weekends by hunting at old churches.

Unpaved parking lots seldom receive enough attention from treasure hunters. When items are lost on such spots, they are soon pressed into the ground by tires and feet and quickly lost from sight. If you frequent any place of business that has such a lot, you should have little trouble getting permission to search it.

New construction may also offer opportunities. Millions of relics—and probably as many dollars—lie buried beneath the buildings of our cities and towns. When old buildings are torn down and the site excavated, huge amounts of treasure are sometimes unearthed. All too frequently, the bottles and other valuable relics are discarded as junk or hauled away to be used as landfill. Get to know one of the workers on the site, ask him to get permission for you, and invite him to help you in the search—on a fifty-fifty basis, of course.

If your job involves any excavation, as in farming or construction, your opportunities may be even broader. Once the surface of the earth has already been disrupted most objections to treasure hunting vanish. If you ask your boss for permission to go over the area on your own time, he may grin at you a little oddly, but he will likely give his okay. You can be sure the grin will vanish if you have only reasonable success.

You may do far better, though. Treasure hunters going over an urban renewal project in Vallejo, California, took away more than $50,000 in artifacts, many of them silver crafted by Mexican artisans, in a single week of searching, and a similar project in the heart of Detroit allowed treasure hunters to reclaim more than 30,000 relics and historical artifacts. One California heavy-equipment operator has literally filled his home with treasures he has gathered from places his work has taken him. The collection includes one vase worth more than $10,000.

Such urban renewal projects almost always take place in the poorer, more blighted, rundown sections of a city. But it is important to remember that these areas were not always as they are now. They are simply older, and the worst section of your city today may well have been its finest a century or more ago. And even after its decay began, riches may have been stashed by a tax-dodging bookie or his next-door neighbor, that successful madam.

In most cities, after the buildings in a section have been torn down for urban renewal, the land stands vacant for long periods while planning is done. During this period, if you are willing to wade through the red tape thrown forth by the bureaucracy, you may be able to search these areas. And because cutting the tangle of red tape is so difficult, thus discouraging most of your competition, these areas may be even more fruitful.

But there is an easy way to cut that red tape—try joining your local historical society. In most cities, after the buildings are leveled for such projects, historians and archaeologists are given first chance to go over the land. They are often concerned only with finding items relating to local history, and more often, they have time to search only a small part of these areas, hoping to find a cross-section of artifacts typical of an era. They will usually welcome you and your helpful metal detector.

You may be asked to sign over to the society all unique artifacts relating to local history, but you will be allowed to keep a good percentage of everything else. The local government will demand that you sign a waiver releasing it from responsibility in the event you are injured or killed.

There are other good reasons for joining the local historical society. The folks you will meet by doing this are the ones who really know local history. They know where the old buildings stand, where others once stood, and who owns them. They know of sites that deserve a good search, and after you become a member, they may ask you to do just that. Most successful treasure hunters are deeply involved with their historical societies. As a matter of fact, you will find that most successful treasure hunters are involved, to varying degrees, in a wide range of community affairs.

Many small-town police forces, for example, cannot afford a metal detector or a person trained to operate it, yet these have proved to be very useful tools in police work—they have been used in locating stolen goods, guns, knives, weapons, and other important criminal evidence. By offering your services to the local law enforcement agency, you will not only be fulfilling a civic responsibility and helping to improve the image of treasure hunters in general, but you will also find that this volunteer work makes local officials much more receptive when you approach them for permission to hunt on public property.

Other public service can be just as rewarding. By helping with the work of planning and holding a festival, fair, horse show, or other community event, you almost assure that you will be given permission to go over the grounds after the event is held—permission that may not be given to other, less thoughtful treasure hunters.

Each and every community in America has enough sites similar to those described to keep you and your detector profitably busy for a lifetime. You may want to add a little more excitement to your sport—and pick up some tips from experts—by joining a treasure hunting club and using your detector in competition.

Treasure Hunting Clubs

There are about 150 treasure hunting clubs in America. Some are small, with only a dozen members. Others have memberships numbering in the hundreds. Many are listed in the appendix to this book. But the sport is growing so fast that new clubs are being created almost daily, so you may want to obtain a more recent list by writing to The International Treasure Hunting Society, Dept. T, P.O. Box 3007, Garland, Texas 75040. Members of these clubs are joining together not only to share their common interests and learn more skillful use of their metal detectors, but also to lobby against laws they feel are unfair and discriminatory.

No two clubs are alike. In some the members just get together to show their discoveries, perhaps trading and selling a few items, while helping one another identify and evaluate the more obscure pieces they have found. Other clubs sometimes band together to research—and then search—treasure-laden sites. Each member usually profits because of the increased thoroughness of the effort, and some of the biggest finds in recent history have come about through the efforts of club members working together. Still other clubs may limit their activities to annual or semi-annual get-togethers, perhaps meeting at some known "hot spot" for a picnic followed by a little treasure hunting. But no matter what its size and the range of its activities, in each and every one of these clubs you will find experts who will gladly help you learn the finer points of using your metal detector.

Joining such a club will also give you a chance to try your hand at metal detector competition, one of the fastest growing sports in the country and another opportunity for you to strike it rich.

Competition treasure hunting is a fairly recent innovation. It began in a small way, with some of the clubs simply visiting a good spot and offering a trophy or other prize to the member who found the most coins. Then some of the larger clubs began charging entry fees, offering slightly larger prizes, and adding a little spice to the sport by stashing on the hunting grounds a few valuable coins for the entrants to seek.

Metal detector companies, quickly seeing an opportunity to advance the sport, then stepped in and began sponsoring these events and offering more prizes. From small local events sprang statewide, regional, and finally, national events. These prizes offered are big, and the purses are going to continue to grow in the years to come.

In June 1979, with newspaper, magazine, and television reporters from around the world looking on, the biggest treasure hunting competition in history was held at Traders Village in the heart of the Dallas–Fort Worth area. It was the First Annual International Championship Treasure Hunt, and it attracted thousands of amateur, semi-professional, and professional treasure hunters from Canada, Great

This treasure hunter searches for buried coins and tokens while competing with hundreds of others at the World Championship Treasure Hunt sponsored by the International Treasure Hunting Society in Garland, Texas. COURTESY OF GAR-RETT ELECTRONICS, INC.

Britain, Mexico, Australia, and New Zealand, as well as from all parts of the United States.

They came to attend the informal seminars on metal detecting and treasure hunting, the Texas-style chili and barbecue dinners, the square dances and displays of new equipment set up by manufacturers, or to buy, sell, and barter at more than 2,000 flea market stalls set up on the grounds. And to spend, of course, three days competing for well above $75,000 in prizes.

Indications are that the number of these contests will grow, with bigger and better prizes being offered each year. You can compete in many without belonging to an organized club, of course, but belonging to such a club will keep you better informed about when and where the events are being held.

Other Metal Detector Uses

During the summer months, try keeping an eye on the shallow streams in your area, looking for the spots most heavily fished. In the fall you can return, search around and under the banks with your detector, and come up with boxes full of lost fishing lures. New, those lures cost as much as $5 each; used, bait stores may offer you only a dollar or so apiece—hardly enough to make you rich, but more than one treasure hunter has paid for his detector by this method.

Local firing ranges offer the chance to earn small sums from scrap. Thousands of brass shells, all worth some money, can be recovered around the firing lines; these bring even better prices if they can be sold to gun shops for reloading.

Some treasure hunters actually specialize in hunting lost items and claiming the reward. A few even keep their eyes on the lost-and-found columns in the newspapers, then call the person running the ad and offer their services for an hourly fee. Others print up notices or business cards and post them at beaches or swimming areas, where people are always losing things.

If your detector has full underwater capabilities, and especially if you are a scuba diver, you might try letting a few marinas know that your services are available. Outboard motors, often costing $1,000 or more, all too often end up under the water instead of on it, and the unhappy owners will pay you handsomely for recovering them.

The detector is also going to be useful in recovering items lost by your own family. About twenty years ago, as a private in the Army, John Paquette was stationed near Stuttgart, Germany. While out riding his new motorcycle, John and his fiancée were involved in a minor accident and she lost the high school class ring she had been wearing in lieu of a more proper engagement ring.

The two returned to the scene of the accident several times, hoping to recover the ring, but were never able to locate it. Finally deciding that someone else had found and kept it, they gave it up as lost forever.

Then, in 1978, they returned to the scene with their son, John, Jr., who had been given a metal detector as a birthday present and who'd heard the story of the lost ring many times. He was eager to see if he could find it.

Fifteen minutes after starting the search, the instrument gave off a "bleep," and digging down with a shovel, young John found the ring under a few inches of dirt. Resting beside it was a World War II hand grenade, which experts were called in to remove.

The defused grenade is now displayed in the Paquette home, while young John proudly wears the ring. Mrs. Paquette is not wearing it, because, as her husband explains, "The last time I let her have it she lost it, and it took nearly twenty years to get it back. I'm not taking any more chances."

3

Research—The Key to Success in Treasure Hunting

Tales of buried treasure are as old as mankind. The most romantic stories are usually associated with plundering pirates, the ones who supposedly came ashore at night to secrete their ill-gotten treasure, then murdered those who helped bury the loot, leaving behind a ghost or two to frighten away anyone who would try to recover the hoard. Such tales abound throughout the western hemisphere. Some have a basis in truth. Others exist only in imagination. Sorting out truth from fancy is the first step in going after any really big treasure, and the distinction can be made only through proper research.

Consider the time that has been wasted searching for the treasure that, according to old legends, the pirate Henry Morgan buried after his sack of Panama City in 1670. That attack was launched from the island of Old Providence, which lies not far off the coast of Nicaragua. At least two dozen major expeditions have gone over virtually every inch of that tiny dot of land, searching for the millions in treasure that legend places there—yet historians long ago established that Morgan had no treasure to bury, not a single doubloon. After paying off his crew and creditors, and handing over a share of the booty to the king of England, Morgan had to borrow money to finance his later ventures.

Compare those futile searches to the tremendous success of Pennsylvanian Bart Webber, who recently made headlines by locating the sunken wreck of the seventeenth-century Spanish galleon *Concepción*, probably the richest treasure ship of them all.

The *Concepción* existed—the exact date of its sailing is known, as is the date it sank. The captain and the crew survived, even carrying ashore with them some of the vast treasure held by this ship. Spanish salvage crews had returned to the scene and recovered even more. A century or so later, a crew of Englishmen located the site and took from it a small number of gold and silver bars. So the *Concepción* really did exist—but where?

For about fifteen years Bart Webber tried to solve that riddle, traveling time and again to Spain to dig through dusty archives in search of any clue about the wreck. Then, just as his efforts looked hopeless, Webber was contacted by a man who had a diary belonging to one of the Englishmen who had previously located the wreck. With this, Webber was able to pinpoint the exact location of the old galleon, in waters just off the Dominican Republic. He and his investors are presently tapping it for gold and silver bullion, coins, priceless jewels, and relics they expect to be worth a total of about $700 million!

You don't have to become an expert researcher in order to strike it rich. Simply because they are out there and using their metal detectors on such a regular basis, recreational treasure hunters make some of the biggest and best finds. Perhaps like Bill Baxes, a seventeen-year-old beginner from Marin County, California, you will hit it big without spending a lot of time on research.

In 1979, just on the remote chance that it held something of value, young Bill decided to sweep his new detector over a pile of sand that trucks had dumped close to his home. He quickly got a reading and unearthed several old coins, including a silver Willow Tree shilling dated 1652 and worth at least $11,000. He has been told by experts that this coin may be only one of a large number struck without the knowledge of the king of England, and for that reason he hopes to find the source of that pile of sand—and perhaps a treasure that will set him up for life.

Very few treasure hunters are so lucky. Most strike it rich in one of two ways—by quietly and steadily accumulating small treasures until, one day, they look around and see that these small treasures have added up to real wealth, or by selecting one or two known treasures and tracking them down through painstaking research.

The mention of buried treasure always prompts certain questions from the skeptical: why do people bury treasure? And if people really do bury treasure, why don't they come back and dig it up again? People bury treasure to keep it out of other hands, or to prevent others from having knowledge of it. If it remains there, it does so because the one who buried it either died before it could be recovered, forgot its exact location, or was just unable to reclaim it.

Some of our most important treasures were hidden away by honest folks of the Revolutionary era. There were almost no banks, and most people kept their money hidden somewhere on their property. Even those who kept the money in the house were quick to bury it at the first indication of attack by the British or Native Americans. If the family failed to survive and the attackers went away without finding the cache, it probably remains buried today. During the Civil War people in the South buried their possessions not only to keep them out of the hands of the invading Union Army, but also to avoid having to hand them over to the Confederate Treasury to bolster the weak economy. Even before the War Between the States, these people faced the possibility of a slave uprising or other attacks, so the family money was kept in a hole in the ground—the only safe bank of its time.

Westerners faced threats even more deadly than those faced by their friends in the East. There were so many vicious cutthroats preying on these early settlers that they had to take extraordinary precautions to protect their valuables. Farmers, miners, and gold prospectors all faced the threat of being bushwhacked at work or while heading to town for supplies by marauding thieves who infested the land. Since a prospector had no desire to advertise a strike by showing up in town toting a fortune in nuggets, the bulk of his wealth usually remained back at the claim-site.

Often, of course, attacks occurred when the family was away from the property and so the family survived. But even when this happened, they sometimes returned to find their home so ravaged by fire that they were unable to locate the family wealth. There it remains, waiting.

When bandits struck at stagecoaches, banks, or wagon trains, saving their own necks often became more important than saving their booty, so they frequently stashed away the heavy loot in order to escape a pursuing posse. Since soldiers had no way of sending their pay—which usually consisted of gold or silver coins—home to their families, this too sometimes became a part of America's vast hidden treasure. So did the winnings of some gamblers, who were often victimized by robbers, and the more honest earnings of those shop- and saloonkeepers who lacked a sturdy safe, or had no faith in the local bank.

One estimate says that about half of the more than $4 billion in treasure now concealed around the United States was stashed away in the years since 1929. Many of the owners of this new treasure are still alive and waiting to reclaim their wealth. But others have passed away, leaving fabulous hoards for someone to find.

Some years back, near Reno, Nevada, hundreds of bags of silver dollars were found hidden under piles of trash in the mansion of the late

LaVere Redfield, a reclusive millionaire. According to documents later filed on behalf of his widow, he left behind an estate of between $70 and $200 million in gold and silver mixed with uncashed checks—all of it concealed in various places on or around his property.

In 1961, on Long Island, New York, another $200,000 in paper currency turned up in the garden of an estate belonging to the late Bernard MacFadden, who, according to his wife and several others close to him, habitually placed his money—a total of about $7 million—in waterproof metal containers and buried it on his various properties around the country. Much of it remains hidden.

The owner of another vast treasure revealed its whereabouts as he lay dying. R. S. Altman, owner of several grain mills near Troy, Ohio, had concealed $500,000 in cash beneath a grain elevator, protected from the elements by milk cans. In the last moments before his death he told a workman where it could be found. Altman had developed a great fear of banks after losing a fortune during the Great Depression.

Not all treasure is intentionally buried. Natural disasters often cause great wealth to become lost. No one knows how much valuable property lies buried because of such disasters as the San Francisco earthquake of 1868, the great fire that swept Portland, Oregon, in 1866, the Chicago fire of 1871, or the deadly Johnstown Flood of 1889—but it must certainly be a tremendous amount. Disaster on a smaller scale has touched hundreds of communities, and often it has left vast wealth waiting to be claimed.

If you are convinced that great treasures are waiting for you, the next step is to start the research necessary to locate them. There are a number of ways to get started and valuable tools you can use.

Determining the area—and the specific treasure—to research depends on many factors, especially the amount of time you have and how much money you want to spend. You might decide to concentrate on treasures believed to exist near your hometown, or you might want to go after one in the area where you intend to spend your next vacation. Even if you decide not to go after a specific treasure, general research about the area where you do your treasure hunting will lead you to better hunting grounds and vastly improve your chances of striking it rich.

But most experts suggest that you concentrate on a specific treasure. Thousands are known to exist around the country, and while it would take a lifetime to try to document and pinpoint the exact location of each and every one, I have listed some of the more probable ones in the appendix to this book, with a few bits of information about the history, general description, and likely site of each. More information about these can be found in the books mentioned later in this chapter. By selecting a single one and going after it with all you have, the experts say you stand a fair chance of finding any treasure that truly exists.

There are other advantages to this concentrated research. By selecting a small area and putting it under the microscope, you increase your chances of finding other riches. In going after a cache known to have been buried near your hometown, for example, your historical research might also disclose that gold or gems were once mined in the region, and that bit of information could lead you to other riches.

Maps and Charts

The most important thing to remember about treasure maps is that nobody sells a real one. In a few treasure hunting magazines you may see them offered for sale, but they are mass-produced novelties, good only for decorating the wall of your den or study. The big X marking the spot of the treasure usually indicates an area of something like 50 square miles, sometimes more, and the description of the treasure site is so vague that you may have trouble locating the right country. There are, however, certain maps and charts that can be as useful as your metal detector.

Among the very best of these are the remarkable topographical maps produced by the U.S. Geological Survey. They are remarkable because of their unbelievable detail. They show roads, bridges, fencelines, mine shafts, houses, barns, and old windmills. Even if you are not on the trail of a specific treasure, these maps can be incredibly useful. If the map shows a house where a house no longer stands, for example, you could reasonably expect to find something of value by locating the site and searching around the foundation.

These maps are offered in six scales, from 1:24,000 (meaning that every unit of measurement on the map corresponds to 24,000 units on the surface of the earth) to 1:500,000. On the 1:24,000 map, an inch equals about 2,000 feet; on the 1:50,000 scale the inch equals about 8 miles, or 42, 240 feet.

Since at a scale of 1:24,000 even a map of Rhode Island would cover several hundred square yards, these topographical maps are offered in sections called quadrangles. Each quadrangle map costs 60¢ to 75¢.

The first step in securing one is to write to the U.S. Geological Survey, GSA Building, Washington, DC 20242, requesting an index to the topographical maps of the state in which you are interested. You may also obtain such an index from any of several U.S. Geological Survey map distribution centers around the country. After the index is obtained, you will get faster service by placing your order with one of the regional offices. If you are interested in an area east of the Mississippi, the address is Distribution Section, U.S. Geological Survey, Washington, DC 20242. To obtain maps for areas west of the Mississippi River, write Distribution Section, U.S. Geological Survey, Federal Center, Denver, Colorado 80225. For maps of Alaska contact U.S. Geological Survey, Map Office, 520 Illinois Street, Fairbanks, Alaska 99701. Expect at least a month to go by before you receive a reply.

By studying these maps, you can develop a fairly accurate idea of an area's terrain. This is possible because these maps include precisely drawn contour lines, the lines coming together at points of equal altitude. Here and there the lines are broken by figures showing the height in feet above sea level.

These contour lines are spaced at intervals representing 10 to 80 feet. This makes it possible to tell at a glance where high and low points are located, even the steepness of ascent. You can sometimes just look at such a map and determine the probable route that might have been taken by an old wagon train, or the spot where a prospector might logically have located his cabin.

Cartographers are constantly at work to keep these maps current, a fact that can work to your advantage. Many of the maps were produced as long as thirty years ago. Some of the older ones remain available, even though a new map for the same quadrangle has been drawn and produced. By ordering two maps for the same quadrangle—one old, one new—you can sit in the comfort of your home and locate the sites where buildings once stood and valuables may remain.

The Army Corps of Engineers also offers a series of maps of various areas of the United States. Many of these contain data not shown on the topographical maps of the U.S. Geological Survey, and they are widely used by treasure hunters. You can obtain a full catalog and price list by writing Commanding Officer, Army Map Service, 6500 Brooks Lane, Washington, DC 20025. Maps and photostatic copies of plat books showing the layout of old military bases and abandoned forts are available from Adjutant General's Office, Historical Branch, U.S. Army Headquarters, Washington, DC 20025. The latter are invaluable.

From the Superintendent of Documents, Government Printing Office, Washington, DC 20403, it is possible to obtain thousands and thousands of maps produced by all the agencies of the federal government. You can get current catalogs showing what is available by writing to the Printing Office. Request lists of maps dealing with geology, transportation, mines, historic sites, soil surveys, abandoned settlements, military sites, Native American reservations, and minerals.

The Bureau of Land Management, Department of the Interior, Washington, DC 20240, issues a large number of charts it calls "Public Land Maps," which are updated from time to time. They are essential in determining if the site you want to explore is on public or private land. The Forest Service also produces very detailed maps showing the land under its jurisdiction.

Aerial photographs can be enormously valuable, especially in searching out old ghost towns, abandoned mines, or ancient ruins. These, too, can be had from a number of government agencies. To get a better idea of exactly what is available, write to the U.S. Geological Survey, Department of the Interior, Washington, DC 20244, and ask for its free publication *Status of Aerial Photography*. This pamphlet tells you where you can obtain the photos related to your area of interest. By obtaining a few photos and going over them with a magnifying glass, you will quickly realize why these are used by so many successful treasure hunters—you will see lines where fences and buildings once stood, perhaps a strange formation that will beg for your personal inspection. The photographs must, of course, be used in correlation with maps of the same region.

Many states have geological survey departments that produce and distribute maps that are equal, if not superior, to those offered by federal agencies. In many instances, these maps date back a century or more, sometimes showing the exact locations of mines and mining camps. Similar maps may also be offered for sale by local historical societies, perhaps showing historical ruins of the region and even towns that have long since vanished.

Original copies of old maps and charts can be a great deal harder to come by, but many can be studied at state archives and libraries, or at the Library of Congress in Washington. Many universities also allow treasure hunters to study the charts in their collections.

Old sailing charts are the most difficult of all to obtain. Hundreds of thousands of these lie uncataloged in dusty rooms in Europe, making them very difficult to find. The greatest depository for these records is the Archives of the Indies in Seville, Spain, which houses records dating back centuries, while another great storehouse is the Academia Real de la Historia. Treasure hunters have generally found these two institutions to be less than cooperative, however.

The best sources for information about English ship movements in American waters are *Gentleman's Magazine* and *Lloyd's List,* both of which have been published since 1740 and devote themselves to maritime trade, commerce, insurance, and news, following the movements of all ships of British registry and frequently describing the intended route of a departing ship and its cargo. Both are available at major libraries, such as the Library of Congress and the main branch of the New York City Public Library.

Authentic sailing charts for British ships prior to the year 1666 are nearly impossible to come by. That year, a great fire swept London and destroyed most of the documents related to shipping and the Colonies. More were lost during the bombing raids of World War II. On this side of the ocean, nearly every major city suffered devastation from fire during its early years, so the authenticity of any sailing chart or map dated prior to 1740 is questionable at best. But a few authentic ones probably do exist, and tracking one down might be the clue that leads you to a sunken ship holding a fortune.

Books, Magazines, and Newspapers

Well over 1,000 books have been published on treasure hunting and topics related to it. Some tell tales of fabulous lost mines or outlaw caches; many others deal with sunken ships and buried pirates' treasure.

Yes, they make exciting reading, but that is what they are for—to curl up with when the days are cold and the fire is warm. No writer in his right mind is going to reveal the exact location of millions of dollars in buried treasure, and even if he did, his editor, publisher, or printer would beat you to the site.

Robert Marx, one of the most famous and successful treasure hunters ever, says that years ago, when he first began searching for lost, buried, or sunken treasure, he took these books literally and wasted years searching for 150 "authentic buried treasures" they described. Later after he had gained experience, he was unable to find a shred of evidence to indicate that any one of these treasures had ever existed.

Books on treasure hunting—listed under "treasure trove" in the card file at the public library—should be regarded as secondary sources, ones that can lead you to treasure only if you use them as a starting point and research the original clues. By going over the bibliography and the references at the back of such a book, you can find the names of books and other publications that the author used as his sources. By obtaining these you can sometimes move closer and closer to the authentic source. Where an old newspaper article is mentioned in the book, you may be able to obtain a copy of the newspaper and dig out important clues that the book's author overlooked, or the article might put you on the trail of even better sources.

But even as secondary sources, many treasure hunting books are utterly worthless. In the appendix to this book, I have listed some treasure hunting books that are generally held in high regard. But please don't expect any of them to pinpoint the exact location of a hidden fortune.

Certain books are so worthwhile that they deserve special mention here, especially since the library may have them listed under some heading other than "treasure trove." If any book is not in the collection at your local library, remember that it can be obtained through an interlibrary loan.

Shipwrecks in the Western Hemisphere 1492–1825 by Robert Marx, is primarily devoted to ships lost in the southern part of the hemisphere. It is by far the best compilation of information on ships lost during the era mentioned in the title. Marx has spent a lifetime researching lost ships and going after their treasure, and his book gives good general information on about 8,000 sunken wrecks—the date they went down, where they went down, and what they carried.

For researching American shipwrecks of the American Revolution, you might start by asking the librarian to obtain *Naval Documents of the American Revolution,* a ten-volume series published by the Department of the Navy. A similar work is now being compiled by the Coast Guard on ship losses in the years following the Revolution.

For information on shipwrecks that occurred after 1800, you should consult *A Guide to Sunken Ships in American Waters* by H.R. Kaplan and Adrian Lonsdale or the *Encyclopedia of American Shipwrecks* by Donald G. Shomette. For information concerning shipwrecks of the Civil War era *The Official Records of the Union and Confederate Navies in the War of the Rebellion,* published in 1894 by the Government Printing Office, is unsurpassed.

Books dealing with treasure buried on land are far less reliable. However, as a good starting point and purely for the sake of interest, I suggest that you take a look at *The Explorers Ltd. Guide to Lost Treasure in the United States and Canada.* Compiled by the well-known group of adventurers, it will certainly not "guide" you to the treasures it lists, but it provides worthwhile information about nearly 300 major treasures that this group has studied, and, in each case, they have found some evidence to show that the treasure does exist.

Unlike modern books on treasure and treasure hunting, old books can be incredibly good sources of information. Footnotes were more commonly used in the early days of publishing, and often these can lead you to old letters and documents, which could conceivably put you hot on the trail of a major treasure.

Especially useful for purposes of research are the old privately published books—local and family histories, and so forth—that you may be able to obtain at your library. Frequently these are not in the stacks but are stowed away in some dusty corner of the library basement, and you may have to ask the librarian to look around and see what is there. These books are often loaded with incredible amounts of detail about family movements and eccentricities, and they sometimes contain accounts of events that may not have been reported elsewhere.

Histories published by local historical societies can also be very valuable—they are detailed and accurate. If they contain old photographs, they are even more helpful to you.

Locating old ghost towns requires only the most basic research, for most states show these on their official maps. But there are a few books and booklets that can be of further help to you in finding old settlements to go over with your metal detector. If you intend to hunt treasure in Arizona, you will want *Ghost Towns and Lost Treasure,* a free booklet that can be obtained by writing the Department of Economic Planning and Development, 3003 North Central Avenue, Phoenix, Arizona 85015. For information about ghost towns in Colorado, send a request for *Colorful Colorado Invites You* to the Division of Commerce and Development, 602 State Capitol Annex, Denver, Colorado 80203.

The best way to start researching the old ghost towns is through a series of books published by White's Electronics (see page 20). They offer individual guides for Arizona, California, Colorado-Utah, Montana-Idaho-Wyoming, Oregon, Nevada, New Mexico, Texas, and Washington. The guides cost $2.95 each. White's address is 1011 Pleasant Valley Road, Sweet Home, Oregon 97386.

Books, especially the older ones, sometimes also contain information that may help you locate an old mine or prove to you that valuable minerals do exist in your area. They can reveal not only where the mines are located but also the precise routes taken by the gold-seekers, thus making it possible to find old relics left at campsites along the trail. Generally regarded as the best of these, for purposes of research, is *The Prairie Traveler, a Handbook for Overland Expeditions with Maps, Illustrations and Itineraries of the Principal Routes Between the Mississippi and the Pacific,* written by E. B. Marcy in 1859. It has been reprinted many times, so your library may be able to obtain it for you.

Articles that have appeared in magazines offer another starting point for your research. Articles on any subject are easily located by using the *Readers' Guide to Periodical Literature,* a standard reference work available at most libraries. It indexes approximately 135 publications from the year 1900 on, by subject matter as well as by author. Those related to treasure hunting are found under the heading "Treasure Trove." In looking for articles published prior to this century, consult the *Nineteenth Century Guide to Periodical Literature,* which indexes, by subject and author, articles published from 1800 to 1899, or *Poole's Index to Periodical Literature,* which lists those published between 1802 and 1906.

If you locate the titles of articles that might be helpful to your research and find that your local library does not have a copy of the magazine, your next step is to consult the *Union List of Serials,* a catalog that provides the locations and inclusive dates of the holdings of periodical publications in all American and Canadian libraries. If the magazine containing the article you want is not available at a nearby library, you can probably obtain a Xerox copy by writing to one that does have it. Most libraries charge about 15¢ a page for this service.

Treasure hunting magazines, like the modern books on treasure hunting, have only limited value as research sources. Most contain articles about ghost towns, lost mines, and successful treasure hunters. A complete list of treasure hunting magazines appears in the appendix. They will keep you informed on what other treasure hunters are doing, where competitive events are being held, what new equipment is available, and what research methods are being used by others—but don't expect them to contain any really worthwhile clues about that fabulous lost treasure you are after.

There are two publications you might find of special interest. The first is called *Discover,* and it's a free bimonthly magazine offered by White's Electronics. Not only does it provide a wealth of information about coins, buttons, artifacts, and relics, as well as stories about the activities of treasure hunters, but its columnists will help you identify and evaluate any really odd items you turn up. To have your name put on the mailing list, just send a request to White's.

The second is more of a service than a magazine. *The Treasure Index of Current Finds,* which began operation in 1974, offers information about where recent discoveries have been made. These are noted on state maps. So if you accept the theory that no good treasure hunting spot is ever truly exhausted, as many treasure hunters do, these maps can lead you to spots that might be worth checking out. For current information, including the cost of subscriptions, write to *Treasure Index of Current Finds,* P.O. Box 101, Bronx, New York 10468.

In doing general research about the history and topography of an area, few magazines are more valuable than the *National Geographic,* a publication held in the highest esteem by treasure hunters. Because of the way this publication is funded, its writers sometimes spend years working on a single project. They are able to treat a subject with a thoroughness few other magazines can afford, and facts are checked and checked again before anything goes into print. If this magazine prints something as fact, you can be reasonably certain that it is so—and that makes it a valuable tool for the treasure hunter.

This magazine is dear to the hearts of treasure hunters for other reasons. More than one treasure hunting expedition has obtained at least partial funding from it, and dozens of successful treasure hunters have added to their good fortune by telling their story in its pages or on one of its television specials. So keep the *Geographic* in mind—it might offer another way for you to strike it rich.

Old newspapers are better sources of information than either books or magazines. But you must always bear in mind that newspaper articles have always been written for public consumption, not for use by those hunting lost treasure. This means that newspaper accounts, like those in books and magazines, should be used as a secondary source, and you should always attempt to verify them with original documentation. Your librarian will be able to tell you exactly when the first newspaper appeared in your area of interest, as well as where copies or microfilms can be obtained. Usually they will have to be borrowed from state archives, state or university libraries, or state historical societies. However, most major city newspapers are on microfilm, and your librarian can borrow them from the Library of Congress or the main branch of the New York City Public Library. Further help in locating old newspapers can be had from the International Newspaper Collectors' Club, Box 7271, Phoenix, Arizona 85011.

Such old newspapers are often the only source used by those treasure hunters who specialize in going after the loot stashed by outlaws of the Old West. Sometimes just an account of a robbery can be enough to lead to the spot where the escaping robbers stashed the loot, but more often it will only be the first in a series of clues that leads to the treasure.

In these old newspaper accounts, the most useful of all are articles about treasure that was *found* in the past. Why? Because if the treasure was found in the days before the metal detector was invented, the odds are excellent that part of it was missed and lies waiting to be discovered.

You may also come across old newspaper accounts that tell of mines being closed. This could be a real find, for the mine that was unprofitable to operate at yesterday's prices could be worth a fortune today, with the price of gold and minerals climbing to the sky. The same is true of accounts of gold or silver (or whatever) being found in an area, even though the strike might never have been an operating mine.

Although books, newspapers, and magazines can put you hot on the trail of a treasure, you should always try to verify your facts by looking up original documentation. Most documentation can be found in the National Archives; Manuscript Section of the Library of Congress; Historical Sections of the Departments of Defense, the Interior, Agriculture, and Justice; or, sometimes, through agencies below the Cabinet level.

Closer to home, documentation can be found in state archives, state libraries, state universities, secretary of states' archives, state treasurers' archives, state land office archives, and at state historical societies. On the county level, documents exist in the offices of county attorneys, clerks, surveyors, tax assessors, and sheriffs, as well as historical societies. Old city records can usually be scrutinized in the files or archives of mayors, clerks, engineers, police departments, and street commissions. Private libraries and museums will also sometimes allow you a look at their old records. You may find gaining access to these records is easier if you are a member of a local historical society or a similar organization.

Historical Societies, Clubs, and Other Organizations

Historical societies are the best thing that ever happened to treasure hunters, though that is certainly not the major reason for their existence. In every state, these groups have been responsible for erecting thousands of markers showing the exact spots where events of historical significance took place. The sites of vanished settlements are revealed by such markers; so, too, are the spots where military forts once stood and the birthplaces of the famous, the infamous, and those largely forgotten. Often the marker is the only indication that the spot is anything more than ordinary.

These markers can save you a lot of time. Though you may not be permitted to hunt and dig in the immediate area of the marker, you can often use them to locate good sites nearby. Some of these simply reveal the campsites used by long-ago travelers and cowboys on cattle drives, for example, and by following such a trail you can reasonably expect to be on good hunting ground. Around an area where a fort once stood, you could also assume that there is a fair chance of finding old artifacts, perhaps weapons lost in some past skirmish.

Where these markers stand and are related to events of relatively recent times, you may also find good hunting spots by making personal inquiries of a few residents in the area. Some may know of related spots or incidents—usually through information passed down from one generation to the next—that deserve no historical marker but hold interest for you. Just be aware that such information may be grossly exaggerated.

But placing these markers is far from the only service rendered to treasure hunters by the historical societies. They can be the most useful source of research material available. State historical societies are listed in the appendix; but to contact those on the local level you should visit the library and check the *Directory of Historical Societies and Agencies in the United States and Canada,* which lists more than 5,000 associations, giving a brief description of the services provided by each.

Many of these societies will open their archives only to those involved in scholarly research and offer little or no help to the treasure hunter. A few others serve only as a depository for certain types of records, so they have little to offer. But most are veritable warehouses of helpful information and have a permanent welcome mat out for anyone with an interest in seeing it.

Much of your success in obtaining material from these associations depends on your approach. They are generally willing to assist, but you must provide specific information that will give them an idea of what you are looking for.

A representative of the Darke County, Ohio (where Anthony Wayne signed the Treaty of Greenville, and birthplace of Annie Oakley) Historical Society remarks: "We have an excellent collection of maps, manuscripts, and printed material related to the past in this part of Ohio. We offer these resources to all responsible persons and there are many, I am sure, that would be helpful to treasure seekers."

In Florida, where treasure hunters are almost as numerous as tourists, the Florida Historical Society, which operates out of South Florida University at Tampa, offers similar advice to treasure hunters seeking information. "The resources in our collection are available for use by any interested party, including treasure hunters and amateur archaeologists," says the librarian of their special collection. "The collection includes old Florida maps, the earliest dating from 1584, nautical maps of Florida waters, and records from early towns and old forts. They are used quite regularly by people looking for treasure, but there is so much material that any request has to be fairly specific. At the very least, we need to know what part of Florida the researcher is interested in, or what era."

Two national organizations are of special interest to treasure hunters. The first is the National Treasure Hunters League, which may be contacted by writing to P.O. Box 53, Mesquite, Texas 75149. The League publishes an information-packed quarterly magazine for its members, and also provides a telephone information service that will, when possible, answer your treasure hunting questions. Membership costs $5 a year.

The Prospectors Club International, operating through P.O. Box 68069, Indianapolis, Indiana 46205, has as its sole purpose the exchange of information between members. This information goes into an eighteen-page quarterly newsletter, which goes to all who pay a $6 annual membership fee. Membership also entitles you to call club headquarters for the answers to your treasure hunting questions.

4

Treasure on the Beach and Beneath the Sea

Before the great new boom in treasure hunting really got started in 1948, a building contractor named Kip Wagner was strolling the beach near Sebastian Inlet, Florida. Sebastian lies about halfway between Cape Kennedy and Fort Pierce, in the very heart of what may be the great treasure hunting region in America. Wagner found seven Spanish silver coins partially covered by the sand. He had never been a treasure hunter, but this find converted him for life. The conversion finally led to some of the most amazing and valuable recoveries of treasure in history.

Wagner spent all his spare time that year and part of the next walking up and down those beaches with a noticeable lack of success—he did not find a single coin. Reasoning that someone had lost the coins there in recent times, or perhaps even planted them as a joke, Wagner grew discouraged. Then a friend loaned him a surplus World War II mine detector, and he found more coins resting under just a few inches of sand. During the next year he turned up several dozen coins, many made of gold. Over a period of years he built up a tidy collection of gold and silver coins, most coming from the sunken wrecks of a convoy of twelve treasure-laden galleons that went to the bottom during a devastating hurricane in 1715.

Wagner soon realized that these coins must be originating from wrecks that were lying reasonably close to shore and, bringing together a group of investors, he formed the Real Eight Company to locate and salvage the ships. Real Eight met with quick success—recovering at least $10 million in treasure and artifacts during its first decade of operation—more recently it has located a ship that may yield a staggering $190 million in bullion and coins.

When radio and television stations began broadcasting reports of the treasure being salvaged by the divers of Real Eight, they set off a frenzied rush that has not been equaled in this country since gold was found at Sutter's Mill in 1848. Thousands of treasure hunters scurried for the beaches opposite the wreck sites. Over the past 200 years, each storm had carried some of the treasure ashore. Those with metal detectors quickly began turning up valuable coins, jewelry, and relics. A small city of tents, campers, and house trailers sprang up along the beaches, and nobody knows how much treasure was carried away by those beachcombers—but one newspaper account estimated that it was worth hundreds of thousands of dollars.

Beaches: Where to Search, When to Search, How to Search

During the heyday of the great sailing ships that carried treasure from the New World to the Old, approximately 95 percent of the ships lost in the western hemisphere sank or ran aground in waters close to shore. Some, caught in hurricanes, were actually tossed far up on the beaches, then covered by sand as time passed. One estimate says that ships lost in Western waters carried at least $22 billion in treasure! And most experts agree that at least half the gold mined throughout history has been lost at sea, certainly a great part of it along the American coastline.

In Florida between Cape Kennedy and Fort Pierce, many experts feel that the amount of treasure found by beachcombers may actually exceed that found by the professionals who dive down to the sunken wrecks. Beaches around Sebastian Inlet alone have yielded hundreds of thousands of dollars in gold and silver coins, and *Playboy* magazine recently carried an account of one man in that area who, over a period of years, had amassed a small fortune by beachcombing in his spare time.

But the Florida beaches are certainly not the only ones that put money in the pockets of treasure hunters. The beaches of North and South Carolina, especially those near the treacherous waters of Cape Hatteras—that infamous "Graveyard of Ships"—have been giving up treasure for years. A cache of eighteenth-century gold and silver coins found near Nags Head, North Carolina, was worth just under a quarter of a million dollars to the lucky finder.

Along the shore at Brigantine, New Jersey, less than five years ago, a fisherman spotted a $100,000 cache of treasure that had been exposed by high winds; and farther down the New Jersey coast, in the area around Cape May, gold and silver coins are found with regularity.

Across the Delaware Bay, around Cape Henlopen, Lewes, Rehoboth, and Dewey Beach—an area that once provided a base of operations for numerous pirates—treasure hunters frequently find gold and silver coins from the long-sought treasure ship, *De Braak*, as well as from several other wrecks. One man in that area is said to have collected more than 1,000 gold and silver coins along the beaches.

Treasure hunting at the beach is booming. New finds are constantly discovered in Florida, North Carolina, and other shore areas. COURTESY OF WHITE'S ELECTRONICS, INC.

A stretch of shore below Ocean City, Maryland, has produced so much treasure that it is known locally as Money Beach, a name it shares with another piece of shoreline not far from Cape Charles, Virginia. The "Money Beach" designation almost always refers to a place where coins have been found and sometimes appears on state and local maps.

Not all this treasure washes ashore directly from sunken wrecks. Survivors of those wrecks often buried their valuables on the beaches. Bodies from the wrecks also washed ashore, or were buried there, sometimes along with jewelry and weapons. Near Cocoa Beach, Florida, one skeleton was found with a gold pendant around its neck, fingers covered with rings set with emeralds and diamonds, and a rotting leather pouch beside it that held gold Spanish coins minted two centuries ago.

Remember, too, that beaches once served as highways for travelers, who lost, discarded, or buried items as they went. Many early settlements were also near beaches; their remains are now eroded almost completely by wind, sand, and time. These can yield artifacts of great value.

There is also modern treasure that is constantly lost at public beaches. Skin shrivels and becomes slippery when one enters the water; rings and other jewelry are easily lost, and the beaches probably yield more jewelry than any other hunting grounds.

The point of all this: there are really no bad beaches on which to use a metal detector. Thousands and thousands of shoreline sites—including many on the Great Lakes—hold old and extremely valuable treasure; even where no treasure from the past turns up, modern coins and jewelry will be plentiful enough to amply reward your efforts.

There are still other reasons why the beaches are so popular among treasure hunters—they are rarely required to obtain permission from the government or anyone else before searching on them. Tourism is important in most coastal areas, and officials do not like to offend tourists by restricting their activities. The treasure hunter usually gets to keep all that he or she finds—which may not be the case in other treasure hunting situations. In Florida, for example, you can keep all the coins you find on a beach above the waterline, but if they are found in the water they fall victim to the salvage laws, and the state gets a hefty share. Beaches are also easy to reach, easy to walk, and fun.

Hunting modern coins and jewelry on the beaches is easy. Select a beach that is always crowded, and then move in when the people leave or early in the morning before they arrive. Remember that most beach towns and resort areas have clean-up crews, and you will have to beat those crews to the punch if you are to have any luck.

Check the areas around the refreshment stands or where people rent chairs, beach umbrellas, and other equipment. These spots will almost certainly turn up a handful of coins at the end of the day.

When working in soft beach sand, most treasure hunters prefer to use a screen scoop instead of a garden trowel. Most bait and tackle shops sell several kinds of scoops that are used for catching fishbait at the shore. With these you can sift large amounts of sand very quickly.

Low tide gives you the largest possible area to search, but the tides are subject to seasonal variations. Spring tides, which cause the greatest fall and rise of the water, occur just before and after a new moon—when the moon, sun, and earth are in closest alignment. The shrewdest treasure hunters keep track of these tides and plan to visit the beaches in accordance with them; they almost always result in the dunes above the beaches being cut down, sometimes exposing old hulks or even long-buried treasure caches. Tide tables are regularly published in coastal newspapers, or you can obtain a set of annual tide tables for either coast by sending $2 to the National Ocean Survey, Distribution Division, Riverdale, Maryland 20840.

Beer cans, pull-tabs, bottle caps, and bits of aluminum foil are the nuisances that plague the treasure hunter on beaches, so you will want your discriminator set to tune those objects out—or work with a great deal of patience.

One good way to locate potentially good spots is to go over old issues of local newspapers. Before treasure hunting on the beaches became so competitive, people who found gold coins were much more likely to publicize the find—and where currents have swept coins ashore in the past they are likely to do the same again. Ask local residents if they have seen objects from shipwrecks come ashore, or if they know where the partial remains of any hulks lie. Fishermen, local scuba divers, and surfers may also be good sources of information. There is one area on every beach where your chances are best: right where the waves break against the shore there is usually a pocket or trough. This is where shells, debris, coins, and other objects collect as the surf batters the beach. Just by screening the debris from this trough it is possible to locate coins and other treasure without using a metal detector, but experienced hunters take the detectors right into the trough. Caution is the rule here, for more than one treasure hunter has been swept out to sea while working these troughs. Never turn your back on the sea and allow a giant breaker to catch you in the water.

In a few instances, storms may also work against the treasure hunter. Unless the beach is in a cove or some other protected area, the level of sand keeps shifting as a result of the tides. More and more sand is deposited and coins become buried and difficult to detect. The most common effect of a storm is to carry away tons of sand and expose new levels holding wealth. But there are occasions when the pattern reverses itself and several feet of new sand may be dumped on the beaches. Always, of course, there is the possibility that more coins and other treasure may be carried in along with this sand, so the wake of a storm remains the very best time for treasure hunting.

Beachcombing, despite the minor nuisances of litter and bothersome insects, is probably the most pleasurable form of treasure hunting. And the odds are excellent if you stay with it long enough that you will one day find yourself looking at the brilliant beauty of a gold coin minted in the long-ago past—a coin that will certainly be worth at least as much as you paid for your detector and perhaps a great deal more.

Equipment and Skills Needed for Underwater Detection

The underwater search is not for everybody. It requires special equipment not used by the average treasure hunter, good health and stamina, and special training. But it opens new vistas to all those who love the excitement of treasure hunting, for the amount of treasure under dry land pales in comparison to that which lies underwater.

Until recently, the equipment needed for underwater detection was so expensive that only the professionals could afford to buy it and go after the enormous profits that can be made in underwater treasure hunting. But in the last few years, White's, J. W. Fisher, and Garrett Electronics, as well as other manufacturers, have introduced hand-held underwater detectors weighing less than 3 pounds and costing no more than other detectors or a good scuba outfit.

Constructed of heavy-duty plastic, these underwater detectors are about the size and shape of a megaphone. The diver uses a pistol grip to hold the device in front of him as he swims along the bottom with the search coil held parallel to the sand or mud. Audio signals are transmitted through earphones, although some units transmit visual signals by means of a flashing light or meter. Audio signals are preferable because visibility is not always good near the bottom.

Most of the underwater detectors currently available are of the beat-frequency oscillator (BFO) type, emitting a constant beepbeep sound that changes when metal is detected. They are operated much the same as the detectors used on dry land.

Exceptions to this are the models offered by J. W. Fisher, Anthony St., Taunton, MA 02780 which appears to be the leading manufacturer of underwater detectors. By utilizing some unique electronic circuitry, their devices are capable of detecting both ferrous and nonferrous metals, and may be used in either fresh or salt water.

These underwater detectors use solid search coils that are available in sizes as small as 11 inches or as large as 18 inches in diameter. They are capable of detecting a penny buried to a depth of 4 inches and large objects to depths of about 4 feet. Power is provided by a 9-volt battery system. The control box is a cylinder, with a meter for visual signals and earphone jacks for audio. Hand-held Fisher underwater detectors range in price from $149 to $285, while a larger model designed for towing behind a boat will set you back $528.

States Electronics Corporation, through its Bludworth Marine Division, 10 Adams Street, Linden, New Jersey 07036, distributes a sophisticated underwater detector capable of perceiving any kind of metal in fresh or salt water. This also works when the metal is buried in sand or mud or encrusted with coral. The strength of its response is based on the conductivity of the metal as well as the size of the object and its distance from the search coil. This detector is said to be capable of locating a silver dime buried under 12 inches of sediment, or larger pieces of metal, such as old cannons, at depths of 4 feet. It can be used by divers at depths of even 180 feet and sells for $1,475.

In going after sunken wrecks the basic tool is the magnetometer. By the time a diver locates a wreck, its wooden hulk has long since deteriorated into nothing, leaving behind only a few metal guideposts as evidence of its existence—weaponry, anchors, cannonballs, etc. These are almost always so coral encrusted that they are unrecognizable, and it may take the best metal detector to get a reading from them.

The magnetometer does not respond to gold coins but only to ferrous metals. It is an instrument that compares the intensity and direction of one magnetic field to another. It is adjusted to zero for the normal magnetic field of the region in which it is to be used. If the probe of the instrument is then passed over a site that holds iron—perhaps an anchor or a cluster of old cannonballs—the magnetic lines of force are disturbed, and the meter on the instrument makes the diver aware of the disturbance.

The magnetometer was developed during World War II, when it was towed suspended under a blimp and used to locate submerged enemy submarines. It was at first a large and complex device, requiring a team of technicians to operate it. For many years its cost was so prohibitive that most treasure hunters could only dream of having one— $16,000 to more than $50,000.

The magnetometer is no longer bulky nor difficult to operate. Modern ones are completely portable (often hand-held) and no more complex than a good metal detector. It has two basic components: a probe, which is usually a slim metal cylinder about 18 inches long and as thick as your forearm, and a control box linked to the probe by a submersible cable.

Cost is no longer totally beyond reach, though the magnetometer is admittedly an investment you will not want to make unless you are very serious about your treasure hunting. Prices of portable units start at $500 and range to well above $1,000. The devices are available from all the firms that manufacture underwater metal detectors.

Generally, the magnetometers are used in partnership with the underwater detectors. Most professional treasure hunters use the type of magnetometer that can be towed over the bottom behind and below a boat, thus allowing them to cover very large areas of bottom in short periods of time. The area being searched is marked off with buoys, to avoid going over it more than once. Iron, even small pieces that are deeply buried on the bottom, will register abruptly on the magnetometer—sometimes at a distance as great as 20 feet. When such a signal is received, scuba divers with hand-held metal detectors go below to investigate further.

Underwater treasure hunters are also using sound to locate sunken wrecks with sonic depth finders, also known as echo sounders. These send sound waves to the ocean floor, bouncing them back to be picked up by a receiver. The time lapse between the transmitted sound and the signal received translates into distance covered, or depth. Any variation in the interval means a variation in depth, which could be caused by a peak in the ocean floor, a reef of coral, a natural undulation, or the long-buried hull of a ship. Some of these sound devices report changes in depth on a moving roll of graph paper and do it so accurately that they can reproduce the silhouette of a ship or any other object on the ocean bottom.

Once too large and too expensive for all but professionals, these sound devices are now portable and in a price range that more amateurs can afford. One, called Scuba-Eye, is hand-held, and sells for $349.50. The manufacturer is Fishmaster Products, P.O. Box 9635, Tulsa, Oklahoma 74107.

Devices such as Scuba-Eye are especially useful where visibility is limited, as it often is in the murky waters of lakes and rivers. The instrument reports to the diver the distance between the bottom and the device itself, as well as the composition of the bottom—weeds, rocks, coral, or remains of a sunken wreck.

Rebounding sound waves are converted into visible readings on a brightly illuminated depth meter. Different types of bottom give off different signals. Even a school of passing fish can be distinguished. Experience is required to differentiate between the variety of signals and tell what is causing them, of course, but several users report the art is easily mastered.

Scuba-Eye will accurately scan bottoms at distances as great as 200 feet, which means that you don't necessarily have to be a diver to use it—it can be suspended over the side of a boat. But it works only when completely submerged.

When a treasure site is located—by whatever means—somebody is going to have to go in the water to investigate, confirm and recover the treasure. This means you must be schooled in, and conditioned for, scuba diving.

For an idea of what scuba diving involves, you might take a look at *The New Science of Skin and Scuba Diving,* which is the textbook used in most courses, including those offered by the YMCA. It is available at bookstores or can be ordered for $2.75 from the National Council of YMCAs, 291 Broadway, New York, New York 10017.

Researching and Locating a Site

Florida offers the greatest possibilities for striking it rich in underwater treasure. According to authorities at the Florida Board of Archives, between 1,200 and 2,000 sunken vessels lie in the relatively shallow waters within reasonable distance of the state's coastline. The Board has detailed information on several hundred of these, at least 250 of which are believed to have gone down with considerable quantities of gold and silver.

Certainly the coastal waters off Florida are not the only place worthwhile for underwater treasure hunting. Submerged wrecks are found all along the major shipping lanes of the United States. As many more can be found on the treacherous coral reefs of the Caribbean, if you're heading that way. The St. Lawrence River and the Great Lakes are known to hold at least 13,000 wrecks, perhaps 15,000. Nearly 1,000 sunken vessels lie off Cape Hatteras, including at least four Spanish galleons—one is known to have gone down in 1750 with a cargo of 400,000 pieces of eight. The waters off Hatteras are also the graveyard for dozens of Confederate blockade runners, many of which probably carried gold and silver due to a lack of trust in Confederate currency.

Picking a general area in which to search is no problem, but after that it becomes a little more complicated. The amount of research you do depends on how much time and money you have to spend, as well as on the size of the treasure you are after. It is safe to say you can never do too much—even after the wreck is located. For example, if it can be proved beyond a doubt that a coin or coins came from a specific wreck, historical interest will cause the numismatic value of that coin to soar. It is for this reason that coins recovered directly from sunken wrecks are usually worth far more than coins of the same mintage that wash up on beaches. Even after a wreck has been located, further research may be needed before the wreck can be identified, and you will certainly want to identify it and determine what it held before you go to the expense of a salvage operation.

Treasure Salvors, a major treasure hunting group, for example, maintains its own salaried historian in Seville, where the Casa de Contratación (the Spanish government agency that controlled all trade between Spain and the New World) was headquartered more than four centuries ago. Not only does this historian assist in the research that guides the group to treasure sites, but when the wreck is found, the first coins, bullion, or artifacts recovered are sent to him for evaluation and identification. His confirmation that the items came from a specific ship known to have gone down with worthwhile treasure is used by the group to attract investors willing to share the financial risk of raising the treasure—and the profits that follow.

You probably cannot afford the upkeep of your own Spanish historian, or even the cost of a trip to Spain, but you should be able to do the research that will put you hot on the trail of a specific ship known to hold treasure. Some of the books mentioned in the chapter on research will help, as will the ones listed in the appendix. The idea is to pick the general area in which you intend to search, find out what ships have gone down in that area, choose a specific one to go after, and then give it all you've got.

For ships that went down in fairly modern times, contemporary newspaper accounts can be a good starting point. Survivors may have mentioned the exact location of the wreck in those accounts, or you might be able to locate some survivors' descendants who can provide diaries or other firsthand accounts of the loss. Bear in mind that libraries in large cities often maintain bound or microfilm copies of major foreign newspapers, many dating back a century or more.

Always try to find some official report of the wreck. If it is a fairly recent one, try to obtain the ship's manifest, its listing of passengers and cargo. This may be available from the files of the shipping line, or from the agent at the port where the cargo was loaded. Check the records of the insurance company, if possible. These should describe the cargo and place a value on it. Lloyd's of London, through hundreds of brokers around the world, has insured many thousands of seagoing vessels. It has records dating back to 1838; all those prior to that were destroyed in a fire.

Naval archives usually contain detailed accounts of naval engagements; and when a naval vessel has been lost, for whatever reason, most navies either hold court-martial or board-of-inquiry proceedings, and records of those can be especially helpful.

Maps and charts that may be useful in your underwater search are available from the government for either coastal waters or the Great Lakes. These provide detailed information about the water's depth, the prevailing currents, the locations of reefs and shoals—and they also pinpoint the exact location of many sunken wrecks.

The best of these are available from the National Ocean Survey, which is part of the National Oceanic and Atmospheric Administration Oceanographic Office, Department of Navy, Washington, DC 20373. Some chart long stretches of coastal waters, while others devote themselves to tiny coves, bays, harbors, or inlets. To find out what is available obtain a catalog listing the charts for the region that interests you.

Charts for the Atlantic and Gulf Coasts of the United States, plus those for Puerto Rico and the Virgin Islands, are listed in Nautical Chart Catalog Number One. Nautical Chart Catalog Number Two lists charts for the U.S. Pacific Coast, Hawaii, Guam, and the Samoa Islands. The catalogs are free upon request from the National Ocean Survey,

Distribution Division, Riverdale, Maryland 20840.

The chart catalog for the Great Lakes and connecting waterways can be obtained by writing the National Ocean Survey, Lake Survey Center, 630 Federal Building, Detroit, Michigan 48226. Like the other catalogs it is free. In order to understand these charts and the symbols they use, you will need a pamphlet titled "Nautical Chart Symbols and Abbreviations." It costs 50¢ and can be ordered from any of the sources listed above.

The Library of Congress has some charts that may also be of great help. These are from a "Wreck Information List" compiled by the U.S. Naval Oceanographic Office during World War II. They show known wrecks in U.S. coastal waters. While the charts have been out of print for many years, photographic reproductions of sections are available. For detailed information on how to order, write to the Library of Congress, Washington, DC 20402.

You might also want to order from the Library of Congress, at a cost of 45¢, a bibliography titled *A Descriptive List of Treasure Maps and Charts*. This gives background information on treasure maps, books, atlases, and charts. It has long been a standard reference for diving treasure hunters, and when it was revised five years ago a great deal of new information was added.

If you have decided to go after a specific ship that went down after 1875 but prior to 1940, your starting point should be the National Archives and Records Service of the General Services Administration, Washington, DC 20408. If you can provide them with the name of the ship and the date and general area of the disaster that claimed it, they will conduct a search of their records and refer you to sources that may provide further information.

This same agency also compiles a summary of wreck data from various years, drawing on information from many different sources such as the Navy, Coast Guard, Merchant Marine, and even newspaper accounts. Copies cost $1 per page. The summary is called the *Reference Service Report*. Ask about it at the address provided above.

Photostats of wreck charts for the Great Lakes are available from the Cartographic Archives Division of the same agency. These were compiled by the U.S. Weather Bureau, and are available in three series covering the years 1886–91, 1893, and 1894.

Once you've done your research and finally dropped overboard to attempt to locate the wreck that holds your fortune, don't expect to see the sharp outline of the ship's hull and spars, unless the vessel went down recently. Marine creatures, especially the boring teredo worms, quickly do away with all exposed wooden parts of a vessel, and metal parts are rapidly covered by silt and, in warm waters, coral.

Look instead for the straight lines and symmetrical shapes that indicate the handiwork of man. If the ship went to the bottom in the nineteenth century or before, it would almost certainly have had cannons for its own protection, like all other merchant ships of that era. The straight, slowly tapering line of the cannon stands out even when covered by mud, silt, or coral and is the guidepost that most often leads a diver to treasure—and of course, the cannon can be treasure itself, if it is brass.

Underwater Salvage

Even in the preliminary search for an underwater wreck you will never be alone, because the first rule of underwater safety is that you always dive with a partner. But after the wreck has been located and the salvage operation begun, it is likely to seem downright crowded down there. Modern salvage is almost always a big operation. How big and how expensive depends on the nature of the wreck, the treasure it holds, and other factors.

In bringing up treasure that lies in less than 30 fathoms of water, the air lift is the device most frequently used. An air lift is very much like an underwater vacuum cleaner, so powerful that it can lift even coral-encrusted cannonballs. Most treasure recovery teams build their own because the parts are relatively inexpensive and the design simple.

The air lift conveys material upward from the bottom through a long metal tube or reinforced rubber hose, usually 6 inches or more in diameter. A second, smaller hose runs parallel to this one, creating suction by its attachment to an air compressor aboard the diving vessel. Compressed air coming down this smaller tube is sent into the larger tube at its lower end, creating a mixture of compressed air and water that has a much lower specific gravity than the water surrounding the tube. It is this difference that creates the powerful sucking that sends material rushing up to the diving vessel where it can be screened.

The lift is often used along with a water jet, a hose that is used to blast away sand, mud, and relatively thin layers of coral. But in tropical waters and on very old wrecks, where the coral may be several feet thick, special jackhammers and underwater chain saws may be needed to do the job. The recovery of *Concepción* is a recent instance in which such tools were needed. For small operations, a basket or net is suspended from a rope, filled by divers working the bottom, then hauled aboard the diving vessel and screened by the crew members.

A variation of this is far better. Inflatable pontoons are filled with water and sunk to the sea bottom. Objects to be raised are attached to the pontoons. The pontoons are inflated and rise to the surface, carrying the treasure with them. These also were used in recovering the treasure of *Concepción*. Oil drums can be used in this fashion, with half a dozen 50-gallon drums, when pumped full of air, capable of lifting about a ton of debris.

Salvage operations can become expensive, lamentably expensive. Costs typically run into the thousands, even hundreds of thousands, of dollars. One major treasure recovery firm has said that it cannot afford to undertake a salvage operation unless the treasure is worth $10 million! Before allowing you to salvage a ship of historical significance, authorities in most areas will probably require that a trained marine archaeologist participate in the recovery operation.

To go after a sunken treasure of real size, you obviously are going to need financial backers. This is why careful research and documentation is so important, even after the site is located. Gone are the days when the only treasure hunters were wind-burned adventurers with pirate blood flowing in their veins and a gold earring in the lobe of one ear. The treasure hunter of today is just as likely to wear a Brooks Brothers suit and have an office on Wall Street. Not only are you going to have to convince him that the wreck exists and you have found it, but also that it holds enough treasure to give him and other backers a fair return on the money they invest. The only way to do this is to provide all the documentation possible—legends and folklore just won't serve when dealing with bankers and brokers.

Even then, getting them to listen to you might be a problem. But Mel Fisher, founder of Treasure Salvors, and a man who has recovered treasure worth millions, used a little trick during his early days, when money was a problem, that is almost guaranteed to get you a fair hearing before any investor. Fisher would set up a meeting, walk into the investor's office, then reach into his pockets and start covering the money man's desk with gold and silver coins, including a 7-pound gold disk he held on to for just that purpose.

It worked for Mel Fisher. It may work for you.

5

Coins and
Coin Shooting

More than $115 million in coins are lost each year according to an article in *Wheels Afield* magazine. To those who regularly practice coin shooting—by far the most popular type of treasure hunting—the $115 million estimate would probably seem low.

According to Charles Garrett, owner of Garrett Electronics and a man who has been deeply involved in treasure hunting throughout the full period of its enormous growth in popularity, at least 65 percent of all metal detector buyers use their instruments primarily for this purpose. Those who practice coin hunting on a regular basis should, according to Garrett, find about 5,000 coins per year, with a face value of $250 and a numismatic value far above that—more than enough to pay for a very good metal detector. These figures are based on regular weekend use of the detector, with an average weekend yielding about 100 coins. After a reasonable amount of practice with the detector, most treasure hunters reach a point where finding 200 coins per day is considered a good average, and many do far better.

Kay Modgling, a retired nurse in southern California, is a good example; she was more than a little bit dubious about finding coins when she first took up the sport.

"I'd had a heart attack and as I was recuperating, the doctor told me to get out and walk slowly," she recalls now. "I was bored to tears until I got my first metal detector."

Her boredom soon ended. During the first four years she owned her detector, while using it about eight hours a week, Kay Modgling found more than 82,500 coins and about 1,000 rings. Some coins dated back to the early 1800s, and the rings included one worth $7,500. In a single hour she has found more than 250 coins, including a valuable $5 gold piece. She has used all this treasure to finance several treasure hunting vacations, even one that took her from California to the East Coast, and she has made all those trips in a new Pinto she bought with the money she earned treasure hunting.

"If someone had told me years ago that I'd be metal detecting in parks, digging around old buildings, and searching pre-turn-of-the-century dumps, I wouldn't have believed it," says this one-woman recovery squad. "It just wasn't like me. I was even afraid to go camping. But now, next to my family, treasure hunting is the most important thing in my life."

Like Kay Modgling, many folks take up this sport for the mild form of healthful exercise it offers and are content to quietly go about adding a few coins to their own collection. But always, in the back of the mind, there is the knowledge that the next "bleep!" of the detector could be caused by a coin or coins worth many thousands of dollars.

That is precisely what happened with George Banks, an electrician for the Potlatch Corporation in Lewiston, Idaho. Banks had been using his metal detector just four years when he took it with him on a vacation to the nearby state of Washington. While using it to go over the grounds of a long-abandoned racetrack, he came up with his first gold coin, a $20 piece minted in 1855 by the private firm of Blake and Agnell. Only two others like it are known to exist, one owned by the Ford Foundation, the other held by the Smithsonian Institution. The coin is worth $300,000! An isolated incident? Certainly. But similar incidents—although usually on a smaller scale—occur often enough to make coin shooting one of the most fascinating and profitable types of treasure hunting.

The Where and How of Coin Shooting

The question most frequently asked by new coin shooters is what kind of coins can I expect to find? No matter how long you stay with this sport, and no matter how experienced you become, the penny is the coin you are going to find with greatest frequency. The reason for this is that the lower the value of the coin, the greater the number minted. The greater the number minted, the more that are available to lose. But there is another reason almost as important. When a person drops a larger coin—a quarter or half dollar, for example—it doesn't get hidden in the grass or dirt as easily as a smaller coin. When a larger coin does become lost, its owner is much more likely to get down on his hands and knees and spend a little time looking for it.

There is also a sound scientific reason why a large percentage of the coins you find will be pennies. Copper is the least stable metal used in the minting of coins. If a penny drops in wet or damp soil, it begins to corrode almost immediately. The wetter the soil the faster the corrosive action. As this corrosion takes place over a period of time, the soil surrounding the penny becomes saturated with copper salts and creates a large area that will cause a signal when the search coil of a metal detector passes over it. A penny that has been buried for a long time in damp ground therefore gives off a signal that is at least as strong as that caused by a half dollar buried to the same depth.

Gold coins are not subject to such corrosion. Even though buried for a century or more, a gold coin usually remains bright and shiny, with engraving that stands out in bold relief. Gold coins found on beaches, however, may be badly scoured by the abrasive action of waves and sand that, of course, also erodes all other types of coins.

If buried in a dry place, silver coins are likely to retain at least some of their brilliance. But when exposed to dampness or soil with a very high mineral content, silver coins are more apt to be badly tarnished and corroded. Many a beginner has passed over a blackened disk on the beach without realizing it was a badly tarnished coin made of silver.

The kinds of coins you find also depend on where and how you hunt. If you concentrate on slowly, carefully, and thoroughly searching the ruins of abandoned houses or ghost towns, for example, you are almost certainly going to find fewer coins than if you search crowded parks and beaches—but the odds of finding old coins at the former sites are better than at the latter.

On the whole, however, you will find this sport far more enjoyable if you are realistic with yourself about what you can expect to find—and that does mean a high percentage of pennies among the coins you collect. A treasure hunting club in Ohio kept a careful tabulation of all the coins found by its members over a period of years and developed a statistical breakdown. Out of each hundred coins recovered, 72 were pennies, 13 were dimes, 10 were nickels, 4 were quarters, and the last was a half dollar.

The kind of coins you find will also be determined, in part, by the search coil you use. With only a few exceptions (such as old coins that wash up on beaches), the newer coins are closer to the surface and so will be found more easily.

Which brings us to the second question frequently asked by beginners: how deeply will a detector find coins? This is a complex question, the answer depending not only on the quality of the detector and your skill in operating it, but on other factors as well. A major factor is how the coin happens to be resting in the ground.

When a coin drops to the ground it can either become deeply buried or remain right on the surface. How deeply it becomes buried is determined by many things—the amount of sand and dirt that blows over the area, the quantity of rainfall, the amount of foot traffic by people and animals, and even the normal, natural settling caused by the weight of the coin.

Most coins, as they settle and become covered, remain nearly parallel to the surface of the ground. This is fortunate for the treasure hunter, because *all* metal detectors are surface area detectors and will produce a greater signal if the coin is flat than if it is lying at an angle or standing on edge. You can prove this by conducting a simple test with your own detector.

A coin is detected on the basis of its surface area. The larger the physical size of the coin, the more deeply it can be detected under most conditions.

How deeply a coin can be detected also depends to a great extent on how long it has been buried, for newly buried metal of any kind cannot be detected as readily as metal objects that have been buried at least one year. Generally, the greater the length of time metallic objects have been buried the deeper they can be detected. This is especially true of copper, lead, zinc, nickel, and silver. But the detectability of gold increases only during the first year or so it is buried, then levels off and remains approximately the same.

How deeply a coin can be detected also depends on the size of the search coil and on the metal detector itself. A search coil of 8 inches in diameter has long been standard in coin hunting, and with a coil of this size you should be able to easily detect newly buried coins at a depth of 4 inches or so, reaching down to about twice that depth for larger coins or for ones that have been buried at least a year.

Wet weather will also help you to detect coins at slightly greater depths. Damp ground causes the detector to transmit its signals with greater than normal facility, not only reaching the deeper coins but obtaining stronger responses from those closer to the surface. For this reason, you will see many coin shooters working in damp or even rainy weather. If you plan to work in rainy weather and your search coil is not waterproof, simply enclose the coil in a polyethylene bag held in place with a rubber band. This will have no effect on the signals.

Any type of detector can be used for coin hunting by a person who really understands its operation. But as I have mentioned, the transmitter receiver (TR) detector, because of its faster response, has long been favored over the beat frequency oscillator (BFO) for use in this type of treasure hunting. For example, when using a BFO detector, the slowness of its response makes it all too easy to pass over a coin standing on edge.

The introduction of the new very low frequency transmitter receiver detectors has caused the TR detectors to lose their favored position among coin hunters. These VLF-TR detectors not only offer fast response coupled with the ability to tune out ground minerals, but will also detect a coin at far greater depths than the older detectors. In doing comparison tests, I found that when using a quality VLF-TR detector, a buried coin could be perceived at depths almost twice as great as with the other detectors. One disadvantage in using the VLF-TR type for coin hunting is that it also detects all other small bits of metal, such as nails, at greater depths, but these can be avoided by using an instrument with the discriminator feature and tuning them out.

When using the discriminator feature on any detector for hunting, however, it is best *not* to use the setting that tunes out the troublesome pull-tabs from soda and beer cans. If these are tuned out, the detector will also pass over nickels, costume jewelry, campaign buttons, and metal tokens, which means you could miss out on some items that you really want for your collection. Even a ring holding a diamond or another precious stone, if the mounting has a low enough content in precious metal, could be passed over with the discriminator on this setting. Digging those pull-tabs from the ground can be a real headache, but it is better than passing over items of real value. You will be able to recognize the difference in signal strength with experience and no longer need to waste time on those scraps of aluminum.

When using the detector over ground that is relatively free of minerals, hold the search coil approximately 1 inch above the ground. Adjust the tuning control according to the manufacturer's instructions until a slight sound is heard in the speaker. Scan from side to side or move the search coil in a straight line in front of you, while holding the coil at the same level above the ground. If the speaker sound remains fairly steady, the ground is relatively free of minerals and you can operate at this optimum setting. If you encounter mineral interference, however, you will have to adjust the detector to operate without sound or try using the scrub method of searching.

To employ this method, you place the search coil in direct contact with the ground, adjust the audio to operate so that sound is emitted only when a coin or other metal is under the search coil, and then slide the search coil over the ground in front of you. When you operate with the coil in direct contact with the ground, you achieve greater depth penetration and also avoid much of the interference from large above-ground metallic objects such as swings and slides on parks and playgrounds. The biggest problem with this type of silent searching is that the detector will need to be retuned almost constantly. With some of the newer and better models, however, the push of a button is all that is needed to retune, and so this is no problem. When using the scrub technique you should also protect the search coil by using a cover; these expensive coils can be worn out with surprising speed, especially when used on beach sand or rough terrain.

If among your family and friends or the members of your treasure hunting group there is both a standard TR detector and a detector that discriminates, you can team up to employ a technique that allows you to quickly search any area to its maximum depth while leaving virtually all of the trash behind.

Carry with you a few dozen nonmetallic markers—golf tees, poker chips, or whatever. Have one treasure hunter move ahead with the TR detector and a handful of the markers, marking the spot each time a signal is received. The other treasure hunter, with his detector tuned to discriminate, then comes along and "reads" each of these locations. If the indicator shows the signal was caused by trash, just remove the marker. After the area has been swept by both detectors, you then go back to the remaining markers and start your digging. The discriminator may misread a few objects and cause you to dig up some junk, but most teams who use it report that it greatly reduces wasted time while increasing their returns.

When using the scrub technique described above, you will encounter interference if you move the detector very, very close to large metal objects. Few treasure hunters have taken the time and trouble to learn how to tune out this interference—yet the areas around swings, slides, and similar objects are the very places that are likely to hold a large number of lost coins. If you will take a few minutes to master the technique, you will be able to double or triple your profits by going over the spots that must be avoided by those treasure hunters who do not know the method.

Rings, coins, and other valuable items at Daytona Beach, Florida. COURTESY OF
WHITE'S ELECTRONICS, INC.

Follow the normal search procedure until the detector begins to
respond to the metal object, which will surely happen as you move very
close to it. When the interference begins, you can do one of two things.
If the interference is caused by a fence, truck, trailer, or other long
metal object, turn the detector so that the search coil is parallel to the
line of metal. The detector should then begin to give a uniform signal,
which will rise sharply as buried metal is encountered. This takes some
practice to master, but it is the best way to overcome the interference
caused by great lengths of metal.

When it becomes necessary to search within just a few inches of
interfering metal, adjust the detector down until only the faintest sound
is emitted. Again, try scanning while holding the search coil parallel to
the nearest line of the interference-causing metal, listening for the
faintest change in the signal. This technique takes a great deal of practice to master, but learning it could result in a real bonanza in coins.

As you begin coin hunting in parks, playgrounds, and other places
where people congregate, you will quickly learn that within these areas
there are certain hot spots—areas that gather more coins than any
other. The areas around picnic tables, swings, bleachers, and vending
machines are the obvious ones.

The best way to locate the hot spots in any given area is to drive by and look it over during the time when the crowds are heaviest. Just try to pick out the spots that seem to attract people in the greatest numbers. Often people will gather where you might least expect. By locating the spots that hold attraction for people, you can almost assure yourself of success when you return during a quiet period to do your coin hunting.

Trees, especially the very old ones, will almost always be the sign of good hunting ground. Not only do people picnic on the shady ground beneath them, and not only do youngsters sometimes climb among their branches, but this shady ground often serves as a dining spot for workmen on their lunch break. There is something about settling down in the shade of an old tree that produces a temptation to remove one's coat or jacket. Writers for *Treasure* magazine once attempted to see if a spill pattern existed beneath such trees—to learn if more coins were lost under certain parts of the branches than under others. They began by choosing a tree that looked as if it might be worth searching around, then used twine and stakes to mark off a rectangular grid of 15 by 30 feet. This was divided into columns and rows, thus establishing fifty 3-foot squares. One square at a time was methodically searched, the treasure hunters digging each time a signal was received (even when the signal was quite obviously caused by a pull-tab or other junk). Each find, not including the junk, was carefully marked on a chart corresponding to the grid laid out beneath the tree. A very definite pattern began to emerge.

The day yielded a total of 149 coins, 1 pink shell cameo ring, and 685 pull-tabs. The ring was valued at $100. The coins included 116 Lincoln wheatback pennies dated 1920 to 1957; 10 Lincoln Memorial cents dated 1959 to 1973; 3 Jefferson nickels dated 1946 to 1972; 5 Mercury dimes dated 1925 to 1943; 1 Roosevelt dime dated 1963; 3 Washington silver quarters dated 1940 to 1944; and 1 Washington quarter bearing a 1973 date.

The grid pattern was surprising. It might be expected that the ground very close to the trunk of the tree would yield the greatest number of coins, but this was far from the case. Almost 75 percent of the coins were found in the squares between 10 and 15 feet away from the trunk. Of course, it is evident that the conditions which created the pattern under this tree would apply only to that particular tree—which was frequented by high school students taking their lunch break—but the results of this experiment are interesting and worth keeping in mind. By making careful observations or by keeping adequate records, you can establish the spill pattern under trees in the places you search.

In searching over public places with heavy traffic, you should also remember that junk can be your best friend. It is a sad fact that many treasure hunters buy the best detectors made, then never learn to use them properly, and therefore have to avoid all places that hold a lot of trash. By becoming thoroughly acquainted with a good detector and learning the use of its discriminator, you will be able to take any number of coins from the trash-cluttered areas that less experienced treasure hunters must avoid.

A good way to start searching around these trashy areas is to use the smallest search coil possible. Look for the little nooks and crannies that are not obviously cluttered with foil, pull-tabs, bottle caps, and other trash. Search around the perimeter of the trashy areas. The very small coil will make it easier for you to isolate the coins from the trash. You should also remember that lost coins are sometimes concealed under trash. Robert Marrs, a coin shooter in southwestern Ohio, had been visiting an old amusement park for several years with his detector before this fact was drawn to his attention. One spot there always yielded several coins, but the spot also held a great deal of trash.

"There was this flattened tin can that I had detected, I guess, at least fifty times. I knew what it was by the strong 'trash' reading I always got when I passed over it, so I never bothered digging it up. Then one day—and I still couldn't tell you why—I just decided to dig the darned thing up and be rid of it for good," he recalls. "I passed the detector over the hole after the can was out, got another reading—and dug out the first gold coin I'd ever found."

In public areas that attract many other coin hunters, bushy spots can often be productive. Most coin shooters probe around the edges of bushes and shrubs, but few take the time and trouble to search carefully beneath heavy foliage. Keep in mind that a bush may not have been there a few years ago, and search beneath every bit of it you can reach. Treat it like virgin territory—that is what it is likely to be. Areas adjacent to roads may also be untouched. Coin hunters seldom seem to touch them because they are bothered by traffic noises, embarrassed to be seen by those in passing cars, or perhaps because these areas often contain so much litter. The few who do work these areas report excellent results.

The most successful coin hunting of all is being done *in* the water at public swimming areas and beaches, though it is being done by only a small percentage of coin hunters. The special techniques for doing this on ocean beaches are described in Chapter Four, but here I am talking about searching the bottom in shallow lakes, swimming holes, and other popular spots that can be found all across America.

You must have a detector with completely submersible search coils, preferably one that allows the control box to be remotely mounted. One of the new lightweight underwater detectors designed for use by scuba divers would be even better. For retrieving coins and jewelry from the bottom you will need a long-handled scoop of some sort, with holes drilled to let the water pour out.

Why is this type of coin hunting so worthwhile? Well, not only do people lose coins in the water or at the water's edge, but young lovers and others toss them in for good luck. When we humans are in water for any length of time, our fingers pucker and shrivel, becoming slippery and making it very easy for us to lose our jewelry. Even when we remove this jewelry and leave it ashore for safekeeping, it has an uncanny knack of finding its way into the water—and treasure hunters like Allan Darby, a young schoolteacher from Delaware, are really cashing in on this bonanza.

In the summer of 1978, with his former college roommate Dave Thompson, Darby set out on a trip he had been dreaming about for years: a treasure hunting trip through several Southern states, concentrating on retrieving coins and jewelry from swimming areas.

At their first stop, in Florida, they managed to choose an area that had almost certainly been searched recently, for several hours of searching turned up only a few coins. Then, just as they were about to give up and move on, Thompson came up with a diamond ring worth about $400, and a Mexican $20 gold piece worth at least that much.

At a private swimming lake in Alabama they were given permission to search for a single day. Their finds were amazing.

"Upon entering the water our metal detectors never ceased bleeping," says Darby. "We worked that area, off and on, for the whole day. We found one hundred sixteen rings, fifty-six of them gold or silver, two with diamonds. Our coin total had a face value of eighty-six dollars, about half in fairly old coins. We also found a pretty good assortment of medals, watches, and bracelets."

By the time the trip ended the duo had collected boxes of coins, hundreds of rings and bracelets, and diamonds that, alone, had a value in excess of $2,000. The face value of the coins far exceeded the cost of their metal detectors.

Not all coin hunting is done in public places such as these. Coins are where you find them. Some coin hunters find them in the most unexpected places, such as in the bindings of old books offered for sale at flea markets, or secreted in hollow doors in old houses, which, it seems, once served as the bank for many families. But most coin hunting is done on soil of some sort, which means there are two things you must be able to do: dig without doing permanent damage to the soil, and dig without harming the coins.

Recovering Coins

Once you are fairly sure that you have detected a buried coin, get it out of the ground with the least possible effort and damage to soil or coin. If you damage someone's lawn, you can say good-bye to that treasure hunting spot, and if you damage the coin, you can say good-bye to at least part of any numismatic value it might have.

No matter what type of soil you are searching, the first step is to pinpoint exactly where the coin lies. Go over the area with the search coil several times until you are sure of the exact location of the coin. The procedure you follow next depends largely on the type of earth in which the coin is found.

In loose beach sand, recovery is the easiest of all, but there are a few techniques that will speed up coin recovery. Most coin hunters who work these areas use a small trowel and a sifter. If the sand is loose and fine, the coin can be recovered just by passing a scoop of sand through the sifter. When working nearer the water's edge, where the sand is likely to be wet and packed, the trowel can be inserted into the sand, twisted, and the coin brought up in a plug. In these sandy areas, it is easy to extract a coin without damaging it, and nature quickly covers the signs of your digging. But in other types of earth you must be a little more cautious.

After a coin has been pinpointed in a grassy area, you can use a heavy knife or bayonet, thrust about 3 inches into the ground, to cut a half-circle around it. Fold the turf back. If the coin is not in the part of the turf that has been folded back, cut a second and deeper plug, making sure the loose dirt falls back in the hole. Throughout this process, you must be cautiously feeling for the coin with the knife, easing off if contact is made, so as not to damage the coin. After the coin has been extracted, fold the sod back into place and step on it. Cutting just a half-circle in tall grass, according to those who use this method, assures that it will not be killed.

Others cut a full plug. Use a hunting knife with a blade at least 7 inches long. Place the tip of the blade about 2 inches to one side of the detected coin, then insert the knife gently the full length of the blade. With the knife slanting slightly inward, cut a full circle, so that a cone-shaped plug with the point on the bottom is formed. Run the search coil over the plug to determine if it holds the coin or if the coin is still in the ground. If the coin is in the plug, carefully knock the dirt from the plug back into the hole until the coin is located. Then replace the rest of the plug and stomp it down. Cutting a plug of this size does no harm to most types of grass.

But on very smooth lawns, even these methods may be too destructive—or at least the owner of the lawn may expect them to be and not allow you to use them. For coin hunting in these areas you should learn some of the more delicate techniques.

One coin hunter has become a master at recovering coins from these areas using only a screwdriver. After pinpointing the coin with the detector, he pushes the screwdriver into the ground at an angle of about 45 degrees, sliding it in about 2 inches behind the coin and to a depth of about 5 inches. With the screwdriver thus inserted, he makes a slit of 3 to 5 inches in the ground by pushing forward and to the left. He returns the screwdriver to its original position, then makes another slit of equal length by shoving forward and to the right. These two slits form a V-shaped piece of sod which, with a slight tug forward and a gentle rotation, can be eased from the ground. After the coin has been extracted, the piece of sod falls easily back into the spot from which it came. According to the coin hunter who showed me this method of coin extraction, he uses it because most park caretakers would much rather see a treasure hunter with a screwdriver than with a knife or any other digging instrument.

For extracting coins from those manicured lawns where you will not be permitted to cut a plug or leave a noticeable mark of any kind, you should master the technique suggested by Charles Garrett. It is a little slower than other methods, but it gets the job done, he says, and allows you to take coins from places that might otherwise be off-limits. In addition to the screwdriver, this technique requires an ice pick or similar tool with which you gently probe down until the coin is felt.

After you have located the coin with the probe, insert a long screwdriver about an inch or two out from the probe to a depth that places its tip just below the probe and the coin. Remove the probe, then gently lever the coin up to the surface with the tip of the screwdriver. Garrett says that in some types of soil—but only in some—the coin is easier to remove if the tip of the screwdriver is slightly bent to form a small scoop; this suggests that perhaps you should carry two screwdrivers, one with the bent tip, one without. Be careful.

Cleaning and Storing Coins

You should treat any recovered coin as if it is the most valuable you will ever find, until you learn otherwise. Too many treasure hunters, in their haste to remove corrosion and see a coin in all its shining brilliance, have destroyed any value the coin or coins might have had.

As a general rule, coins found buried in soil are in a much better state of preservation than those found in the sea. The condition in which they are found depends not only on the purity of the metal from which they have been made, but also on the mineral content of the soil, sand, or mud in which they were buried. Even those in the very best condition usually require a certain amount of proper cleaning.

Most gold coins, including those washed up from the sea, will be found in excellent condition, almost as dazzling to your eyes as the day they were minted. But when they have rested in close proximity to iron, gold coins may be covered with a thin coating of iron oxide. Such a coating can be removed with a very light rubbing of baking soda and fresh water. Remember that gold is a very soft metal, and about the worst thing you can do to a gold coin is to clean away any dirt or encrustation by scraping it away with a knife or removing it with some highly abrasive material.

The condition of silver coins found on beaches depends on several factors. Those resting under water will usually have been protected from corrosion by electrolysis, especially if they have been in close proximity to other metals, including coins of the same metal. But in many instances, where an isolated bit of silver has not been protected by electrolysis, a silver coin will be converted to silver sulfide, leaving only a thin sliver of the original metal inside a thick and almost weightless wafer. Coins with a very high content of silver are, unfortunately, the ones most likely to be found in this very poor condition. However, even those made of pure silver are sometimes preserved by the occurrence of certain minerals, such as bauxite, in the muddy bottoms, and may be found in mint condition. Silver coins that contain copper and other base metals—which means most of those you are going to find—will usually be in a far better state of preservation.

Copper or brass coins are affected little by contact with salt water. Most found along the beaches are covered only by a thin green patina or perhaps a layer of coral growth, both of which are easily removed. All coins found in soil can be cleaned by the methods which follow.

One easy way of removing corrosion and discoloration is with a solution of one teaspoon of white vinegar mixed with one-half teaspoon of table salt. Cover the surface of the coin with this solution for not more than one minute, then very gently rub the surface of the coin with a pencil eraser. Badly corroded coins may require two or three treatments to remove all the corrosion. After the corrosion is removed, a gentle coating of silver polish will bring it back to its original brilliance.

You might also try one of the special chemicals made for cleaning coins. One that has been widely used and found to be quick, safe, and inexpensive is Super Coin Clean, a powder that you mix with water to form a solution that removes all dirt, patina, and corrosion from silver, nickel, and copper coins. It is found at most coin shops or can be ordered for $2.95 from the Gem and Treasure Hunting Association, 1493 San Diego Avenue, San Diego, California 92110.

Coin shops also offer several types of electronic devices for cleaning coins. These cost a good deal more initially, but they are extremely efficient and are being widely used by treasure hunters and serious coin collectors. With these devices, nearly all coins, no matter how badly corroded when found, can be brought back to a shininess approaching mint condition. Probably the most popular of these is the Koin-Kleen, manufactured by D-Tex Electronics (see page 19).

Like all the coin-cleaning devices on the market, the Koin-Kleen is basically an electrolysis bath, which reverses the process used in electroplating of metals. It uses standard household current and a bath made of harmless ingredients. A current passes through the bath—in which the coins are placed—and the negative electrons simply eat away all foreign matter that is attached to the coins. Most coins come clean in a matter of minutes. The jewelry you find can also be cleaned by this method, and any gemstones in that jewelry can be safely immersed in the bath.

After your coins have been cleaned you should continue to treat them with care to assure that they do not get scratches or abrasive marks that will reduce their value. Store those that are worth saving in individual coin envelopes, preferably made of cellophane. The individual envelopes should then be placed in special paper coin envelopes or boxes, such as those sold by coin dealers. Store these in a dry place—preferably a bank safe deposit box if you have been lucky and the coins are valuable.

Establishing Coin Values

According to the American Numismatic Association, the number of coin collectors in this country has more than tripled since 1970. Since there is no way that more old coins can be made available to meet this increased demand, the demand creates a shortage that keeps prices moving upward. Now and then, coin prices may go into a brief decline, when some large dealer or collector releases large numbers of a certain date or type into the marketplace, but aside from those brief lapses most coins have been annually doubling in value.

This is especially true of gold coins, the ones most eagerly sought by collectors. As late as 1955, most Spanish colonial doubloons were selling for less than $1,000; many were bringing as little as $100. Today these same coins range in price from $1,500 to as much as $50,000, depending on factors that will be explained later in this chapter. One could fill pages with examples of the rising value of gold coins. Yet it is not only the gold coins that are rising so swiftly in value. In the year 1955, for example, the rare Mexican mint 1724 silver eight real was selling for about $500, but by 1975 the same coin was bringing more than $30,000 at auctions. It is worth much more now. Prices paid for other silver coins have kept pace, with a 1794 silver dollar recently bringing $110,000, a 1792 silver cent, $105,000, and an 1894-S dime with raised edge fetching $75,000. Continental dollars made of pewter often bring bids in excess of $25,000.

Any coin made of silver, no matter what its date and condition, can presently be sold for at least nine times its face value. But to do so would be a mistake, for the metal content of a coin has little to do with the price it may possibly bring in the numismatic marketplace.

The two main factors that determine the worth of almost any given coin are its rarity and condition. The rarity depends on many things, including the total number originally minted, the number lost through the normal attrition of years of circulation, and the interest the coin holds for collectors. As an example of how the last can create rarity in a coin, look at the Bicentennial year of 1976: a pewter coin minted in 1776—which ten years before had sold for $350—brought $25,000 at auction.

More often, however, rarity has existed since the year the coin was minted. There are literally thousands of coins in the world that were originally minted in very small quantities—often fewer than 100 of the particular type were struck—and these coins are so prized that almost any one of them can make you wealthy.

In some other instances, coins have become extremely rare and valuable when a complete issue is lost before any have a chance to get into general circulation. The most famous example of this occurred when, in 1733, a fleet of twenty-one Spanish galleons went down off the coast of Florida, taking with it the entire issue of a silver dollar that had been minted in Mexico City that year. The ships have never been found, but many of the coins have been picked up by treasure hunters using detectors on Florida beaches—and they have been selling for well over $15,000 each.

Now and then, the government takes a common coin and makes it rare. This happens when coins are recalled from circulation, melted down, and then the metal is used in the minting of new coins. The most striking example of this occurred right after World War I, when the U.S. mints recalled and melted down more than 270 million of the highly unpopular 1895-P Morgan silver dollar but missed a single coin and made it among the most valuable coins in existence.

The matter of the coin's age is important, too, from a numismatic standpoint, but it has far less significance than most people believe. This is especially true of coins minted in this century, which will account for the majority of the coins you find with your detector. Between the years 1939 and 1955, for example, the lowest mintage nickel was produced in 1955, a fact that makes this nickel worth far more than those produced in other years of the era. The same is true of the 1955 dime; fewer of it were minted than any other in the Roosevelt series, thus it is by far the most valuable.

If the coin was minted in this country, you can easily find out how many of its type were struck by checking the *Handbook of United States Coins,* an annual publication that is available at all coin shops and most bookstores. More commonly called the Blue Book, it not only provides year-by-year mintage figures for each coin, but also lists the average amount dealers are paying for each. But remember, these are the prices dealers are *paying.*

To find out what dealers are *charging* for the same coins, which may be a better way to determine the real worth of any coins you find, you should check *A Guidebook to United States Coins,* or, as it is better known, the Red Book. It too can be found at most bookstores and all coin shops. Most coin shooters consider these books essential equipment.

But no matter how rare a coin may be, its value is going to be greatly affected by its condition, and determining the condition of a coin is very much a subjective matter. Numismatic dealers use eight different categories in describing coin quality, and often this is a source of disagreement between dealer and collector. What looks "very good" to you may be regarded as merely "good" or just "fair" by a dealer.

These are the coin classifications, which you will want to know before you sell any coins:

Proof • Coins specially made to be sold by the mint directly to collectors and dealers. These have a flawless surface and mirrorlike sheen, and all the design features are extremely sharp in detail. Since the chances of a treasure hunter finding a coin or coins in this condition are almost nonexistent, this category is mentioned only for clarification, not as one of the eight categories you must consider in establishing the value of coins you find with your detector.

Uncirculated • Coins that are in the same condition as when they left the mint. Since such coins may vary somewhat, they are also known as being brilliant, dull, or tarnished. But they always must be without foreign marks of any kind, and they must not have been cleaned in any manner.

Extremely fine • These coins show only the faintest evidence that they have ever been in circulation. They have only the slightest traces of wear on the highest points of the design and retain at least some of the mint luster.

Very fine • These coins retain their sharp features of design and show only slightly more evidence of wear than coins in extremely fine condition, though they are usually not as brilliant in color.

Fine • Coins that remain sharp but are slightly more worn than those in very fine condition. Their overall appearance is the most important consideration, and this is the lowest grade that is considered desirable by those who buy coins for investment purposes.

Very good • These coins are clear in detail but not as sharply defined as coins in fine condition, and the lettering remains visible, as well as the date, if the coin was originally dated.

Good • Coins that must have all lettering and digits visible and readable, but the features can be more worn than on very good coins.

Fair • These coins are readily identifiable as to date, type, and series, but on which all the lettering and digits may not be visible to the naked eye. A coin mutilated by deep marks or scratches would also fit in this classification.

Poor • These coins are usually of no value to collectors because they are badly bent, mutilated, or corroded, or because they are unidentifiable.

Such classifications are also used to establish the value of foreign coins and of coins privately minted in this country, but establishing the rarity and thus the real value of these coins often requires more work. For example, many of the Spanish coins minted in Mexico bore no date but were stamped with a crude likeness of the currently reigning monarch or with the royal crest; the date of such a coin is usually established by identifying the monarch or crest and learning when he or she reigned. For help in identifying most foreign coins and establishing their value, most collectors rely on the *Coin World Almanac*, which is printed by Amos Press of Sidney, Ohio, and can be found at most coin shops.

Coin dealers are in business to make a profit, and all too many of them tend to do this by offering to the seller a price that is only a fraction of the real value of the coin. The worst mistake made by beginners is rushing out to a coin shop and accepting the first offer made by a dealer. One treasure hunter tells of being offered $10 for a coin that eventually brought $700, and another describes the time he was offered $500 for a doubloon that finally sold for $17,500.

Whenever you find a coin that appears to have real value, you should send a clear photograph of both sides of the coin to the American Numismatic Association, P.O. Box 2366, Colorado Springs, Colorado 80901. This prestigious group was founded in 1891 and now has more than 30,000 members. The group welcomes as members all who have an interest in collecting or studying coins, paper money, tokens, medals, and related items, and upon receipt of your photographs, they will put you in contact with a person or group who will advise you of the coin's worth and the best way of obtaining full value.

To get the full value of your coin, you will almost certainly need to have it appraised by an expert—and not just any coin expert, but one who specializes in your type of coin. The great new interest in coin collecting and the subsequent high prices being paid for coins have caused so much counterfeiting of old and rare coins that many dealers and collectors will not even examine specimens without the certified appraisal of an expert. There are two ways to obtain such an appraisal.

The first is to consult the *National Coin Dealers Directory*, a publication that can be found in most libraries and coin shops and which lists hundreds of coin and bullion dealers according to their specialties. This directory can also be obtained by sending 25¢ to *NCD Directory*, P.O. Box 296, New York, New York 10024. After finding a dealer who specializes in your type of coin, you can inquire about arrangements for having it appraised.

Preferable to this, in most instances, is an appraisal from the highly respected American Numismatic Association, which costs only $10. You can have your coin appraised and certified as authentic by sending a check and the coin—by certified mail, return receipt requested—to the American Numismatic Association, Certification Service, Box 87, Ben Franklin Station, Washington, DC 20044. With the ANA certificate in hand you need never accept less than the true value of your coin.

Aside from those extremely rare and valuable coins that all treasure hunters dream of finding, there are many coins of fairly recent mintage that are dear to the hearts of most coin hunters. Most are not so valuable that you will want to spend money having them appraised, yet, in each coin denomination, there are certain ones that are always sought by collectors and of which you should be aware. Knowing them can greatly increase your coin hunting profits.

Modern Coins of Value

Indian Head Pennies • As I have already mentioned, the penny is the coin you are going to find with the greatest regularity. But a surprisingly large percentage of the copper cents you find are likely to be these, one of the most popular of all coin issues. The coin was designed in 1859, then issued each year through 1909. Indian head cents were minted of a copper-nickel mix from 1859 through 1864, then changed to an alloy of copper and zinc. The first bearing a branch mint mark was produced by the San Francisco mint in 1908, one year before the coin was discontinued.

Any Indian head penny dated prior to 1880 is virtually certain to have numismatic value. Among those bearing later dates, the ones most eagerly sought are from the years 1885, 1886, 1894, the 1908-D, and 1909-S.

Lincoln Pennies • These were first issued in 1909, the 100th anni-versery of Abraham Lincoln's birth. The originals had the portrait of Lincoln on the front, wreaths of wheat on the back. In 1959, the wheat design was replaced by a representation of the Lincoln Memorial.

Among those issued in the first year, both the 1909 and the 1909-S were made bearing the initials V.D.B. on the bottom of the reverse, the letters being the initials of the designer, Victor David Brenner. The 1909-S with these initials, even in no better than good condition, brings $100 and more.

That same year the Denver mint produced 7,160,000 cents that were issued without the D mark of that mint. These are the most valu-able of the Lincoln pennies, selling for as much as $750. Other Lincoln cents with high value are the 1911-S, 1914-D, 1914-S, 1915, 1924-D, 1926-S, 1931-D, 1931-S, and 1933-D.

Nickel Five-Cent Pieces • The Jefferson nickel, first minted in 1938, is the one found most frequently by coin hunters. The few of these that have numismatic value include the 1938-D, 1939-S, 1949-S, 1950-D, 1950-P, and 1951-S.

As you probably know, the Jefferson nickel took the place of the Indian head or Buffalo nickel, which was produced from 1913 to 1938. These were actually 75 percent copper, but a "nickel" nonetheless. A few bring very high prices, including the 1921-S and the 1926-S.

Liberty Head Nickels • These were produced from 1883 through 1913. Those produced from 1900 through 1912, when mint runs of them were the highest, bring prices, generally speaking, of less than a dollar. All others are worth at least several dollars each.

Roosevelt Dimes • These are the ten-cent pieces you will find most frequently. First minted in 1946, none have yet become highly valu-able. But the 1950-S, which was minted in relatively small numbers, is one that some collectors are stashing away with an eye toward rising prices.

Winged Liberty Head or Mercury Dimes • These preceded the Roosevelt dime, the mints turning them out from 1916 through 1945. The most valuable is the 1916-D, which can be worth hundreds of dollars. Others to keep a special watch for include 1921, 1921-D, 1926-S, 1930-S, 1931-D, and 1931-S.

Liberty Head Dimes • Known also as Barber dimes after the de-signer, Charles Barber, these were produced from 1892 through 1916. They are all valuable to collectors, but look especially for these: 1894-O, 1895, 1895-O, 1896-S, 1897-O, and 1901-S.

Standing Liberty Quarter • These were produced from 1916 through 1930. Those minted prior to 1924 are especially scarce. Best finds are the 1919-S, 1919-D, 1920-D, and 1923-S.

Liberty Head Quarters • Also designed by Charles Barber, these were made from 1892 through 1916. Without exception, they all have value to collectors, but the 1896-S, 1901-S, and 1913-S are the ones most eagerly sought.

Liberty Head Half Dollars • Another design of Charles Barber, these were minted from 1892 through 1916. Almost all are worth at least a few dollars, but the most valuable are 1892-S, 1893-S, 1896-S, and 1897-S.

Liberty Walking Half Dollars • Made from 1916 through 1947 and once one of our most popular coins for common use, these are found with surprising regularity by coin shooters. Most valuable in the series are 1916-S, 1921, 1921-D, 1921-S, and 1938-S.

Kennedy Half Dollars • Made as a silver coin only in 1964, the first year of issue, then produced as a clad coin, these have no great value to collectors—but people keep stashing them away for sentimental reasons almost as fast as the mints can make them. The 1964 coins appear certain to increase in value as time goes by.

Silver Dollars • Although silver dollars were the first coins authorized by Congress, in 1792, and have been produced off and on since 1794, not many are found by coin hunters. Most turn up as part of a buried cache.

The design of the dollar has changed many times. From 1878 through 1921, they bore a Liberty head design. Any from those years are highly prized. Either the 1893-S or the 1889-CC coin is likely to be worth several hundred dollars, if its condition is right.

The silver dollar you stand the best chance of finding is in the series minted from 1921 through 1935, the one known as the Peace Dollar. Keep your eyes open for the 1921, 1927, 1928, 1934, and 1934-S—all likely to fetch more than $100 each.

Metal Tokens

As you pursue this hobby of coin hunting you are almost certainly going to find metal tokens, especially transportation tokens. Many coin hunters fail to recognize the value of these, yet collecting them is a fast-growing hobby, and any number of them are worth a few dollars each.

They are frequently found in relatively large numbers.

Transportation tokens are stamped from brass, tin, lead, or, infrequently, nickel. They are round, square, triangular, or rectangular, as large as a quarter or as small as a dime. They were sold to transit passengers for a few cents each. Most are of a fairly recent era, but others date back to the days of cable cars and canal boats.

Several thousand kinds of tokens have been issued, some dating back to twenty years before the Civil War. A few had design features very much like our coins, but most were far simpler, usually bearing just a single letter or similar mark. Some of the better-designed ones were actually issued by private mints to be used as substitute money during times of coin shortages caused by hoarding. Congress banned these in 1864.

You may also come across state sales tax tokens. These have been issued by at least a dozen states, first appearing in the early 1930s. Most were turned out in denominations of a few mills, the mill being a monetary unit equal to 1/1000 of a dollar. Most were stamped from copper or aluminum, a few from brass, with a legend stating their purpose, as in "Missouri Sales Tax Receipt." Because of their minuscule face value, people simply tossed them away; thus relatively few are in existence today and their numismatic value appears certain to rise.

Tokens are issued even today, most often as part of a sales promotion by a company. These have no value at present—but they may be real rarities to collectors of the future. Use a little foresight if you come across them.

Most coin books and magazines about coin collecting carry information about the tokens of highest value. But if you really begin building a collection of these and want to sell it or establish its value, you should contact the Token and Medal Society, P.O. Box 82, Lincoln, Massachusetts 01773.

Tokens alone are probably not going to make you rich. But you are going to be surprised at how many you find and at how easily they can produce enough profit to pay all the costs of your treasure hunting.

6

Treasure from the Past

Spectacle Island lies in Boston Harbor. Not too much about its history or its present appearance would indicate that it holds anything of value to the treasure hunter. During the eighteenth century it was home to a few fishermen. In the last century it was a reception center for the immigrants who swarmed to this country from Europe. Two small hotels also stood on the island during those years. After these were closed because of some dubious activities that included gambling, the island became a dump for the city of Boston, where enormous amounts of trash were burned and buried each week—leaving so much metal in the ground that taking a detector there would be pointless because you would get a reading no matter which way the detector was aimed. Not much of interest in such a spot, is there?

Well, it may be one of the very best treasure hunting spots in the United States. It is one spot where, according to treasure hunters who have been working it for years, a metal detector is not really needed. They say you will find something of value almost anywhere you dig. One Boston-area man has taken thousands of pieces of crockery, old tools, watches, toys, banks, and other collectibles from this island and claims that an average day's work nets him more than 100 items that will fetch good money when sold as antiques.

There are thousands and thousands of sites like this across the United States. Not all are as good as Spectacle Island, but many are far better.

Ghost Towns, Native American Settlements, and Other Sites

A ghost town is a boomtown of the Old West that has been completely abandoned. Treasure hunters look for settlements anywhere in the country that people left and which presently stand deserted or nearly so. True, most ghost towns are in the West, in the areas where major strikes of gold or silver were made, but there are thousands more in all parts of the country.

Some of the more famous ghost towns, such as Virginia City, Nevada, have been restored as tourist attractions; some have escaped the ravages of time, nature, and vandals and are remarkably well preserved. When a ghost town or other place where humans once lived has been so ravaged with the passing of time that scarcely a depression or remnant of foundation remains, the treasure hunters refer to it as a barebones site. No one can begin to accurately estimate how many sites of this type exist. Even with the best of research they can be difficult to locate. But they are well worth the trouble. A site of this type has probably not been picked over by other treasure hunters and is much more likely to hold wealth than the picturesque areas that are easier to locate.

Most ghost towns are far easier to locate. Many are shown on current maps and in atlases. Old maps can lead you to many more. Local historical societies can direct you to the ones nearest you. Some sources of further information about ghost towns are listed in Chapter Three, and I have listed some more sites in the appendix to this book.

Some of the most fantastic finds of recent years have been made in these abandoned settlements. The site of Rawhide, Nevada, which in its heyday produced more than 50,000 ounces of gold and millions of ounces of silver, still held $50,000 worth of artifacts—including a pistol with gold handle grips—when it was worked over by two treasure hunters in 1976. In the saloon of a ghost town in Arizona, another team of treasure hunters came across a solid gold cuspidor whose former owner had camouflaged it with green paint.

Many of the mining camps failed to become boomtowns. They were never more than a collection of tents and crude cabins. Few traces of their existence remain today. Generally, the only clue to their existence is the tailings from the mining operation, or, in some cases, rusting bits of machinery. These camps are exceptional finds, because they had no banks and the miners were forced to hide their money in the ground. When the miners broke camp and moved on, they would discard things that were of little value to them but which can be enormously valuable in the modern marketplace. In a single day of working such a camp in the high country of Colorado, one husband-and-wife team recently found dozens of crystal whiskey glasses, half a dozen hurricane lamps, a copper still, hundreds of valuable bottles, two dozen old whiskey flasks, several ounces of gold, and many other interesting artifacts. There are tens of thousands of these sites scattered from Georgia to Oregon. All hold something of value, and a few hold enormous treasure—such as the tumbledown adobe shack in Arizona that held half a ton of gold and silver ingots until it was unearthed by a lucky explorer in 1954.

Aside from the ghost towns one can find in the United States, there are thousands upon thousands of isolated and abandoned houses, most of them only ruins. Those in the New England region, which sometimes date back to colonial years, are real targets for treasure hunters. Within the last decade, one house site at Sassafras Point, near Boston, gave up $50,000 in coins, pearls, iron artifacts, and other treasure.

Private homes are not the only buildings that have been abandoned. There are old schools, shops, churches, taverns, and bordellos. The girls who worked in the latter establishments—perhaps because they were so frequently victimized by their customers, perhaps because they were so out of touch with family and friends—were notorious for hoarding money, jewelry, and other treasure. Many a girl who toiled in such houses of pleasure and sin found herself in virtual bondage. For that reason many of them stashed away money that might someday allow escape.

In the past there were thousands of stagecoach stations, not just in the West but throughout the nation; some date back to the days of the colonists. These sites can usually be located through research or by asking a local historical society. These almost always hold some interesting artifacts.

In addition to the many forts that are now national monuments and off-limits to treasure hunters, there are thousands of others in ruins. In some instances, not a single trace of the original structures remains. Like the ghost towns, these forts generally had private dwellings, shops, stores, trash dumps, and all the other structures needed to maintain life on the frontier. Where these structures once stood treasure hunters find weapons, cooking and eating utensils, buttons, buckles and early military decorations, knives, bottles, old watches and jewelry, and even a few old coins. Soldiers had no banking system available to them in the early days, so caches of money often are found around these old forts. Battlefields hold large numbers of artifacts lost or buried by opposing armies. Often, too, large treasures were buried to prevent the enemy from claiming the riches. But weapons and other materials of war are the items that really cause treasure hunters to go looking for old battlefields.

The Encyclopedia of the American Revolution by Mark Boatner is the reference most treasure hunters use as a starting point for locating obscure battlesites of that war. *The Civil War, Day by Day, an Almanac* by E. B. Long lists many obscure battlesites of the War Between the States. Keep in mind that most major battlefields are now monuments or parks where treasure hunting is prohibited, and concentrate on finding sites that have been forgotten by history.

If you happen to live in the Southwest, you are probably within reach of hundreds of abandoned Spanish missions and settlements scattered throughout that region. Any artifact found in one of these is likely to be very valuable, and some of them almost certainly hold vast hoards of treasure. Often they were abandoned hastily because of the threat of attack, so whatever treasure they held at the time was simply left behind. More and more of these are being protected as historical sites, so be careful about getting permission before you start exploring, or you could face a fine, a jail sentence, or both. Your best bet is to seek out those on private land and ask permission of the present owner.

Between the U.S. coasts there are many thousands—some say millions—of caves, the vast majority of them unexplored, at least in modern times. In these you may find shards of ancient pottery, stone tools, primitive cookware, or other items of little monetary value but of great archaeological importance. When such items are found the proper authorities should be notified, a very real service treasure hunters can provide to others.

But a cave may also hold vast treasure. Jesse James and his gang were among the outlaws who used caves as hiding places. So were Butch Cassidy and the Wild Bunch. Cronies of Al Capone are known to have stashed $300,000 worth of bootleg whiskey in an Illinois cave, then blasted the entrance shut—it has never been found.

Caves may hold treasure of any sort, not just that hidden away by outlaws. They often served as temporary living quarters for trappers, mountain men, hunters, miners, and even the first who went west to farm and settle the land. Because most have only one entrance and were thus easy to defend against attack, they were frequently the last stronghold—and of course they provided countless little nooks and crannies in which things might be hidden from the attackers.

Trails and roads used by early travelers sometimes yield old items that are valuable to modern treasure hunters. Those who used these trails were in almost constant danger. When they came under attack, they were likely to bury their valuables and most important possessions.

Top: Civil War relics are actively sought by treasure hunters. COURTESY OF
FISHER RESEARCH LABORATORY, INC. *Bottom: Spanish coins found on the Florida coastline.* COURTESY OF GARRETT ELECTRONICS, INC.

If they failed to survive the attack, these remained hidden in the ground.

Most of the old trails of the East that were used during colonial days are gone now, obliterated by progress and buried under ribbons of concrete; often the new roads follow the exact routes of the old, as U.S. 40 follows the old National Road. But some old roads are as unspoiled and as picturesque as ever. Daniel Boone's Wilderness Trail, which cuts through the hill country of eastern Kentucky, is one—many a family under attack is known to have buried and left all its worldly goods there.

The trail of Lewis and Clark is preserved and marked along much of its length, and, since it was followed by many others as they headed west, probably holds many valuable artifacts at old campsites. But the famous—or infamous—Oregon Trail is the route that draws treasure hunters like a magnet. Its wealth of artifacts is so great that it will probably never be exhausted. This trail has put money in the pockets of thousands of explorers who specialize in going after treasure from the past.

Known also as the California Road, the Emigrant Road, and the Mormon Trail, the route began at Independence, Missouri, and was already well established by the time of the California gold rush. But between the time when gold fever struck, in 1849, and the start of this century no fewer than 350,000, and perhaps as many as a million, miners, settlers, and pioneers endured its hardships to seek new lives in the West. Around campfires along the way they discarded millions of items that are valuable as artifacts today. Many had left home with items that were far too cumbersome for such a journey and, as it became necessary to ford rivers or climb steep hills and mountains, the wagons were lightened by tossing such items away. Varna Enterprises, P.O. Box 2216, Van Nuys, California 91405, offers a booklet titled *Map of Pioneer Trails*, which has detailed maps of many old roads and trails, including the Oregon. The booklet costs $3.95.

If you live in the northeastern part of the country, you might want to investigate an even older transportation network: the canal systems. At one time this part of the country had more than 3,000 miles of canals. During the fifty or so years that they served as a primary means of transportation, the canal barges carried millions of passengers and billions of dollars worth of consumer goods.

Like the famous Erie Canal, which once carried passengers through the part of Ohio in which I now live, most of these waterways are gone now, long since filled in, and forgotten—except by the small number of treasure hunters shrewd enough to realize that those who rode the canal boats, like the travelers of today, were litterbugs, and that yesteryear's litter may be today's treasure.

The routes of the old canals are commonly shown on maps. Along these routes coins were tossed overboard by those passengers who thought the gesture brought good luck. Some few of the canal boats sank, their rotting hulks were left in place when the canals were filled, and artifacts from these might be extremely valuable today. Countless thousands of empty bottles were tossed overboard after travelers had quenched their thirst, all of them likely to have some value.

Finding the old buildings once associated with the operation and upkeep of the canals is only a little more difficult than locating the waterways themselves. But doing the extra bit of research could be well worth your time, for it is around the locks and toll stations where people once congregated—losing and discarding things—that you can find the really worthwhile items.

Old Native American settlements are another matter. With the exception of tribes such as the Cherokees, who once lived in well-established communities, most Native Americans left behind almost nothing to show where and how they once lived. Amazingly little is known about their way of life as it was before the first Europeans arrived—largely because they lacked an alphabet and written language. There were many thousands of camps at one time, but most were temporary and built of materials that returned to the soil with the passage of time. They used far fewer metal items than did the early European settlers, and so their camps are rarely found by treasure hunters using metal detectors.

There are exceptions, of course. In 1978, an Alabama treasure hunter using a metal detector got a reading and dug up dozens of priceless relics, including a crown fashioned of silver and set with valuable early American coins, probably once worn by a princess of the Creeks. But such finds are rare.

Most early encampments have been found by accident, as when a field is plowed or a road built. In November 1979, for example, workmen leveling a stretch of land for a new interstate highway near Akron, Ohio, began turning up stone tools, weapons, and other relics that may be as much as 5,000 years old. Archaeologists were called in to exhume the spot.

That is as it should be. Few relics have great monetary value. They are easily destroyed when handled by untrained persons. But any one could provide the key that will allow archaeologists to unlock some of the mysteries of the early Native American existence. So if your treasure hunting does lead you to one of these sites, please do the right thing and notify the nearest museum or historical society.

Techniques for Searching

In old towns and abandoned buildings that have not been picked to pieces, your eyes may lead you to almost as much treasure as your metal detector. Valuable items can be found right on the surface of the ground, or with some part protruding from it. Almost anything you find around a really old ghost town or dwelling place is likely to have some value, be it jewelry, horseshoes, keys, locks, bottles, buckles, tools, pieces of harness, or whatever. Some old towns have yielded literally thousands of these items—and if they fetch only a dollar apiece, so what? That still adds up to thousands of dollars. Never discard anything you find in this type of treasure hunting. One Nevada treasure hunter casually walked by a huge pile of old auto license plates; they were picked up by his companion, who promptly sold them for more than $1,000.

Treasure hunters in the West sometimes make these visual searches even more productive by using wind machines—huge fans that are powered by generators and mounted on a jeep or dune buggy. They use these fans to blow away the thick dust that has accumulated on deserted streets and around old buildings, then move in to harvest the coins and relics that were hidden by that dirt.

The visual search of a barebones sight is more difficult, requiring the use of imagination. The idea is to try to visualize how the site once looked and determine the best places to search. If the site is now farming land that has been recently plowed, look for bits of metal that might give you some clue. Old ash piles will stand out from the surrounding soil, and soil that holds old iron or rotted wood is likely to be discolored. Fencelines are a certain clue, and vegetation will be greener and more lush if it is growing on soil made more fertile by the long-ago existence of outhouses, barnyards, or chicken coops. A long line of trees almost always indicates a spot where humans once lived.

Whether you are working abandoned houses, ghost towns, old trails, or battlesites you will want a detector that is tuned not to discriminate; you are interested in anything that will cause the device to give a reading. You will also want at least two search coils—a small one for locating smaller items on or near the surface and a large coil for penetrating deep into the ground. In addition to digging tools you will need a probe of some sort—a long thin metal rod will do—that you can thrust into the ground to help determine the nature of your discovery before you start to dig. Careful digging is the rule here, for some of the most valuable artifacts are fragile and easily damaged.

If you are exploring a ghost town, locating the dump should be one of your first projects. Most of the really old ones will be covered by several feet of sediment, but you can find them with little trouble because they rise above the surrounding ground. Where gullies were used as dumps they can be harder to spot, but the metal detector will quickly reveal the exact location. Most early business places had dumps right behind them, or, in the case of Western saloons that were raised a few feet off the ground, beneath them. Only the most avid treasure hunters are willing to crawl and dig under these buildings, so they can be real mines of treasure.

Old bottles are among the objects most commonly recovered from dumps—one reason why cautious digging is suggested. The collectible bottle market is a very good one today, but not for broken bottles. Remove these with caution, as did the husband and wife who, four years ago, recovered 5,000 old bottles from the town dump of Goldfield, Nevada, and you may be able to cash them in for thousands of dollars.

Bottles are not all you will find in dumps. That dump at Goldfield also yielded thousands of other artifacts that included pocket watches, toys, tools, crockery, and even some nineteenth-century coins that must have been lost there or tossed away by accident.

Wells and cisterns were often used as hiding places by misers or people under attack. When a well ran dry, its pit was sometimes used as a trash dump. These were, of course, situated as close to buildings as possible and can usually be located by using a probe or detector. In one old cistern in Ohio, a treasure hunter found a cast-iron kettle filled with coins dating back almost to the time of the American Revolution, a Bible that was partially bound in brass and amazingly well preserved, and an old flintlock gun. Look also for spots where outhouses once stood.

Different types of buildings require different search techniques. Older buildings may be constructed of logs, sod, rock, brick, or adobe. Those made of rock, brick, or adobe are the easiest to search, for they do not have many nails, spikes, or other bits of metal to plague you with false readings, and it is easier to spot any place where the walls have been tampered with and treasure has possibly been stashed. The nails used in construction in wooden buildings will give you any number of false readings and so more patience and experience are needed to search them. Buildings of wood also have more cavities for hiding things, and so one must move very deliberately in searching them.

There are certain spots in buildings that are likely to have been used as hiding places. Look under stairways and stair treads, under windowsills and doorsills, behind baseboards and up chimneys. Look for removable bricks in foundations, fireplaces, and walls, and check for hollow places in any old furniture left standing around. See if any floorboards can be lifted. Heavy hollow doors in older homes sometimes served as safe deposit boxes, as a California treasure hunter was delighted to learn when, taking one apart, he found 500 gold coins that had been stashed there nearly a century ago.

In ghost towns, gold and other treasure have turned up in places so unlikely that only the most imaginative treasure hunter would think of looking there. A bottle from an old pharmacy was filled with gold dust, and four whiskey bottles from an old well were full of the same precious metal. The banister in an old brothel was hollow and held hundreds of gold coins, and a counterweight from a dry goods store turned out to be 50 pounds of pure gold.

But finds like these are rare, and to do well in this type of treasure hunting, you should remember that most of your money will come from the sale of relics and artifacts—which means almost anything in and around these old buildings. Kay Modgling, the treasure hunting retired nurse has found thousands of coins and pieces of jewelry; she has found gold and silver nuggets and small caches of money. Her biggest stroke of luck came when she located what had once been the pharmacy in the ghost town of Frisco, Utah, and took from it thousands of old medicine bottles and antique medical instruments.

If the building has been more recently abandoned and still holds scattered bits of its furnishings, check inside all urns and vases, the bottoms and backs of drawers, the fireboxes and ashboxes of old stoves, between the picture and the backing of old photographs and portraits, in trunks and books, especially family Bibles. Run the detector over everything in the house. One treasure hunter did this recently and found four old and rare gold coins hidden in the spine of a book.

In checking around old farm sites, go carefully over the outbuildings and all they contain, including feed or seed bags, toolboxes, and rusting machinery. If the farm is fenced, check to see if any fenceposts are marked in an unusual way—such as by having an extra loop of wire around the post. A favorite trick was to hide money in the posthole before the post was set, marking the post in some way that heirs could later identify.

Use common sense when searching old buildings. Folks who hid valuables intended to retrieve them at some later time, and they also liked to hide them where they could be kept under fairly constant watch. Put yourself in the place of the person doing the hiding, and you have put yourself much closer to adding caches of money and precious goods to the valuable artifacts you can recover from these sites.

The Cleaning and Evaluating of Relics and Artifacts

Those who use their metal detectors on a regular basis never cease to be amazed at the number and variety of items they find. A full list would be longer than this book, but it would include lanterns and lighters, spurs and spoons, nails and knives, buttons and bells, cleavers and keys. No book could possibly tell all there is to know about these items, but the following paragraphs examine some of the categories in which treasure hunters specialize. Items not included in these categories can usually be identified and evaluated with the help of local museum historians, historical societies, or antique dealers, or through the use of books suggested by your librarian. A photograph of the item sent to the manufacturer of your metal detector will also result in tentative identification or referral to an expert who will provide identification.

BOTTLES

Next to coins, bottles are probably the items most commonly collected by treasure hunters—not only because they are found with such regularity, but also because they can so quickly add up to a very real fortune. They are worth their weight in . . . well, bottles.

If you have doubts about the price bottles are bringing, visit some antique shops and see what they are getting for the collectors' bottles made by Jim Beam whiskey and Avon cosmetics. In each line there are numerous bottles worth several hundred dollars apiece; you could retire if you had a complete set of either line in mint condition—and yet these bottles are not even old as collectibles go.

Age is an important factor in determining the value of a bottle, though of course rarity is also, as well as condition. One way to estimate the age of a bottle is to examine the mold mark. This is the seam caused by the joints of the mold. If made prior to 1860, the seam will extend up the side of the bottle to a point just above the shoulder; if turned out between 1860 and 1880, the mold seam will run up the full length of the neck. Bottles made between 1880 and 1910 have a seam that extends up the neck and over the lip of the bottle.

The bottles you find will need a safe and thorough cleaning before you can even hope to identify them. Start by soaking them overnight in a tub of water to which you have added a little household ammonia. Bottles that are badly encrusted with minerals may need to soak for several days. When they are removed from the water, most of the dirt will fall away, and the rest can be removed with a stiff brush.

Use a bottle brush for scrubbing the inside, then rinse the bottle in warm water, polish it with a soft cloth, and you are ready to see what it will bring in the collector's market.

Many excellent books are available on the subject of bottle collecting, and they provide the best way to determine the value of your glassware. One of the best available is *The Collector's Book of Bottles* by Marian Klamkin, which has 400 illustrations and contains helpful information on all bottles of American origin.

RELICS

As early as 1621, forges and furnaces were busy turning out the items of iron needed to build a new nation, and relics from those very first forges continue to be found by modern treasure hunters. Iron was the single most important metal in the early days and it continues to be the metal most often found by treasure hunters who search ghost towns and abandoned buildings.

Any item of iron produced before 1900 will have some value to collectors, sometimes even if it is no more than a piece broken off the whole. The possibilities are too numerous to list here, but the following are items that are especially sought by collectors of Americana.

Cooking Utensils • Kettles and pots; spiders, which are pans with three legs and short handles; trivets, which are three-legged stands that could be set in the fireplace to hold pans and keep food warm; spoons, forks, ladles, and skimmers; and the S-hooks upon which cooking pots were hung.

Fireplace Equipment • Pokers, tongs, shovels, and irons; and trammels, which are long, notched bars of iron that were once used in the fireplace to allow cookpots to be suspended at varying heights.

Lamps • A few were made of tin but most were of iron. They were simple in the early days, a bowl that held fuel and a wick, but sometimes they had a hinged cover. All old lamps have high value.

Flatirons • The first were iron boxes into which hot coals could be placed. Later ones were designed for heating on stoves and had handles that were decorative as well as useful. A type known as the sadiron was larger and heavier, with a point at either end. Any of these move fast in the marketplace.

Door and Shutter Hardware • Locks and keys, hinges or hasps, especially if they are large, heavy, and decorative, bring good prices from buyers of antiques.

Nails • At least 2,000 types were made of iron. The hand-wrought ones with square heads are most valuable. One Georgia treasure hunter came across 25,000 of these in a batch. He moved them all by selling them to tourists and through the mail. The individual price was small but it added up to thousands of dollars.

There are many relics of value that you can find in or near abandoned houses or settlements, and a great deal of them can be identified only with difficulty. Your librarian can suggest several authoritative guides to any class of antiques, but the one most recommended as a guide to identifying iron, copper, brass, and pewter pieces used by early colonists, New Englanders, and ranchers of the West is Katherine McClinton's *Complete Book of American Country Antiques.*

If you are working the old ghost towns, the market is good for all Old West memorabilia—not just relics made of iron. Certain types of barbed wire have become so valuable that many Western treasure hunters specialize in looking for it. More than 1,200 kinds were made, and single strands of rare types no more than a few inches in length have sold for as much as $3,500. If you find any of this and want to check it out, ask your librarian for the *Barb Wire Manual with Pricing Guide* by Gary Fountain.

Almost anything you find on a battlefield is going to be valuable. Regardless of condition, all weapons, cannons, rifles, swords, bayonets, and even knives are eagerly grabbed up at high and rising prices by collectors. If a large weapon such as a rifle or cannon is found in good condition and bears markings that identify the owner or manufacturer, a price of $25,000 or more might be obtainable in today's market.

But weapons are not all you can recover from battlefields. A button, token, canteen, snuffbox, belt buckle, or other seemingly innocuous item may turn out to be worth a surprising sum. At least two excellent guides are available to help you identify such items, handle them properly, and establish their monetary value: *The Civil War Collector's Encyclopedia* by Francis Lord and the *Care of Historical Collections* by P. E. Guldbeck, which contains information on the proper handling of relics of all kinds.

When an item has been properly cleaned and identified, you should get at least half a dozen offers before you finally decide to sell. Appraisals can vary enormously in the antiques market, so be careful.

7

Hunting for Gold

Around the California mining camps during the gold rush days, the Argonauts told a story about a miner who died and went to heaven only to be refused admittance because, according to Saint Peter, heaven already had far too many gold miners.

"Look, if you'll let me in," said the late Argonaut, "I'll get rid of those other diggers and panners for you." So he was admitted and promptly began spreading rumors of a gold strike in hell. Within a matter of hours he was the only forty-niner left in paradise.

This pleased Saint Peter no end, but only a day or so later the guardian of the pearly gates was befuddled to find the last miner standing at the gates, struggling under the weight of his mining gear, announcing that he was bound for hell to make his fortune.

"But that makes no sense at all," said the saint. "You're the one who started that rumor about a gold strike in hell."

"I know I am," responded the grizzled prospector. "But I've been thinking it over and, you know—there might just be some truth to it!"

A new gold rush is at hand. Not just in California where, according to recent estimates, as many as 100,000 amateur prospectors head for the mother lode country each weekend, but in other parts of this country and around the world. This new gold rush is very real, it is growing by leaps and bounds, and it is making many of the new Argonauts enormously wealthy.

With the price of gold very high (as compared to $16 per ounce during the 1850s) and likely to go even higher, and with much more efficient equipment available for locating and recovering the precious yellow metal, prospecting for gold may be the quickest and surest way for a treasure hunter to strike it rich.

World reserves of unmined gold appear to be far from exhausted. In 1979, two Australians, Don Peters and Peter Culverson, were using their metal detector near Sydney when they unearthed a 13-pound nugget worth $100,000. That same week a 22-ounce nugget was found in the Australian desert, and one worth $16,000 was reported from South Africa.

Late in that same year, CBS's "On the Road" filmed a television special in the mother lode country of California. They interviewed a trio whose claim was producing an average of $500 per hour in gold and is believed to hold as much as $12 million in unmined wealth. They also met up with a young lady who earns a pretty fair living scuba diving for gold in icy mountain streams.

Recent years have produced many other remarkable finds of gold, including a single nugget of 351 grams from Washington, the largest ever found in that state, and another of 77 ounces from a creek bed near Whitehorse, Canada, the largest found in that area since the gold rush of 1898. As nuggets go, however, all those mentioned are small compared to some that have been found in the past: a 2,340-ounce specimen in California; a 408-pound chunk of gold in Chile; a 200-pound nugget from Australia; and at least six of more than 100 pounds apiece found in Alaska before the start of this century. Hundreds of nuggets in the 10- to 25-pound range have been found in California, Alaska, and other places over the years, and probably hundreds or thousands more are waiting to be discovered.

At one time there were at least 10,000 gold mines in the United States. Most of these closed down because of economics, not because they ran out of gold. Simply put, the cost of extracting the metal became greater than the profits derived from the mining operation. It is easy to see how this came about. During the entire period of the gold rush days, the price of an ounce of gold was seldom higher than $18, and not until 1933 was it officially raised to $35, but during that entire period the costs of mining were steadily rising, while the amount of gold that could be mined was declining. Even when the price of gold doubled it was not economically feasible to operate most of these mines, but when it doubled again, and then again, treasure hunters began looking at these abandoned claims with new interest. Perhaps you should do the same.

Abandoned Claims

"Gold is where you find it," experienced prospectors used to tell greenhorns during the gold rush days. While that is true, your best chance to find gold is in areas where it has already been found by others.

This does not necessarily mean that you should load up the wagons and head west, for gold is far more widespread than most people believe. It has been found in more than 450 counties in 39 different states, not counting Alaska. Leading gold producers in the western part of the country are, in order of thier production, California, Colorado, South Dakota, Nevada, and Montana. East of the Mississippi River, North Carolina is the biggest producer, but mining is also done in Maine, Vermont, Michigan, Indiana, and Massachusetts, to name just the leading Eastern states. To find out exactly where gold is being mined in your state, and in what quantities, just write to the Director of the U.S. Mint, Department of the Treasury, in Washington, DC 20228, and request a copy of the annual report entitled "Domestic Gold and Silver," which will be sent to you without charge.

With gold selling at an unusually high price, new mining firms are being formed almost as fast as the investors can think up names for their companies or mines. The costs of establishing and working a gold mine can be enormous, so later on in this chapter I'll tell you how to get government backing with almost no financial risk to yourself. But with or without such backing, your chances of striking it rich may be far better if you go after an abandoned mine, with the idea of selling the rights to work it to an established mining firm. I have listed the general locations of some mines in the appendix to this book, but there are literally thousands more worth going after.

Most of these abandoned mines are located west of the Mississippi, and of these about three-quarters are believed to contain gold in worthwhile amounts. Though many are classified as "lost" mines and have been sought for years by treasure hunters, the locations of others are known and can be obtained by consulting books on mining and mineral resources for the individual states. You can also obtain the names and exact location of most mines by consulting the geological survey department of the state in which you intend to go prospecting.

You can turn a real profit by working almost any of these old mines with modern equipment. The sluice boxes and other primitive equipment used by miners of the past recovered only about half the gold from the ore that was handled, and even before the price of gold went soaring, treasure hunters using metal detectors and other modern equipment were taking thousands of dollars worth of gold from the mining debris around these old camps.

During the first three years of the California gold rush, almost all gold was extracted by panning the gravel in stream and river beds. The gold found there had eroded from deposits in the high country and had been carried down into the lower waters over centuries. Soon these deposits appeared to be exhausted—at least by the standards of that day—and so a new process called hydraulic mining came into being. In this type of mining, high-pressure hoses were used to cut away vast amounts of gravel from mountainsides, exposing gold beneath the surface; the loosened gravel was then run through sluice boxes to extract what gold it held.

Hydraulic mining was destructive—entire mountains were nearly leveled by the technique. By 1893 its use had been greatly restricted, and all the states had passed laws prohibiting the debris from being dumped into any body of water. As a result of these laws, there are thousands of piles of mining tailings that hold vast quantities of gold you can recover using the techniques described in this chapter.

Before you start looking for gold around an abandoned mine, check carefully to see that no one holds the legal rights to it, or you might end up with a pack of trouble instead of a saddlebag full of gold. Claim jumping is no less serious today than in the past, when countless men were shot for it. The best way to determine the status of a mine that appears to be abandoned is by consulting property records in the nearest city or county offices.

Exploring old mines can also be dangerous. Tunnel timbers are likely to be so decayed that the slightest movement could cause them to collapse. Use extreme caution when entering any of these old shafts, do so only in the presence of a companion, and always let someone know where you are going and when you can be expected to return. Dozens of lives have been lost in recent years as the result of accidents in these mines.

Don't expect to find a bright vein of gold staring you in the face. Most treasure hunters find gold in these old shafts by using a good metal detector and digging in the loose dirt and dust that covers the floors in the mine shafts and side tunnels. These old mines were usually worked at a hectic pace. As the ore was being trundled out for milling and processing, many small pieces—and some surprisingly large chunks— were accidentally dropped and pressed down into the dirt floors. Use a small search coil when going over these shafts, and even a small bit of gold will make the metal detector sing.

About the only minerals possible to confuse with gold are iron pyrite (fool's gold) and yellow mica, but there is a simple test that will enable you to tell them apart. Just tap the sample with a hammer. Pyrite or mica will shatter; gold is soft and will resist shattering. It is so soft and malleable that it can be hammered into sheets thin enough to see through, and a single troy ounce of it can be drawn into a wire than 50 miles long. The difference in weight will tip you off, too, for gold is far heavier than the two other minerals.

Placer Gold Deposits and How to Find Them

Most amateurs concentrate on finding and recovering alluvial deposits of gold, more commonly known as placer gold. It is much easier to find gold in this form than to locate the vein from which it originates, for the placer deposits are much more widespread. As mountain streams and rivers sweep through the gold-bearing high country, they cut away flakes, chunks, and minute particles of gold and carry them downstream. The process is a continuing one, with gold constantly being broken loose from the lodes and carried away during the spring runoffs. Placer gold is never truly exhausted, and it can be profitable to work areas that have been gone over heavily in recent years.

The upstream ends of bodies of water closest to the original source of the gold—well back in the hills or mountains—are by far the most productive areas to work when searching for placer gold. In these areas, look for places where high water has washed over ground not normally covered by water, as in the inside of a bend in the river or stream. Expect better chances of finding it also on sandbars or in sharp depressions. Since gold is relatively heavy, placer deposits are usually found down close to bedrock, unless the gold is intercepted as it sinks by clay, thick mud, moss or other vegetation. Look especially for bedrock with a highly irregular surface, for on such surfaces the gold often collects in small pockets. Gold also gathers in pockets around boulders and other obstructions such as tree roots, and moss-covered banks are especially good collectors of alluvial gold.

Places where the velocity of the water slackens are also likely spots, for here the slower water allows the gold a better chance to sink. Whenever the stream widens, where there is a sudden reduction in its downward gradient, or where a small stream enters a larger one, such reduced velocity occurs and gold is likely to gather.

Above all, look for concentrations of magnetic black sand, probably the single most important key to locating deposits of alluvial gold. The magnetic properties of the sand are not capable of drawing gold, but the gold and the sand have similar specific gravity—about nineteen er—and so they tend to accumulate in the same

e hunters capitalize on this natural phenomenon by
ors to locate pockets of black sand on creek or river
he magnetic black sand is located, it is lifted from the
a portable dredge—described later in this chapter—or
shov , then panned or run through a sluice box. In very shallow
waters u black sand is simply panned at streamside.

Nearly every manufacturer of metal detectors makes at least one
model specifically intended for gold prospecting, some very sophisticated. Most of these have a special gold probe that allows you to reach
back into nooks and crannies too narrow to admit regular search coils.
But your ordinary metal detector can be nearly as effective, if you know
how to use it.

When working in streams or other water, as most prospectors must
do at times, the detector's control box should be body-mounted, strung
around the neck or fixed to a belt loop to keep it out of the water. The
search coil must be immersible and, in this system, is linked to the
control box by a flexible cable several feet in length.

The body-mount system is important because it allows you to
move about easily in the stream and extend the probe or search coil in
every possible direction. It also permits you to reach deep down in the
water without running the risk of getting the control box wet.

The size of the search coil needed is determined by the conditions
you encounter. If the stream is rough and strewn with rocks you will
want the smallest search coil possible—no larger than 4 inches in diameter. This will allow you to get in between those rocks, where black sand
deposits are likely to occur. The detector should be tuned to the metal
mode when using the smaller search coils, for the black sand will also
cause a reaction in this setting.

If the bottom is smooth and thickly covered with ordinary sand,
you should use a larger search coil—one with a diameter of 8 to 12
inches. The larger coil will help penetrate the ordinary sand and detect
the mineral deposits that lie below. Use the mineral setting with the
larger search coil, for this assures optimum results in tracking down the
possibly valuable deposits of black sand.

When black sand has been located, be sure to dig it out until you
have reached bedrock, for it is at that level that most gold is found, as
well as the gold of highest quality. And as you start extracting the gold
from the sand, be aware that placer gold does not always have the

traditional color and appearance of gold. It can vary in color from a deep red-yellow to a pale silvery white. In the upper streams it is more likely to be very coarse, and in the lower portions of those same streams it may be as fine as dust.

Panning for Gold

In the mother lode country of northern California, which stretches from the Yosemite foothills about 200 miles north into the high country and the icy rivers of the Sierra Nevada range, it is not unusual to see motorists parked beside a mountain stream using the wheel covers from their automobile to wash out a few panfuls of gravel and black sand. Actually, the hubcap is probably no less efficient than the pans used by the forty-niners.

Panning for gold is still one of the easiest and least expensive ways to find gold. The forty-niners often used pans carved from wood or forged iron frying pans and skillets. Later, they used steel pans, 12 to 18 inches across the top, with flat bottoms and sloping sides that were intended only for extracting gold. Pans today are only slightly different. Most are made of lightweight plastic. They are painted black, thus making it easier to spot a tiny flake of gold. The pan's inner wall is fitted with small ridges known as riffles that run parallel to the rim and trap tiny gold particles as the water and black sand in the pan is agitated.

You should have at least two pans. Most prefer pans 12 to 14 inches in diameter. Some oldtimers use pans as large as 18 inches, but these require a greater degree of skill and are very tiring to handle. Plastic pans will cost about $4 each; copper pans, or iron pans with copper insets, are much more expensive.

In addition to the pans, your basic equipment should include a small pick, a round-pointed shovel, a small magnet, a pair of tweezers (long with flat points), an ear syringe, a piece of canvas with a tight weave, several buckets, a small plastic funnel, specimen bags or containers, 2 or 3 ounces of mercury, several plastic pill bottles or other containers for holding gold dust—and a good metal detector with a submersible head. Panning can be done, of course, without the metal detector, but it greatly improves your chance of finding gold.

There are several approaches to panning. No matter how you approach it, you are using a method that takes advantage of the fact that gold is seven or eight times heavier than the sand and gravel in which it is found and nineteen times heavier than water. The idea is to get rid of the lighter material but not lose any of the gold or the black sand that may hold minute gold particles. The beginner can learn the basics of panning in a matter of minutes, but real skill and efficiency come only with experience.

After you have used the detector to locate a deposit of black sand, carefully dig out every bit of sand down to bedrock. If it is a very large amount, shovel it into the buckets and set them aside until you are ready to start the panning. If the amount is a single panful or less, then you are ready to go to work on it at once. Be sure to save all the black sand after you are through. Refineries, which can extract more gold from it than you can, will gladly pay you several dollars a pound for it.

Place some of the black sand in one of the pans. Pick out any debris and any pebbles that are obviously not gold. Place the pan under-water and shake it vigorously a few times. This will cause all the heavier material to settle at the bottom of the pan. Pick out the gravel and other obvious foreign matter. Now submerge the pan once again, gently rocking it and rotating it in such a way that the movement of the water washes away the lighter matter, leaving the heaviest material clinging to the bottom of the pan. As the pan is rotated, gradually increase the angle of the tilt by moving your hands away from the midpoint.

Transfer all that remains to the second pan. Repeat the entire process. When you have done this, you will find that only black sand remains in the pan, and perhaps a few shiny traces of the gold you seek. Use the tweezers to pick out any nuggets large enough to be handled with them. Put a little water in one of the pill bottles and place the nuggets into the container. Use the syringe to carefully extract the flecks that are too small to be handled with tweezers.

Even tinier flecks of gold may still be visible in the black sand. If so, fill the syringe with water and use the water to rinse away the black sand, leaving the gold behind, or use your magnet to separate the two. This is best done by wrapping the magnet in a plastic bag and moving it around what remains in the pan. It will pick up the remaining black sand, which is actually magnetite. When the magnet has attracted a fair amount of black sand, hold it off to one side and remove the plastic bag, breaking the magnetic field and allowing the sand to fall away. A few repetitions will leave only gold in the pan. Place the end of the funnel in a pill bottle filled with water, tilt the pan over the funnel, and let the gold trickle down. The entire process takes about fifteen minutes.

A more modern method of panning calls for the use of copper pans, or at least pans with copper insets, and mercury. The pans cost a little more, but the method is faster, more efficient, and allows you to get even the finest dust, the "flour" gold that might be missed by the method described above.

Choose an area in the copper pan, or the complete copper inset, and clean it until it shines brilliantly. Follow the panning process already described. When only black sand remains in the pan, rub a small amount of mercury onto the cleaned spot. The copper will hold the mercury, and mercury will absorb gold up to 86 percent of its own weight. Pour the black sand—from which you have already picked the largest pieces of gold—onto the spot of mercury. Hold the pan under water and rotate it gently, tilting it just enough to allow the black sand to wash out slowly. As this is done, the gold will be immediately absorbed by the mercury. The process can be repeated until the mercury, having absorbed all the gold it can hold, begins to thicken and finally reaches the consistency of putty. Then the mercury amalgam should be carefully removed to a container.

When you have a fair amount of this amalgam, place it in the center of a piece of canvas with a tight weave. Draw up the four corners of the canvas and hold the cloth over a container. Twist the canvas above the mercury amalgam, so that the cloth tightens around the mixture and forces it into a tight ball. Twist until no more mercury seeps through the canvas. Now you are ready to separate gold and mercury.

The simplest and safest way is to follow a procedure that was used in the last century and is still used by many prospectors today. Slice a potato in half. In one side carve out a depression large enough to hold the lump of mercury amalgam. Set the lump in a heavy iron skillet, cover it with the potato, and press down until the potato is in complete contact with the skillet. Set the skillet over low heat for forty-five minutes. When you lift the potato, you will find a chunk of gold in the center. To recover the mercury, place the potato half in a small amount of cold water and mash it completely. The mercury will then convert back to its liquid form, separate from both the water and the potato mash, and may be used over and over again.

ANY PROCESS THAT INVOLVES THE HEATING OF MERCURY SHOULD ONLY BE DONE OUT OF DOORS! INHALING MERCURY FUMES OR INGESTING MERCURY ITSELF CAN BE FATAL!

Before you head off to the goldfields to seek your fortune, you'll want to practice first and get the techniques of panning down pat. A good way to do this at home is to half fill a large tub with water, then dump in some sand and gravel and a few handfuls of BBs or buckshot from shotgun shells. The mixture will be similar to what you will be panning in the goldfields. If you follow the panning procedure described, you should end up with only the BBs or buckshot in the bottom of the pan.

Panning is hard work, but it is necessary to every type of small-scale gold mining. Even when you use a sluice box or more sophisticated equipment, panning is still necessary to refine the black sand trapped by the riffles. It can even be used to recover gold not found in water.

Dry Gold

Gold is also found in dry river or stream beds, which most people refer to as arroyos. While the wet-washing techniques for gold recovery (more of those will be discussed later on) are the best known and most popular, a large and growing number of prospectors prefer to work arroyos and desert areas. They feel the rivers and streams are being overworked, and so the chances of a big strike are best in the gullies and small canyons where rivers once ran. Often these overlooked dry washes are just a short distance from riverbanks crowded with eager fortune seekers who do not know the techniques of recovering dry alluvial gold.

Once you've located a promising spot where a stream once ran, or where water runs intermittently, go over it with your metal detector. Locate and mark all the concentrations of black sand. Select those that give the strongest reading, then dig down to bedrock, cleaning out every crack and crevice. Now you are ready to start extracting the gold.

The oldest and simplest method is by a process known as winnowing. Place some of the black sand in a large pan, remove all rocks and coarse gravel, and hold the pan high in the air. Tip it so that the remaining sand trickles slowly into another pan on the ground. The lighter material will be carried away by the slightest breeze, allowing only the heavier material to reach the lower pan. After the process has been repeated several times only gold will be left behind. In a variation of this technique, the black sand is tossed upward from a wool blanket; a slight electrostatic charge builds up in the wool, thus causing the gold to cling to it while the magnetite is carried away.

The electrostatic concentrator is a much more effective means of recovering gold found in dry washes. These weigh about 80 pounds, cost about $300 and are available from most mining equipment companies, including Keene Engineering, 11483 Vanowen Street, North Hollywood, California 91605. The folding devices are relatively easy to transport into gold country.

In using this device, sand and gravel are shoveled into a hopper at the top, which consists of two tilted trays, one mounted above the other. A gas-powered fan creates an electrostatic charge in the lower tray, which is equipped with riffles covered by a synthetic cloth. Coarse material is screened out as it passes from the top tray to the lower, where the gold is attracted and held by the electrostatic charge. The device will process sand and gravel as fast as you can shovel it in, as much as 2 tons in an hour.

Some prospectors prefer the dry-recovery methods even when working in small, shallow streams. They build a dam to divert the flow of water, allow the area to dry out, and then move in with their dry-recovery equipment.

When you set out to prospect for gold, you will probably want to start with either the dry- or wet-panning method, if only because they are the simplest and least expensive techniques. But once you've seen that first bit of color and perhaps put a fair amount of money in your pockets, you'll almost certainly want to go after that precious metal in bigger, faster, and more efficient ways. Several means are available.

The Gold Rocker

The gold rocker, which early miners fondly called the "Montana Mud Mover," was the first workable improvement on the gold pan. One can be bought for about $50, or you can probably put your own together for about $10. At least twice the amount of gravel can be worked in a day with this device than with a pan. It also requires far less physical exertion.

Most rockers consist of a combination washing box and screen, a canvas apron under the screen, and a short sluice with riffles on the bottom and rockers underneath the sluice. The washing box is made of sheet metal punctured with large holes to allow water to flow through. Gravel is shoveled into the washing box, and while water is poured over the gravel, the rocker is rotated back and forth, causing the smaller bits of material to fall through the holes onto the apron. The matter that remains above is scanned for nuggets, then discarded. The riffles catch and hold any gold that reaches the apron, and the water pouring through sweeps away the black sand. Gold is removed from the apron periodically and the process goes on.

The Sluice Box

A sluice box is essentially the same as a rocker except that no motion is used. It is an inclined trough which is placed at a shallow depth in the flow of a stream or river. In the past some were several hundred feet long and were used by dozens of men at a time.

The incline of the sluice is such that water flows through at a fairly rapid rate. The bottom of the trough has a series of transverse obstacles, or riffles. When gravel is shoveled into a hopper at the upstream end of the trough, the water washes it over the riffles, which trap the black sand and flakes of gold, while the lighter material is carried on out the other end of the trough. A layer of carpet covers the bottom of the trough below the riffles, and this captures even the tiniest flakes of gold. This is one type of recovery in which the river does at least part of the work.

Modern sluice boxes are far smaller than those used in the past, and they are also highly portable. For instance, Keene Engineering offers one 36 inches long and 10 inches wide, with removable riffles. It is made of aluminum, weighs 5 pounds, and costs less than $30. A larger model—10 inches wide, 52 inches long, and weighing 10 pounds—can be yours for just under $50. Aside from the sluice box, you'll also need a bucket and shovel, as well as the equipment for panning from the black sand any very fine gold that might escape the riffles.

Sluice boxes perform better in areas of high gravel content than they do in regions where there is a lot of ordinary sand. In these gravel areas you can simply dig out the pockets of black sand, shovel the magnetite into the upper end of the trough, and watch the pebbles and stones flow out the other end.

The sluice box should be placed so there is about an inch of incline for every foot of the trough's length. The incline—and thus the water flow—is about right when it takes thirty seconds for gravel to work its way down the length of a 3-foot sluice box. The material should break up gradually, not flow straight through.

Larger chunks of gravel will sometimes become trapped in the sluice, and you'll have to pick those out by hand. As you go over them for nuggets, keep a lookout for precious and semiprecious minerals, especially garnets, which sometimes turn up in gravel in gold-bearing streams.

When the riffles have trapped all the black sand they will hold, set the sluice box up on dry land and remove the riffles. Use tweezers to take out any larger pieces of gold, then scoop out the black sand and pan it carefully or set it aside to be panned later. Remove the carpet and very carefully transfer any gold to a pill bottle partially filled with water. You'll usually have to repeat this process about three times a day, but if you make that really big strike, you may find yourself happily doing it every hour or so.

A sluice box will cost somewhat more than equipment for panning, but its benefits are obvious. It requires little skill to use, and even an inexperienced prospector can process up to 10 cubic yards of material a day with the smallest box—about ten times as much as he would be able to process by panning.

The Surface Dredge

After you've had some success with the simpler techniques of gold mining, you might want to modernize your efforts by using a surface dredge in connection with the sluice box. The gas-powered surface pump is either set ashore on the stream bank or mounted on a float. The operator wades in the water or works from a small boat, directing the suction end of a vacuum hose over the bottom; it sucks up the gravel, black sand, and gold. This passes through the dredge and on into the sluice box. The running water washes away the lighter debris, leaving the gold and black sand trapped in the riffles of the sluice box.

It is important to choose a dredge of appropriate size for your mining operation. They are classified according to the inside diameter of the suction hose: 1½ inches, 2½ inches, 3 inches, on up to those that use hoses of 6 inches in diameter. For working most stream beds, a smaller diameter hose is preferable, 1½ inches or so. The larger hoses are needed only when tackling large sandbars or gravel banks. Smaller dredges are obviously preferable when you have to make a long trek to reach a good area. A typical 1½-inch dredge, for example, weighs only 25 pounds and uses just a single gallon of fuel in six hours of operation.

Complete with floating platform, hoses, and sluice box, a dredge of this size can be bought from Keene Engineering for $195.

If you've got a really hot spot and decide you need a larger dredge, you'd better start thinking of a partner, if only to help you carry in the equipment and share its cost. The 2½-inch dredge offered by Keene weighs 77 pounds and costs $319 complete with all accessories, and it uses a gallon of gasoline in three operating hours. Weight and fuel consumption increases drastically, as does cost, in the larger dredges, but if you reach the point where one of these monsters is needed, you'll probably be sitting around your corporate offices while hired miners are out in the hills doing the work of dredging your gold.

Underwater Gold

One of the hottest things in diving or treasure hunting today is underwater dredging for gold. A few adventurers began trying it at about the time scuba gear first became available early in the 1950s, and even when gold was worth just $35 an ounce some of these aquatic Argonauts were quietly taking thousands of dollars in yellow riches from the bottom of icy mountain streams. Diving for gold really caught on when California newspapers began carrying accounts of the fortunes being made by divers up in the mother lode country—including a tale of one diver who supposedly brought up $75,000 worth of dust and nuggets during a week-long vacation in the back country of northern California. This was when gold was still bringing that lowly price of just $35 an ounce.

Some time back, when the price of gold was beginning its steady climb but had not yet hit $300 per ounce, divers working those same California waters were reportedly averaging more than $100 per day in gold. At present, only God and the divers know for sure how high those earnings have gone, though the Internal Revenue Service probably has a fair idea.

Two types of dredges are used in the search for these underwater riches: the surface dredge described above, and a special submersible dredge that has fewer mechanical parts.

With only the simplest diving gear—a snorkel and a face mask—and moderate swimming skills, you can work a dredge in relatively shallow water. Drift slowly downstream with the current, towing the dredge as you go, and clean out all the likely spots with the suction nozzle. Material packed tight and deep in crevices can be loosened with a small pick. For working deeper water and using the submersible dredge, scuba gear and diving skills are needed.

The cost of getting started in this can be relatively high. Aside from the cost of diving lessons, the scuba gear, wet suit, and related items will set you back about $500. Then you'll need the submersible dredge, which will cost about the same as a surface dredge, your final investment depending on the size dredge you select.

The only major difference between a surface dredge and an underwater dredge is that the submersible dredge is guided over the bottom by a diver who has a partner keeping a sharp eye on the sluice box at the edge of the stream. The surface dredge is guided along the bottom by a wading treasure hunter.

The diver who operates the dredge must be experienced and a strong swimmer. He has to hold the apparatus in place, fighting the currents while guiding the suction nozzle over cracks and crevices and looking out for any large nuggets that might turn up. The job is something like riding a wild Brahma bull—fighting all these forces at once is no task for the novice. In addition to all the forces just mentioned, the swimmer may have to wear as much as 50 pounds in diving weights to hold him on the bottom, and there is always the possibility of cave-ins and falling rocks.

While one partner is underwater directing the nozzle of the dredge, the other partner or partners keep(s) a sharp eye on the exhaust end of the sluice box, watching for any gold that might be blown through along with the debris. The backup man or men must also periodically check the small sluice inside the dredge for gold and keep the surface pump running. This type of prospecting is not for everyone, but for those with the needed skills and the necessary funds, it can be the most profitable prospecting of all.

Financial Assistance

Unknown to most prospectors, the federal government will actually help grubstake you if you have a valid claim on a site with good potential. This applies to other minerals as well as to gold.

It's not really a handout, because you have to show proof that you can provide 25 percent of the funds yourself, but the program offers some very tangible benefits—the most important being that if you find no gold or minerals you are not obligated to pay back a single dime of the money loaned.

To obtain funding under this program, you must demonstrate that monetary backing is not available to you at reasonable interest rates from any bank or commercial lending institution. You must also prove that you would not ordinarily make such an exploration at your own expense.

If you receive a loan, you'll have to agree to pay Uncle Sam a royalty of 5 percent on whatever the claim produces. But, advises a bulletin from the U.S. Geological Survey, "There is no requirement to produce and if there is no production, no repayment is required."

Several million dollars have been loaned under this program, and the government has been repaid on slightly more than 10 percent of the loans. But government bulletins say that for every dollar loaned, at least thirty dollars in mineral wealth has been located.

To see if you qualify for such a grubstake, write to the Field Office of Minerals Exploration, U.S. Geological Survey, 345 Middlefield Road, Menlo Park, California 94025. Ask for the booklet called *Exploration Assistance*. It's free, and they'll even send along application forms.

Where to Look

If you want to be almost sure of success on your first trip to gold country, head for the shores of the Bering Sea in the vicinity of Nome. It's probably the richest gold country in the western hemisphere. When the first strike was made there in 1899, at least 20,000 sourdoughs worked the area during the six months that followed, and every single one of them met with at least some success. Average earnings during that first year are said to have been $850 per week, and one claim produced $750,000 worth of gold in twelve months—at a time when gold was bringing only $16 per ounce. The area is so rich in gold that until recently tourists were offered the chance to go out with guides and pan for gold and were not charged for the tour unless they came back with at least a few flecks of gold. Today you'll have to go looking on your own, because the skyrocketing price of gold has caused all the guides to grab their gear and head for the back country, and they're not about to direct you to favorite streams.

But probably you're not quite ready to chuck it all and head for

Alaska. Your next best bet, then, is California, just as it was the best bet for the Argonauts of 1849.

Most productive of all is the famous mother lode. This is not, as most people think, one great vein of gold; it is actually a series of small vein systems, running parallel to one another. The richest of these veins are found in an area about 1 mile wide and 50 miles long, extending from Mariposa in the south to Georgetown in the north. Gold is being taken from every stream and river along that line.

The mountains just north of Los Angeles provide the runoff that feeds the rivers Kern and San Gabriel, both famous for their placer

Roy Lagal, noted treasure hunter, searches for lost gold and silver nuggets. With his detector, he scans the floor, ceiling, and walls of this old mine shaft in Idaho. COURTESY OF GARRETT ELECTRONICS, INC.

deposits. Their tributaries are equally rich, and any arroyo in the region is a good spot.

The San Francisco region is even better. In this part of the state numerous rivers converge to flow into the great bays. There is the Sacramento, flowing in from the north and fed by the Butte, Feather, Yuba, Rubicon, and American rivers—all streams that are famous for the gold they produce. There is the San Joaquin, flowing up from the south and joined by the Stanislaus, Tuolumne, Merced, Chowchilla, and Kings. The Consumnes and Moklumnes rivers, which flow into San Pablo Bay, are also famous for placer gold.

The northwest corner of California also has streams that hold great wealth. Ones presently being worked with success include the Klamath, Salmon, Scott, Shasta, Pit, Trinity, and Hay Fork, as well as some of their tributaries.

Colorado is also rich in gold and other mineral wealth. In 1891, a great strike was made just west of Colorado Springs, creating the boomtown of Cripple Creek, where mines once produced $20 million worth of gold each year. The gold rush of today is just as frenzied in that region as it was in 1891, with large amounts of gold being recovered from the tailings of old mines. But remember that placer gold also occurs in Colorado.

The most famous gold-bearing rivers in Colorado include the San Juan, Arkansas, Cherry Creek, South Platte, Eagle, Colorado, and upper Rio Grande. Gold particles are found in virtually every creek in Eagle, Clear Creek, Park, Teller, Boulder, and Lake counties, all of which are in the vicinity of Denver.

In western Nevada, in that strip of land that lies between the borders of California and Oregon, several rivers are yielding large amounts of placer gold, especially those streams around Carson City and Nevada City—rivers such as the Humboldt, Reese, Walker, and Carson. The region is also pockmarked with old mines that may hold vast riches.

Up in Oregon, most weekend prospectors are working the Rogue River and its tributaries, as well as small streams high in the Klamath and Blue mountains. Lode deposits have been found in the northeastern part of the state.

In the state of Washington, head for the tributaries of the Columbia River, which carry gold down from the mountains of British Columbia; if you're over in Idaho, try the Snake and the Kootenai rivers. In Montana, your best bet is the Missouri River or its tributaries, or any stream in Madison County, which is one of the great gold-producing counties in the United States. In South Dakota, work the small streams of the Black Hills, especially those around Deadwood, and try French Creek, which is near Custer.

In the eastern part of the country opportunities are far more limited, but they do exist. Fair amounts of gold have recently been panned from the Swift River in Maine, and in New Hampshire, gold is presently being panned from Indian Stream.

"Other placer deposits in the East may be discovered," says a pamphlet of the U.S. Geological Survey, "but they will be of low grade, costly to explore, and difficult to recognize."

That statement was issued, however, before gold prices were even near their present high, and so those Eastern placer deposits may now be well worth looking for. Best bets are the streams on the eastern slope of the southernmost Appalachian Mountains, especially in Virginia, North Carolina, South Carolina, Alabama, and Georgia. For a complete list of gold-bearing regions in the United States, please see the appendix.

Selling Your Gold

When you've finally collected enough gold to be worth marketing, don't sell it to your dentist or jeweler, for if you do, you'll probably receive far less than its real value. You'll get the best price by selling it to a reputable refiner. Here are just a few of the many firms that are buying gold from amateur prospectors.

Engelhard Mineral and Chemical Corp.
    430 Mountain Avenue
    Murray Hill, NJ 07947

Homestake Mining Co.
    650 California Street
    San Francisco, CA 94108

Western Alloy Refining Company
    366 East Fifty-eighth Street
    Los Angeles, CA 90011

Phoenix Refining Corp.
    1990 East First Street
    Tempe, AZ 85281

Helpful Pamphlets

Numerous informative pamphlets are available on the topics of prospecting and small-scale gold mining. These are some of the best:

Legal Guide for California Prospectors and Miners. This booklet costs $1, but it's absolutely necessary if you're going prospecting in California. The 128-page publication is revised from time to time, and, in addition to an explanation of the state laws, contains many useful hints. It should be ordered from the Division of Mines, Ferry Building, San Francisco, California 94111.

How to Mine and Prospect for Placer Gold, Circular No. 8517, can be obtained from the U.S. Bureau of Mines, Publications Distribution Section, 4800 Forbes Avenue, Pittsburgh, Pennsylvania 15213. It is free.

Suggestions for Prospecting is available without cost from the U.S. Geological Survey, Washington, DC 20242. It is most valuable for its comprehensive bibliography.

Production Potential of Known Gold Deposits in the United States can be ordered from the U.S. Bureau of Mines at the address given above. It is free.

Placer Evaluation and Dredge Selection is a pamphlet that will help you determine the value of your placer strike and choose the right equipment for working it. It costs 60¢, from the Superintendent of Documents, Government Printing Office, Washington, DC 20402.

8

Gem Prospecting

As you have probably realized, your chances of making a big gold strike are far greater if you live in the West. But if you happen to live east of the Mississippi River, don't abandon your pick, shovel, or metal detector. You can still go prospecting with high hopes, but instead of concentrating on the search for gold, you'll probably do best to go looking for gemstones.

As a matter of fact, no matter what part of the country you call home, North or South, East or West, this is a type of prospecting you can pursue with some hope of success.

Amazing strikes have been made in recent years. These include a 34-carat diamond found in West Virginia by a boy who was pitching horseshoes; a diamond valued at $110,000 found by an amateur prospector in Arkansas; a $250,000 opal picked up by a rancher in Nevada; and a boulder of solid jade, worth at least $250,000, recovered by two scuba divers working in just 5 fathoms of water off Big Sur, California. And not all gemstones are found out in the boondocks—several years back, during an excavation project in the heart of Manhattan, workers unearthed a beautifully colored "rock" that turned out to be a garnet weighing just under 11 pounds. Your own strike could be the next to create headlines.

A gemstone is a precious or semiprecious stone that may be used as a jewel when cut and polished. In other words, a gemstone is what precedes a gem.

There are approximately 1,500 mineral species. Of these, only about 100 can be classified as gemstones. Among the 100 or so, four are always considered as precious: diamonds, rubies, emeralds, and sapphires; but dozens of others, such as jade, opal, tourmaline, turquoise, or even garnet, may be worth as much or more to you, depending on factors such as size, quality, and quantity.

Many of the most valuable gemstones are simply colored rock crystals. Millions of years ago, during the great convulsions that shaped the earth, highly heated water was forced up through rock crevices under pressure so great that many minerals in the rock were melted and fused. Upon cooling, these rocks crystallized, much in the way that salt crystals form when a saltwater solution is heated and then allowed to cool. The mineral crystallization occurred only in pockets and crevices in the rock—leaving behind the gemstone deposits that modern prospectors seek. Such a deposit may be as small as a walnut or as large as a Greyhound bus.

There are many areas in the United States where gemstones can be found lying exposed on the surface of the ground, providing, of course, that the gem hunter knows what he is looking for and is willing to spend enough time in the search. But by and large, it is better to look for the pockets in the long pegmatite dikes that run along the sides of hills or mountains in roughly parallel lines. Such hills and mountains consist largely of common granite. The veins that can be seen are the result of shrinking and cooling. These veins are usually filled with a different and coarser granite known as pegmatite, which may be mixed with feldspar and quartz. When such a vein has been long exposed to weathering, the feldspar is the first mineral to break down and decompose. As feldspar decomposes, it sometimes forms a pink, puttylike substance that prospectors know as gem clay. Not every pegmatite dike holds gemstones, but the presence of the pink gem clay is a sure indication that gemstones are around.

If you'd like to vastly increase your chances of success, you might consider a gem hunting vacation in North Carolina, particularly in that part of the Tarheel State known as the Cowee Valley. No state in the Union has a wider variety of minerals than North Carolina. More than 300 types of minerals and gemstones are found there. No fewer than 49 of the 100 counties in the state have deposits of valuable gemstones. Most eagerly sought by gem hunters are rubies, emeralds, agates, sapphires, and the diamonds that turn up very infrequently, but amethyst, beryl, hiddenite, and agate account for a great part of the take.

Most North Carolina gem hunters head for Franklin, the largest town in Macon County. This lies in the western part of the state, nestled in the foothills of the Nantahala Mountains, and is the base for those who hunt gems in the famous Cowee Valley.

It is said that every resident of the Cowee Valley owns at least one piece of jewelry set with a precious stone from the local mines, usually a ruby. Where ancient Cowee Creek cuts through the valley there are at least 75 operating ruby mines. Ruby mining has been going on here since the first blood-red stones were found late in the last century. Vast fortunes were made during those early days, but the main source of the rubies eluded those early miners, and it remains elusive to this day, despite extensive attempts to find it. For a small daily fee—usually be-. tween $2 and $4—you can try your hand at panning for Cowee Valley rubies and keep any precious stones you find.

The Cowee Valley rubies are among the finest found anywhere in the world. They are brilliantly transparent, rich red in color, and six-sided. Many of the better specimens can be seen at the Smithsonian Institution in Washington, D.C.

But you don't have to visit North Carolina to have gem hunting opportunities, just as you don't have to go to Alaska to have a chance at finding gold. Contrary to popular belief, valuable deposits of gemstones exist in all parts of the country. You should be able to get started close to your own home. Perhaps you won't find a diamond the first or second time out, but you may find deposits of other gemstones that are just as valuable. In the appendix I'll provide a state-by-state, county-by-county list of gemstone deposits that will help you decide what to look for; but before you head for the field, there is certain equipment you'll need and certain information you'll want to gather.

Getting Started in Gem Hunting

Aside from the natural appeal of any endeavor that offers an opportunity to strike it rich, there are other reasons why gem hunting is one of the fastest growing hobby sports in America. Not only does it afford the same healthy outdoor recreation enjoyed in all types of treasure hunting, but getting started is far less expensive. You'll need no costly scuba gear or salvage equipment, and even a metal detector is not absolutely necessary, though some gem hunters do use one as an accessory.

If you decide to use a metal detector as an accessory in gem hunting, the BFO detectors are superior to the transmitter receivers, because the latter are likely to react in the same way to any of a number of minerals, confusing you. With the BFO detector, you can acquire a sample of a mineral, such as feldspar, that you know to be associated with one or more of the gemstones, familiarize yourself with the way it causes the detector to react, and then use the detector to locate deposits of feldspar or other associated minerals. Such samples are available, at low cost, at most rock shops.

A great deal of experience is required in order to discern the slight signal variations caused by the different minerals. So many types of minerals are present in gemstone-bearing earth that a detector used over it would almost constantly be emitting signals that you would not want to ignore. For gem hunting, then, think of the metal detector as a tool you'll want to use only after you know it so well that it is almost an extension of your senses.

Other tools are not so optional.

Foremost among these is a good rock pick, or as it's often known, a geologist's pick. These are as basic to gem hunting as the metal detector is to coin shooting. This tool differs from other picks you have seen. It is more like a combination hammer and chisel, usually crafted from a single piece of steel, expertly designed for strength and balance. It ranges in weight from 14 to 24 ounces. The one with a comfortable heft is the one you should choose.

A quality rock pick, with a 24-ounce head, made of polished steel, and with a laminated leather grip to prevent slipping, will cost about $12 to $14. For convenience in carrying it, you'll also want a leather holster or belt-strap, which will increase your investment by just a couple of dollars.

You'll also want at least a small selection of chisels and gads. Chisels, as you probably know, have beveled ends that can be driven into rock, causing it to split along its natural cleavage or along specific directional lines. Gads are field tools with pointed ends that are used to pry rock apart. Chisels and gads cost $2 to $4 apiece. The best have leather or vinyl grips. Sets are available that include holsters. You'll also want a good hammer, preferably one specifically intended for rockhounding. These are of the sledge type, with highly polished faces. The weight of the head can range from as little as 3 pounds to as high as 7. With the heavier hammers, you'll find it easier to break apart rock samples, but you should keep in mind that the incautious use of a heavy sledge could easily shatter fragile gemstones such as opal. The hammer will cost about $10.

Safety goggles are the next essential tool, and be sure you have them on before you strike a rock with a pick or hammer. Unless you've used steel against rock, you'll find it hard to imagine how great the velocity of those shards can be when they break away beneath your hammering. Good safety goggles cost only $5 or so, and they would be cheap at ten times the price.

Other common tools can come in handy. There'll be times when you'll be able to use a shovel, a hand rake, a jackknife, and a bucket or two. You'll also want a good supply of plastic specimen bags. If you're going to be working in remote areas, take along a first-aid kit, several canteens of water, some good maps, a compass, and possibly even a C.B. radio in case you have an accident and need to radio for help.

You'll also need a well-built sifting device with ¼-inch mesh. These are sold at shops that deal in equipment for rockhounds, or you can make your own by removing the bottom of a bucket and replacing it with the screen. Be sure the screen is solid enough to stand a good bit of weight, though, because the purpose of the sifter is to allow you to go through as much sand and gravel as you can in the shortest time period.

There is quite a bit you can do to improve your chances before starting out. Informing yourself about the gemstones in your area is the most important of these. Your library has several comprehensive books on the subject. Two of the best are *Gems and Minerals of North America—A Guide to Rock Collecting* by Jay Ellis Ransom; and *Gems and Precious Stones of North America* by George F. Kunz, which, in addition to providing information that will enable you to identify the gemstones, also includes what is probably the most complete list of gemstone locations ever published.

Some excellent magazines are devoted to amateur prospecting. In addition to their informative articles, these often carry ads for tourist mines, where you can pay to dig and keep any gems you find. A visit to one of these mines is a good idea, because it allows you to see more experienced gem hunters at work, not to mention that some fabulous strikes have been made in such mines.

Gems and Minerals, which is available from the publishers at P.O. Box 687, Mentone, California 92359, is the official magazine of the American Federation of Mineralogical Societies. A twelve-issue subscription costs $3.

Rocks and Minerals is published by the Eastern Federation of Mineralogical and Lapidary Societies. Annual subscriptions cost $3 and should be ordered from the Federation at P.O. Box 29, Peekskill, New York 10566.

Most states publish informative booklets for rockhounds and gem prospectors, especially helpful because of the local data they contain. These can usually be obtained through the Bureau of Mines and Mineral Resources, or the Geological Survey Department, at the state capital of the state in which you plan to search.

If there is a Museum of Natural History in your area, you should visit it. Most museums of this type have displays related to the local geology, and this will allow you to actually see samples in their natural state of some of the minerals that occur in your area. If the museum has a geologist, he or she may suggest some spots for you to try.

It is also a good idea to join a club for rockhounds. You'll not only be able to draw on the experience of other members, but also be able to participate in field trips and rely on their help while you're gaining some experience of your own. There are more than 1,000 of these clubs in the United States.

Most local clubs are affiliates of the American Federation of Mineralogical Societies, which is located at 3418 Flannery Lane, Baltimore, Maryland 21207. The purpose of the Federation is to promote interest and education in geology, mineralogy, lapidary, and certain other sciences. Its local affiliates have more than 55,000 members. Drop them a line at the address above, and they'll gladly direct you to a club in your area.

Your community probably has a rock shop where further information and advice can be obtained. In the *Yellow Pages* you will find these shops listed under "Minerals." Most of these shops are little mom-and-pop operations, with friendly proprietors who share your interests and who will gladly take a few minutes to answer your questions. Besides selling equipment you'll need, and individual mineral samples, these shops usually sell complete mineral collections containing specimens of various ores you can expect to find locally. Each specimen is an inch or two long, numbered, and keyed to an identification chart. These will make it far easier for you to identify specimens you take in the field.

While you're at the rock shop, look over some of the cut and polished stones they sell. You'll see that most are not precious or even semiprecious stones, but simply more common minerals that become relatively beautiful when given the proper treatment.

But gemstones are what you really seek, and now you're ready to go hunting. The laws of treasure hunting also apply here, so you must get permission (in writing if possible) before you venture onto land owned by others. Remember that if you make a big strike and find a spot that looks as if it might continue to produce, you can stake a legal mining claim to the mineral rights just as you would if you struck gold.

Diamonds

This gem among gems is the hardest of all substances. Due to its brilliance and clarity, it is highly prized in all parts of the world and has been since the first ones were discovered in India. For centuries that country was the leading producer of diamonds, but its supply had been nearly depleted by the time diamonds were found in Brazil. That South American country enjoyed a brief diamond boom, but the boom was over by 1867—the year an odd little incident happened in South Africa.

A man named Schalk van Niekirk offered to buy an unusual stone that caught his fancy on a visit to a South African farmhouse. Since the stone was only a child's plaything, he was told by the farmers that he could have it for nothing. The plaything turned out to be a diamond worth several thousand dollars; the great South African diamond rush was under way. South Africa now produces roughly 90 percent of the world's diamonds, those used in industry as well as in jewelry.

That story is pretty well known. What is not so well known is that van Niekirk, who started the South African boom, later visited the gold-fields of California, where miners in Butte County had been finding small diamonds in the streams since 1850. It was his opinion that these diamonds were of excellent quality, a belief that must have been shared by the founders of the United States Diamond Mining Company, which ran a successful diamond mine near Oroville until well after the start of this century. That operation is closed now, but diamonds have since been found in scattered locations around the state in California.

Surprisingly enough, you don't have to head for South Africa or even California to have at least a slim chance of finding a diamond. (You won't have a *good* chance no matter where you look, because if they were that easy to find, they would be far less valuable.) There are several areas in the United States where fair numbers of these precious stones are continually being found.

The most famous site for finding diamonds is the 867-acre crater of Diamond State Park outside the small town of Murfreesboro, Arkansas. The crater is the visible tip of a geological phenomenon not known to exist at any other place in North America—a peridotite pipe containing diamonds. Geologists say the pipe was thrust up from the center of the earth at least 65 million years ago during the eruption of a volcano on an island in the sea that then covered this part of the continent. The eruption drove the peridotite core, or pipe—the diamond-bearing material—up through layer after layer of rock and earth. These layers held jasper and other durable rocks that were shattered and are still found mixed in with the lava from the eruption. The crater also holds chunks of Kimberlite, the mineral frequently found in association with South

African diamonds. Mixed in with the lava and Kimberlite, diggers often find a wide array of other minerals including agate, amethyst, quartz, jasper, garnet, and magnetite, the black sand that commonly occurs near gold. But the diggers are there for the diamonds, by far the most valuable substance thrown up by that ancient volcanic eruption.

Not many of the diamonds found in this field are pure white. The most common color is yellow. But they range in color from black to pale sapphire-blue, with the extremely valuable white ones turning up often enough to keep the excitement going. While not every stone is of high gem quality, the field has produced some incredible stones since the first diamond was found by a farmer named John Huddleston back in 1906.

You will find diamond hunters working the crater at Diamond State Park on any day of the year. There are some who try to "divine" them with peach or willow rods, even one man who claims his dog can spot diamonds. But most people locate the gems by sifting through the top dirt and gravel, which park officials plow weekly so that opportunities for finding diamonds are continually renewed.

Not everyone sifts for diamonds here. L. E. and Pauline Owens of Des Arc, Arkansas, who may be the most successful diamond hunters in this country, prefer to pick a likely looking area, sit on cushions, and very carefully scan the surrounding ground until their vision adapts and they can pick out the faint gleam of a diamond. The method works best after a heavy downpour of rain, they say, for then the water has softened and washed away the dirt that would otherwise be clinging to the diamonds. This is possible because diamonds occur as individual crystals, not as part of larger rock formations, like many other gems. The method has produced more than 200 diamonds for the Owenses, including one 7-carat stone and dozens weighing more than 2 carats a piece. On any rainy day, park officials say, numerous people can be observed working any of the hot spots in the park.

Diamond State Park is open to the public throughout the year. Admission is $2 for adults, $1 for children. You can bring your own equipment or rent it at nominal cost.

While Diamond State Park's crater is the site of the only *known* peridotite pipe containing diamonds, many geologists believe, with very good reason, that another major pipe exists somewhere in the vast wilderness around Hudson Bay. Diamonds have been found in scattered parts of the country, and they could only have arrived there by being carried south by glaciers during the last ice age.

Those glacier-deposited diamonds have been found in West Virginia, California, Indiana, Wisconsin, and Idaho. Most have been found accidentally by gem hunters looking for other minerals, but in a few spots there have been enough finds to encourage prospectors to search for diamonds.

The Kettle Moraine State Forest, near the hamlet of Greenbush, Wisconsin, has produced a small but relatively steady flow of diamonds in recent years, including two stones weighing just over 5 carats apiece, and a giant stone that topped 16 carats. In Idaho, diamonds have been found in Adams County, where gem hunters also find rubies and garnets. Brown and Morgan counties in Indiana have been yielding small diamonds for years, including several in the 5-carat range; and in California, Butte County has been the place to hunt diamonds for well over a century.

Random discoveries have also been made in the sand and gravel of present and ancient stream beds in North and South Carolina, Georgia, Virginia, Texas, Montana, Oregon, and Ohio. It is believed that these originated in the once volcanic Rocky and Appalachian Mountain ranges, or that they were also carried south by glaciers. Only rarely have diamonds been found in the states just listed, and they are not suggested as areas where you would want to put a great deal of time and effort into diamond prospecting.

Unless you're working a known diamond field, such as the ones in Arkansas and Wisconsin, with a very clear idea of what you might find, overlooking a diamond in the rough can be all too easy. A visit to a local museum, where you can view a diamond in its natural state, uncut and unpolished, is strongly suggested. There you will see that a rough diamond has only the faintest gleam to it, looking very much like a piece of quartz that has been coated with a grayish film. A gem cutter appraising the stone makes a minute cut, creating a window in this film, to see what the stone looks like inside. If handled, the raw diamond has a slightly oily feel, which is why mud and dirt seldom adhere to a diamond. As for testing a suspected diamond by using it to scratch glass, remember that several other minerals, including certain types of quartz, are also capable of cutting glass. The only way to verify the worth of a suspected diamond is to take it to a lapidary and have it examined.

Because most of the diamonds found in this country are likely to be very small in size, experts suggest that you use a very fine sifting screen—⅛-inch mesh or so—when hunting them. Take your time in sifting the dirt, sand, or gravel, and carefully examine all pebbles before throwing them away. Diamond hunting probably requires more patience than any other type of treasure search, but if luck is with you and your eyes are sharp, you might end up with a fortune you can wear on your finger.

Emeralds

In guides to gems and minerals, the emerald is classified as one of several gems belonging to a mineral group known as beryl. All beryl has some value but nothing to approach the worth of the magnificently beautiful forest-green stone that is one of the most eagerly sought after jewels in the world.

Other types of beryl are aquamarine, morganite, and goshenite. These are slightly harder than the emerald, but color is the easiest way to distinguish one from the other. Morganite ranges in color from the palest pink to the deepest red. Aquamarine is always some shade of bluish-green. Goshenite is nearly colorless, resembling milky quartz. Emerald, of course, is best described as—excuse me—emerald green in color.

Members of the beryl group of gemstones are found in association with veins of mica. Under the mica there is usually a layer of quartz, and beneath the quartz, if you are lucky, you may find that emeralds and other members of the beryl group have crystallized. The gemstones are usually extracted by sifting the dirt just under the quartz layer.

The emerald is not only softer than other members of its mineral group, it is also softer than most other precious gemstones—which is why great care must be exercised when digging in any area that might hold emeralds. These gems are just hard enough to be used as jewelry, but not hard enough to withstand a solid blow from a metal tool. Softness is a major reason why emeralds are so rare, for the beautifully formed green crystals are easily fractured and destroyed during any geological upheaval.

Emeralds are also relatively light, which is why, unlike many other gemstones, they are seldom found in the sand and gravel of stream beds. Because they have little weight, they have no chance to settle to the bottom and are simply swept away by the currents.

Very few emeralds are completely clear and transparent, but those with these qualities are immensely valuable. The gems usually contain certain irregularities known as inclusions. These inclusions may consist of tiny bubbles of gas, or they may be tiny foreign mineral crystals that were trapped in the emerald when it was originally formed. By studying these inclusions under a microscope, experts can usually determine the origin of the stone.

The value of an emerald does, of course, depend largely upon its color. Unless it is exactly the right shade of vivid green it cannot be classed as an emerald at all. If the mineral is pale green and brilliantly clear, it is not an emerald but simply a green form of beryl. Huge opaque crystals of green beryl—some weighing as much as 2 tons—have been found in various parts of the world, but rarely in the United States.

Aquamarine is the most valuable form of beryl you are likely to encounter while searching for emeralds. These can range in color from pale blue to greenish-blue, and their value as gems depends largely on their transparency, color, and size. The value is greatly reduced if they contain irregularities. Blue stones are the most valuable, and blue-green stones can be changed to blue and made more valuable by careful heating, but this operation must be done by a skilled technician.

Colombia is the leading source of quality emeralds, and there are mines there, still in operation, that produced emeralds for the ancient civilization of the Incas. The Incas hid these mines from the Spaniards who came to plunder their wealth, and some of the mines have never been found. So, if you're ever down Colombia way . . .

But if you don't feel up to braving the jungles of Colombia, not even for emeralds, then I'd suggest you try prospecting around Franklin County, Massachusetts, or the town of Hiddenite, about 25 miles west of Winston-Salem, North Carolina. Emeralds of large size and high quality have been found in both areas, but Hiddenite is the mecca for American emerald hunters.

In 1879, William Hidden, a geologist who worked for Thomas Edison, was sent to North Carolina to search for platinum. He did not find platinum but instead discovered a previously unknown form of beryl. It was not emerald, but a crystal that was named in his honor, hiddenite, as was the hamlet that later sprang up. In later years, Hidden, as well as others, found a few small emeralds, but the emerald fields were considered unimportant until recent years. It is now known that the Hiddenite mines hold emeralds of enormous value, though how many emeralds no one can say.

Emeralds are now mined commercially in this region, but there are plenty of chances for amateurs. Several mines will permit you to do unlimited digging, sifting, and panning for fees ranging from $2 to $3 per day. Of course, you keep any gems you find, and amateurs have been finding plenty in recent years.

The Hiddenite emerald boom really took off after 1969. That year an amateur rockhound named Michael Finger paid to dig in such a mine and walked away with an emerald 2 inches in diameter and 3 inches long—after being cut, the stone sold for $110,000!

The same year a mine near Hiddenite produced an even larger emerald, a whopper the size of a tennis ball that weighed 1,438 carats. This gemstone rested in a local museum for four years and was then stolen; presumably it has by now been cut up into smaller gems.

The following year, 1970, another amateur rockhound, who had been digging in the same mine for two hours, discovered an emerald weighing 59 carats. He quickly sold it for a few hundred dollars. The stone was cut and passed through the hands of numerous owners, then was finally acquired by Tiffany's in New York City for around $100,000. The Carolina Emerald, as it is now known, can be seen on display in that firm's New York store.

Emeralds of enormous value continue to be found in the Hiddenite mines, and geologists say that other emerald deposits almost certainly exist in North Carolina, especially along the eastern side of the Blue Ridge Mountains. Beryl deposits are found in many other parts of the country, so it is likely that a few of these also hold emeralds of gem quality.

The area around LaGrange in Troup County, Georgia, is one that seems worth exploring. To date it has produced no emeralds, but large amounts of minerals from the beryl group have been found here in the last decade, including at least 2,000 pounds of rich blue aquamarine, with many stones weighing as much as 15 carats. The aquamarine here is found in pegmatite dikes in granite rock. Where aquamarine occurs there is always the possibility of finding emerald, but even if no emeralds are found, there are other ways to strike it rich in this region.

Like North Carolina, Georgia is a state rich in minerals, with most of the state offering the chance to find gemstones. Diamonds were found in Hall County more than 100 years ago, but none has turned up in recent years. Gold prospectors of the last century also found topaz in the sand and gravel of the Chattahoochee, Etowah, and Chestatee rivers. Black and gray tourmaline have been found in mica deposits throughout the state. Garnets have been found in large numbers in

Paulding County. But the most eagerly sought stones in this part of the country, as well as in several others, are the closely related gemstones we know as rubies and sapphires.

Rubies and Sapphires

These two gemstones share with the diamond, emerald, and pearl the position of the most precious jewels in the world. Although trends and fashions may cause the value of other gems to rise, it is hard to imagine any set of circumstances that could cause a drop in the worth of any of the leading five. Their beauty and rarity have assured them a permanent place at the top of the bejeweled heap.

Chemically, rubies and sapphires are composed of the simple compound aluminum oxide, known as corundum. Corundum occurs in nature in a startling array of colors, and since rubies and sapphires are chemically the same substance, their names merely indicate their different colors.

Broadly speaking, gem corundum can be divided into two groups: (1) all material that is truly red in color called rubies, and (2) all the many other shades known as sapphires.

Pure corundum is rarely found in nature in a clear form. Moreover, because of its lack of color and sparkle, pure corundum is rarely cut as a gem, and the so-called white sapphires used in cheap jewelry are of synthetic origin. When small traces of a chemical substance known as chromic oxide intrude into the crystal structure of the hitherto colorless corundum, it turns red and is transformed into a ruby. Its beauty, however, does not depend entirely on the red color alone, but involves another of the mysteries of light known as fluorescence. This phenomenon can be illustrated by shining a beam of blue light on a ruby in an otherwise darkened room and then observing it through a red filter. Normally, if you tried to view an object illuminated in this way, almost nothing would be visible because the red filter would have absorbed all the blue light rays and none would reach your eyes. But the ruby is an exception and will glow like a burning coal. This is because the ruby is able to absorb the shorter blue and violet wavelengths of light and re-emit them as red light. The fluorescent glow can also be stimulated by placing a ruby under ultraviolet light—one way to test a suspected ruby—and is stimulated to a lesser extent by the ultraviolet rays present in sunshine.

As with the ruby, the color of sapphires is due to small quantities of chemical impurities, usually titanium oxide and a trace of iron oxide. Few people realize that these impurities can cause sapphires to take on many different hues, and the general belief that sapphires can be only blue is totally incorrect. There are green, yellow, purple, and pink stones, with a large number of intermediate shades.

As is the case with many gemstones, the value of rubies and sapphires depends on appearance, mainly color. The best color in the ruby is the deep, rich red that jewelers call pigeon's blood, while blue is the most valuable form of sapphire, followed, in order, by green, yellow, and black.

The finest rubies and sapphires come from Burma and Ceylon, but the gems are also found in India, Australia, and the United States. They are found in association with other mineral deposits that have been broken down by weather into gem clay, pinkish-brown puttylike clay. Where further erosion has occurred, the sapphires and rubies are frequently found in what are called gem gravels—a multitude of different rock materials that have been collected over thousands of years by rivers and streams and washed into low-lying areas to be deposited in layers and terraces. Deposits of both types exist in the United States, but most of our rubies and sapphires have been taken from gem gravels.

Picking gemstones from gravel may seem a primitive and tedious way to mine, yet it is by far the most productive method, and a little consideration of the nature of corundum will show why.

Mining directly from rock entails the expensive and cumbersome operation of crushing the stones and concentrating them artificially before they will yield their gems. But in the case of the gem gravels, this part of the work has already been done by nature—and without harm to the gemstones.

Corundum is one of the hardest substances known, second only to diamonds. Its perfectly formed, often barrel-shaped crystals are not easily worn down or damaged by the natural erosion that eats away other minerals. And like many other gemstones, corundum is far heavier than the average mineral. This means that as the lighter rock materials are washed away by the natural action of rivers and streams, gem gravels build up a relatively high concentration of the heavier gemstones. Their heaviness also means they may be separated by panning the gravel, very much in the way gold is.

Picking the gemstones from gravel is well worth your time since these jewels can be enormously valuable.

Carat for carat, a ruby of good size is likely to be worth far more than a diamond of the same weight. A 5- or 6-carat diamond is worth only half as much as a ruby or sapphire of the same size, and at the 10-carat level, the diamond is worth only about one-third as much. This is because large rubies and sapphires are exceedingly rare. Small ones are not quite so scarce and, thus, proportionately their value is not so high.

Rubies and sapphires have been found in fifteen states. The guide presented in the appendix will tell you exactly where they have been found nearest you. But if you really want to increase your chances of finding either gemstone, there are certain hot spots you'll want to explore as part of a treasure hunting vacation trip.

Rubies and sapphires have been mined commercially in just two states, Montana and North Carolina. If you're headed out west, or happen to live there, try the Yogo Gulch region of Montana, near Helena. Ask someone in town to direct you to the famous Eldorado Bar Sapphire Mine. Once there, for a small daily fee, you can sift the mine tailings or dig in virgin ground and keep all the sapphires you find.

Most of the Montana sapphires are green, but orange, yellow, red, purple, black, and blue ones have also been found. About 85 percent of the stones are flawed and thus worth only about $150 per carat, but the flawless stones produced by this mine rival any that come from Burma or Ceylon.

Screening out sapphires is hard work. After the gravel is dug up it must first be passed through a ½-inch mesh and then through one of around ⅛-inch; always keep a sharp lookout for the sapphires. The finer material is then put in a pan, held underwater and washed in a swishing motion, tilting the pan very slightly, until the lighter material is carried away. Then only gravel and sapphires will remain. It takes some experience to recognize the sapphires, because they look like ordinary bits of colored gravel, but you can check them by using one to scratch a piece of unglazed porcelain. If it is a sapphire or ruby, it will cut the porcelain quite easily and leave behind a streak of white.

If you're in North Carolina or headed that way, consider a side trip to the famous Cowee Valley, which I have mentioned previously, or the Corundum Hill mine, which is located on the banks of the Cullasaja River, near the town of Franklin. Wear old clothes and be prepared to get dirtier than you have ever been.

Both rubies and sapphires are found here with regularity, as well as occasional emeralds, topaz, gem amethyst, and aquamarine in large quantity. The mines will charge you $2 to $4 a day to dig, furnish all the equipment, and let you keep what you find. Half a dozen lapidaries are nearby to appraise and cut the stones you find.

Rubies and sapphires in this region are often taken from ancient gravel beds that vary in thickness from 3 to 10 feet. You get them out by setting up a sifting screen near the stream or dry stream bed, shoveling in as much mud and gravel as the screen will hold, and then pouring on water to force the mud through the holes in the screen. It is far from the most glamorous type of treasure hunting but is so effective that, according to publicity material sent out by the state of North Carolina, at least one young woman was able to give up her job as a secretary in New York City and move here after she found nine rubies and twenty-three sapphires during the course of her one-week summer vacation. Your own search could be more rewarding.

Pearls

There are five precious gems but only four precious gemstones. That is because the pearl, unlike the diamond, emerald, ruby, and sapphire, is not a gemstone at all, but is an organic product of nature. Beauty—combined with rarity—makes it one of the most treasured of all gems.

Natural pearls are, of course, obtained from shellfish, though not all shellfish are capable of producing pearls. Two groups, the pearl oysters and the pearl mussels, normally give us our gem pearls, although pearls of moderate value have also been found in the conch and pen shells of Florida and the abalone that is found in shallow waters from California to Alaska.

Don't expect to find a valuable pearl in the edible oysters that come from northerly waters such as the Chesapeake Bay. Only rarely do these oysters produce pearls, and even then they are too tiny and lusterless to be of great value. I have a tiny one that came from an oyster I tonged in Delaware's Rehoboth Bay, but it is a keepsake and nothing more.

Pearl oysters occur in the southern waters of the world and thrive only in temperatures of about 25 degrees centigrade. They congregate in vast numbers attached to rock banks in relatively shallow waters. Rarely are they found at depths of more than 30 feet. Most pearls come from the Persian Gulf and Australia, but quality oyster pearls are occasionally taken from the Gulf of Mexico and the Gulf of California. Many of the oyster pearls found in these American waters have been black, with a rich metallic luster, which adds greatly to their value.

Too little is known about the nature of pearls and what determines their color. Their hue is affected by the type of water in which the shellfish lives, by the species, and by the exact spot inside the marine animal where the pearl has grown. An expert can examine a pearl and tell you where it was found, but he cannot tell you precisely why it is of a certain color.

As you probably know, an oyster creates a pearl when it becomes irritated by a bit of sand or a minute worm that has worked its way inside the mantle of the shellfish. The oyster covers the irritant with layer after layer of horny organic material and calcium carbonate. The oyster does not know it is making a pearl—it is simply protecting itself from the irritant—but a pearl is the end result.

Mussel pearls are produced in exactly the same way, yet mussel pearls rarely achieve the luster and iridescence common to the gems found in oysters. Pearls found in mussels were much sought after during the latter part of the last century, but today they have fallen from favor and bring relatively low prices. Still, there are those who do collect them, and there is always the possibility that prices could rise again or that you might find an exceptionally beautiful and valuable specimen.

The first pearl find in America occurred in 1857 when a shoemaker in New Jersey was cleaning some mussels for dinner and came across a gem that today would be worth at least $25,000. Just a few years later a mussel from the upper Mississippi River yielded a pearl that became part of the British crown jewels and is presently worth at least as much as the New Jersey gem. In 1891, fishermen took more than $250,000 worth of pearls from a short stretch of the Wisconsin River in Wisconsin, and just a few years later $500,000 worth were taken from the White River in Arkansas.

In the rivers of the United States there are about 100 species of mussels, about 25 of which have the type of shell linings capable of producing pearls. But one of the great mysteries about them is that they may produce an abundance of pearls one year and not produce them again for many years to come. The best finds in recent years have been made in the rivers and streams of Ohio, Indiana, Illinois, Kentucky, Tennessee, Texas, Maine, and Vermont.

These mussels generally occur in shallow water, so all you really need to go after them is a pair of wading boots and a long-handled rake, though with a small dredge you could really bring them up in quantity.

Pearls often take on the color of the shell's lining, so they may be white, cream, lavender, yellow, orange, pink, rose, blue, or black.

Black, white, rose, or cream are the most desirable colors. Among the many shapes you may find, the most prized are the pear, egg, teardrop, and spherical. Irregular pearls are valuable only when they occur in some recognizable shape, such as the form of a star, when they become known as baroques.

The jeweler will appraise any pearls you find on the basis of size, shape, color, luster, and perfection. A high-quality pearl of 10 grains should fetch about $250, but one of twice that size would not sell for $500—the price would leap to around $1,000.

Other Gems

The gems just described are the ones that head the list of nearly every gem hunter and gem lover alike. But they are certainly not the only gems that could make you rich—about 100 gemstones may be found in America. Some are found in great quantity. Some are of such quality that, carat for carat, they may be worth more than any diamond, emerald, sapphire, or ruby you find in America. To give yourself the best chance of success, you should learn as much as you can about all of these gemstones, not just the ones briefly described in the following paragraphs.

Opals are among the most difficult of gemstones to find, which is one reason the price for them has skyrocketed in recent years. They are also extremely fragile and will shatter at the slightest tap of a hammer; use caution if you suspect opals may be in the vicinity of your digging.

Opals are formed in a variety of ways, most commonly by the decomposition of silicate materials or by the formation of volcanic glass. After the silica is deposited in cracks or crevices, it loses some of its water, hardens, and becomes the iridescent gemstone we know as opal. During the hardening process, more cracks are produced by natural contraction, and these cracks are then filled by additional silicate material. The layering of silicate material creates the play of colors that provides the countless varieties of this gem.

Among the varieties of opal, there are many that are interesting—such as the opal that forms in petrified wood and is marked by growth rings—but not greatly valuable. Opals of greatest value are the white, black, harlequin, fire opals, harlequin pattern, and fiery red.

The best opal hunting is in the Western states, where some opals have been found in the sand and gravel of dry stream beds. In recent years major opal discoveries have been made in the Virgin Valley of Nevada, most of them in an area known as Rainbow Ridge, which is on public land under the jurisdiction of the U.S. Fish and Wildlife Service. Check with the regional director as well as with local authorities about staking a claim.

Most of the Nevada opal deposits have been found along the sides of hills that show ancient watermarks and traces of silicates, as well as around petrified wood and fossil-bearing rock. The largest was a huge black stone worth $250,000, and dozens worth more than $5,000 apiece have been found in recent years. Gem-quality opals have also been found in New York, New Jersey, New Mexico, Oregon, Idaho, and California. Both Idaho and California have producing opal mines where you can pay a fee and dig for opals.

We tend to think of jade as coming only from the Orient, perhaps because that is where it is most highly treasured, but actually the largest jade deposit in the world is in the United States—in Wyoming.

The huge deposit of gemstone is near Jeffrey City, Wyoming, and it was discovered in 1972. It holds literally thousands of tons of the dark green material worth an estimated $65 million. Before you pack your bags and head for Fremont County, where the vast lode is located, be aware that the state of Wyoming has passed laws that require high fees for mining in this county, and even picking up a piece of jade from the surface without a permit can get you in serious trouble. However, jade does occur in other counties of the state, and in those you can prospect without difficulty. Natrona County, in particular, yields large amounts of jade, and who knows—you might be the next to make a $65 million strike.

Wyoming is not the only place to look for jade. Alaska is known to hold several major deposits, and jade also lies in the waters of the Pacific Ocean. Just before the huge jade strike was made in Wyoming, two scuba divers, after six months of effort, managed to raise a 5-ton boulder of solid jade they had discovered beneath an underwater ledge off Big Sur, California. It brought them $180,000! Jade almost certainly awaits discovery in other parts of the country too.

Actually, two types of mineral are commonly known as jade—jadeite and nephrite. Nephrite may be white, gray, yellow, light green, or even black, but the most valuable is the dark spinach-green color the Chinese carve into exotic figurines. Jadeite is much more rare and valuable than nephrite and is either pale green or lilac in color. Very small pieces of jadeite have been found in southern California, but all other

American jade thus far discovered has been nephrite.

Searching for jade requires luck as well as skill and knowledge. On the outside a boulder of jade is black or brown, very much in appearance like any ordinary chunk of rock. Only when the outer matrix is chipped away by pick or hammer will you be able to see the beautiful gemstone that fetches about $100 per pound.

Quartz is the most common mineral on earth, yet some rare forms of quartz can be very valuable. In the world of gemstones, quartz supplies more different varieties than any other mineral. The gem quartzes can be divided into three main groups: crystallized quartz, compact quartz, and cryptocrystalline quartz.

Crystallized quartzes are those that show definite crystal forms. Incidentally, the word *crystal* originates from the Greek word *krystallas,* meaning "ice," for in fact the ancient Greeks thought these transparent rock crystals were frozen water that had turned to stone.

One of the best known of the quartz crystal gems is amethyst, which ranges in color from lilac to deep purple, and which for many centuries has been held in high esteem as a gem of great beauty. Its name comes from the Greek and means "not drunk," since the ancients thought the stone warded off the effects of alcohol. Iron impurities give the gem its violet color. It is found in several parts of the United States.

Rose quartz, which occurs in several delicate shades of pink, is also properly classified as a crystalline quartz, although it rarely takes crystal form and is more likely to be found in massive lumps. It is translucent and will allow light to pass through, but is not clear enough to be transparent. It is relatively common in the United States and is often used as a medium for carved ornaments.

Another form of quartz, known as tiger eye, occurs in large crystals with a silky brown appearance. When properly cut, a single bright line of light appears across the surface, giving it the appearance that causes it to be prized as a gem.

The second group, compact quartz, does not consist of large, individual crystals. The best known gem in this group, jasper, is essentially an aggregate of tiny quartz crystals packed together in a massive lump and given its color by foreign matter such as clay and iron oxide. This form of quartz is opaque, yet it occurs in numerous attractive shades of brown, yellow, red, and green. Jasper has been used as a gem since ancient times, as have several other compact quartzes.

Finally, we have the large group of cryptocrystalline quartzes, which consist of a mass of tiny quartz crystals that have formed together into large lumps and do not appear to be crystals at all. They are most often referred to as chalcedony.

The most valuable form of chalcedony is the apple-green variety called chrysoprase, which is usually found near deposits of nickel, for it is nickel impurities that give it its color. Flawless chrysoprase is extremely rare and valuable, but it has been found in both Colorado and Montana.

Other valuable types of chalcedony are bloodstone, which is green spotted with red; carnelian, which is orange-red and translucent; and sard, a brown translucent form.

Agate is perhaps the best known form of chalcedony, or cryptocrystalline quartz, though agates are formed in a special way that makes them attractive. They consist of chalcedony arranged in curved or circular bands. These bands are made up of various colors of different degrees of transparency. In ancient lava rocks, where the chalcedony was deposited, they were formed in almond-shaped holes. In some agates the holes are not completely filled, and may be lined with the beautiful purple crystals, amethyst.

Onyx is another banded variety of quartz. In this form the bands run in straight lines and usually there is a layer of black adjacent to a layer of white; when the alternating bands are red and white, the gemstone is known as sardonyx.

There is the strangely beautiful moss agate, white or gray with internal black or green markings that resemble strange plants or little trees. All other factors being equal, it is the most valuable of the agates.

The quartz gems, including agate and jasper, are widely distributed throughout the United States, though New Mexico, Colorado, North Carolina, and California seem to have more than their fair share. In New Mexico, some fantastic discoveries have been made along the banks of the Colorado River and in dry streams around Gallup. But no matter where you seek any of the quartz gemstones, you should learn to look for and recognize the geological phenomenon known as a geode.

Geodes are simply rocks, or nodules, to be more scientifically correct, which, when broken open, are found to be hollow and the cavity lined with one or more minerals. Any of the quartz gemstones may be found inside a geode, but amethyst and agate are two of those most often filling the hollow.

A geode is usually recognized only by the fact that it is far too light to be a solid rock, and when so recognized it may be carefully broken. Geodes range in size from the smallest pebble to the largest boulder, and are seldom found alone. When one geode is found, then, you should carefully check around for others—a bed of them could make your fortune.

Of all the so-called semiprecious stones, turquoise is probably the best known and certainly the one most often asked about by beginning rockhounds. Turquoise has grown enormously popular in recent years— our known major deposits of it are fast being depleted. The price is soaring, and finding a vein of it could make you very rich indeed.

Turquoise has been used as a gemstone for centuries. Five thousand years ago the Egyptians mined these beautiful blue and green stones in the Sinai Peninsula and set them in jewelry. Today much of it comes from Iran, but major deposits of turquoise do exist in the southwestern United States and in Mexico.

Turquoise is a complex phosphate of aluminum. The blue color that makes it attractive is the result of the presence of a copper compound. Small individual crystals of it are extremely rare, though some have been found in the United States, but most turquoise is found in masses composed of innumerable tiny crystal grains. Thus, like agate, it is cryptocrystalline in composition.

In earlier days, faultless blue stones of a single color were the only ones sold as turquoise. Today, because turquoise is so difficult to acquire, the so-called turquoise matrix—turquoise interspersed by streaks of green caused by the presence of the mineral limonite—is almost as valuable.

If you do find turquoise, keep in mind that it is extremely sensitive to chemicals and should never be brought into contact with soaps and detergents. The color may also fade if exposed to light for a long time, or, in some cases, a fine blue stone may turn dark green and lose much of its value.

New Mexico is the best American hunting ground for this gemstone and has been since it was mined there by the ancient Navajo, Hopi, and Zuni natives. Turquoise has also been found in Arizona, Colorado, California, and Nevada. Please see the appendix for additional sources on gems and for a state by state, county by county guide to locating gems and minerals.

9

Treasure Hunting and the Law

Too many treasure hunters, especially beginners, operate under the premise of "finders keepers, losers weepers." This is not the case at all. If you set out to hunt treasure under that premise and make a lucky find, it is quite conceivable that you could end up in jail. You could also end up in jail if you walk away with a cache from private property, do damage to that property, tamper with a historical site, fail to abide by the applicable laws, or fail to report your find to the ever-watchful folks at the Internal Revenue Service.

The most important rule you must keep in mind is that all property in the United States is owned by somebody—an individual, a company or corporation, historical society, college or university, or the city, county, state, or federal government. This doesn't mean that you are necessarily prohibited from hunting treasure on these lands; it means, rather, that you must first learn if treasure hunting is allowed on the land you want to explore, and then, where permission is required, *you must get that permission in writing. Never accept just a verbal okay.* Verbal agreements may be perfectly legal but they are notoriously hard to prove.

"No Trespassing" signs mean exactly what they say, and there have been several trespass-related killings in recent years. Most of these tragedies could have been averted with a little bit of common courtesy on the part of the treasure hunter. Eagerness causes all too many treasure hunters to forget or ignore the fact that property owners have rights and want those rights protected. The laws against trespass are probably the most frequently violated laws on the books, but to break them is an act of sheer stupidity. Usually a straightforward explanation to the property owner that treasure hunting is your hobby, and that you will fill in any holes dug, will result in permission to hunt being granted. If it is not granted, and put in writing, then move on to another site. As a matter of law, a trespasser is almost never entitled to treasure or valuables of any sort found on property where he or she is trespassing.

Most local governments have laws requiring treasure hunters to obtain permission in writing before searching and digging on public lands. Many now issue permits which specify where you can dig, how deep you can dig, what repairs you must subsequently make, and how any spoils will be divided. Failure to comply with such laws could cost you your share of treasure you find on these lands.

Nearly every community also has laws that prohibit the destruction of private or public property. If you dig even a few inches into land belonging to another, you are, in effect, committing an act of destruction unless you have permission from the owner. Doing so could cost you a fine or result in a jail sentence. Most experienced treasure hunters can search an area, recover its valuables, and refill any holes so neatly that not a trace of their passing is left behind. But there are also many thoughtless and inexperienced treasure hunters whose actions make it more difficult for the careful to enjoy their sport.

In recent years, as the popularity of treasure hunting has boomed, thoughtless and over-anxious treasure seekers too often devastate good hunting sites—leaving behind bare, gaping craters, piles of trash, bottles, and cans, even tearing down buildings. In one recent Arizona case, a store-owner found his downtown building toppling into a tunnel excavated under it by a crew of treasure hunters searching for old bottles, and he has posted a large reward for information leading to the vandals' arrest. Vandals are causing many communities to pass new and tougher laws or to more rigidly enforce existing ones which restrict the activities of treasure hunters.

The companies that make and sell metal detectors and many of the treasure hunting clubs offer permission forms that are a convenience to use. Add to these the use of common sense, common decency, and respect for the rights of others, and you are on the right path toward successful hunting without legal difficulty.

Treasure Hunting on Federal Lands

The most important law governing treasure hunting on federal land is the Federal Antiquities Act of 1906. This law states that you may not remove artifacts of historical value from protected sites, and it sets forth penalties for doing so. It also states that *any* treasure you take from federal lands without the permission of the proper authority may be seized. The bundle of cash you are looking for on federal property might have absolutely no historic value, but you could conceivably lose it all to the government if you fail to obtain permission to hunt or are otherwise in violation of this act.

Only recently has rigid enforcement of this act—which provides a penalty of a $500 fine or ninety days in jail—begun. Until about four or five years ago, most offenders were let off with a fine of $25 or $50. No more. Because of the great devastation done by thoughtless and uncaring treasure hunters—especially on Civil and Revolutionary War battlefield sites—enforcement officers are cracking down and offenders are frequently landing in jail.

In just one national park, in a single night last year, rangers rounded up more than fifty illegal looters, who had dug more than 500 holes around a historical site—including one crater large enough to swallow a jeep. Fines totaling thousands of dollars were handed down, and several of the culprits received suspended jail sentences.

You can almost certainly forget about receiving permission to search and dig on any land managed by the National Park Service. Although the Antiquities Act sets forth procedures for the granting of such permission, this is given only to qualified historians and archaeologists and is solely for the purpose of recovery and restoration. It was formerly the practice to allow digging on sandy beaches in national seashore areas—where damage could be naturally repaired by the waves—but already Padre Island National Seashore is dotted with signs warning against digging, and such signs will stand along the other national seashore areas before this book is in print.

This may be for the best. Not only do areas of national interest need and deserve protection, but even while permission to search certain parts of the park system was being granted, finders often ended up "weepers," not "keepers." In searching a sandy beach, for example, the treasure hunter might reasonably expect to find gold or silver coins washed ashore from a sunken wreck. But since the Park Service, in granting permission to hunt, required that all artifacts be turned over to them, and since these coins could reasonably be defined as artifacts of historical interest, the finder often ended up with nothing.

It all depends on how artifact is defined. In a classic confrontation over this definition, a pair of treasure hunters in Nebraska spent years butting heads in court with the federal government over ownership of a treasure they had sought, found, and excavated: the remains of a sunken Missouri River steamboat, *Bertrand*.

This riverboat went down more than a century ago, with indications that it held gold and silver coins and vials of mercury worth in excess of $1 million, as well as thousands of bottles of wine, whiskey, and brandy. The two Omaha men had pinpointed the wreck, but because the river changed course over the years, it lay buried under soil in the DeSoto National Wildlife Refuge; so the pair sought and obtained permission to dig from the Department of the Interior.

In the contract that was drawn up, the government retained all rights to any artifacts that might be recovered; but this term was not clearly defined. After many months of arduous labor and after spending a considerable sum of money, the two treasure hunters recovered literally millions of artifacts, including 4,000 antique bottles of considerable value to collectors, but no gold or silver and only $4,320 worth of mercury. The agreement gave to the men 60 percent of the gold, silver, mercury, coins, and, specifically, bottles, but now the government decided that the bottles were also artifacts and refused to share these with the finders.

By the time a judge in the United States Court of Claims finally ruled in favor of the two men, their total expenses had greatly exceeded the $38,000 they received as their share of the price paid for the bottles at an auction. The government received artifacts of inestimable value, which will fill a multi-million-dollar museum the National Park Service is having built on the site of the wreck.

While national parks and national monuments are virtually off-limits to treasure hunters, this does not mean that treasure hunters are totally excluded from searching for, and finding, relics from the American Revolution, the Civil War, or other items of historical interest and value. Skirmishes in these wars also took place in areas not designated as parks or monuments, and often, when troops were captured, their weapons were buried. Other valuable artifacts lie buried around the ruins of buildings dating from these periods. By careful research many treasure hunters can locate these hoards and enrich themselves without coming into conflict with the National Park Service.

Obtaining permission to hunt on the various military bases is not much easier than obtaining permission to search and dig in the national parks. F. Lee Bailey, the famous criminal attorney, did manage to obtain for a group he represents the right to search for $250 million in treasure they believe lies buried on the White Sands Missile Range in New Mexico—but he did so only by taking the case to the United States Supreme Court. Unless you are prepared to do likewise, forget about hunting treasure on land held by the military.

This is the bad news about treasure hunting on federal lands. Here is the good news. Treasure hunters are welcome, or at least not unwelcome, on hundreds of millions of acres of land owned by the federal government.

On most land under the jurisdiction of the Forest Service, the Bureau of Land Management, or the Bureau of Reclamation, treasure hunters are given permission to search and dig as a matter of course. But a few areas are off-limits, so it is wise to check beforehand with the ranger in charge or with the regional office of the proper agency. Since these lands are also protected by the Antiquities Act, all artifacts found on them must be handed over to the government, and if you undertake a major project on these lands, be sure the term artifact is clearly defined.

You will be allowed to keep any treasure you find on these lands, other than artifacts, in accordance with the laws of treasure trove—a concept important to every treasure hunter.

The Law of Treasure Trove

Like much of our common law, the laws regarding treasure are descended from the English. At present, only nine states—Georgia, Indiana, Iowa, Maine, New Jersey, Ohio, Oklahoma, Oregon, and Wisconsin—adhere strictly to the doctrine of treasure trove. But in most other states, the law is descended from this concept, and it usually has a bearing on the legal decisions handed down in disputes over treasure.

According to the treasure trove laws of England at the time America was being settled, all lost or hidden property belonged to the ruling monarch. To take possession of such property was a treasonous act and offenders could be—and were—at times beheaded.

In America, the first laws of treasure trove were slightly more lax, stating that hidden property became the property of the king only when the owner was unknown; and also "If it be found in the sea, or above the earth, it doth not belong to the king, if no owner appears. So that it seems that the hiding of it, not the abandoning of it, that gives the king a property. A man that hides his treasure in a secret place, evidently does not mean to relinquish it; but reserves the right of claiming it again; and, if he dies, and the secret dies with him, the law gives it to the king."

As the law has evolved in America, treasure trove has come to apply to valuables found concealed on the property of another. It usually defines as treasure any gold or silver in any form, and any currency of any sort. The property need not be fixed, as with a house or a piece of land; it can be movable property such as an automobile, a piece of furniture, or even a book. To be classed as treasure trove, the item of value must have been lost or buried so long that the original owner is dead or unknown.

In addition to property classed as treasure trove, found items will fall into one of five other categories. Even in the states that do not adhere strictly to the doctrine of treasure trove, the discovered loot will be classed as one of these if the matter comes to the attention of the courts.

Abandoned Property • Where it is obvious that an object of value has been intentionally, willfully, or knowingly discarded, disposed of, or otherwise abandoned by its previous owner, the object or objects, as a general rule, become the legal property of the finder. If, for example, you have a bad day at the golf course and throw your new set of clubs in the trash can, you have legally abandoned them, and the trash collector has the legal right to take and keep them, though you might change your mind and act to reclaim the clubs. A presumption of abandonment exists unless and until the owner appears and lays claim to the property, but the law also requires the finder to take reasonable steps to notify the owner of the discovery.

If, on the other hand, you were to find a billfold containing documents of identification on the street, it would be unreasonable for you to presume abandonment, and the law requires you to return this *lost property* to its owner, who may or may not, at his or her discretion, give you a reward.

Lost property • This is property the legal owner has unintentionally or inadvertently lost, but which remains his or her property in every sense of the word.

Mislaid or misplaced property • Property that the owner put away or hid with no intention of abandoning, but was unable to retrieve for one reason or another, most often because he or she forgot where it was hidden. The finder is required by law to make a reasonable effort to locate the owner. When the original owner cannot be found, in most instances, the treasure becomes the property of the owner of the land or premises on which it was found, though most courts award a percentage of the value to the person who made the discovery.

Concealed property • Something of tangible value that the owner hid to keep from the observation, acquisition, or posession of others. It remains the property of the person who concealed it, and the finder has no claim on any part of it.

Things imbedded in the soil • A broad class of property that includes many of the antiques and artifacts that are not dealt with as treasure trove. As a general rule in disputed cases, the courts have awarded half of such finds to the property owners, half to the finders—always provided, of course, that the treasure hunter was not violating any law, such as ignoring a properly displayed sign warning against trespassing.

In addition to the nine states which adhere rather strictly to the doctrine of treasure trove, three others interpret the old law in a way that is generally not favorable to treasure hunters. In these three states—Texas, Louisiana, and Florida—all found property is regarded as either lost, misplaced, or abandoned. In the states having no specific laws on found property, each case that comes before the court is settled at the discretion of a county judge, who usually hands down a decision based on the precedents of treasure trove.

Perhaps you read about the treasure hunter in Connecticut who found the broken statue of King George III that had been spirited away by a band of American patriots shortly after America declared its independence from England. If so, you may remember that the owners of the marsh in which this valuable artifact was found sued the treasure hunter over rights to the statue. During the court battle, the landowners established that Tory loyalists had shattered the statue and hidden its pieces to prevent them from being melted down and used as musket balls. In a classic ruling, the court decided that the statue had not been intentionally abandoned, in which case it would have gone to the finder, but that it had been "mislaid" by Tories who clearly intended to retrieve it after the Revolution had been squelched—it was awarded to the owners of the land.

When stolen property is found and it can be clearly shown that it was stolen, a reward is about the best the finder can hope for. In one recent Cleveland, Ohio, case, a young boy discovered nearly $100,000 in currency buried in his own backyard and received not a dime after it was established that this was loot from a California bank robbery.

The reverse side of this coin is brighter. In cases where it can be shown that money or treasure was hidden by a known criminal but there is no solid evidence linking it to a specific robbery or crime, the finder almost always receives at least a percentage of the stash, if not its full value. Perhaps this is why the fortune allegedly buried by John Dillinger on an Ohio farm is one of the most eagerly hunted treasures in America; linking it to a specific crime, after more than four decades, would be difficult.

Nearly every state treats it as a criminal offense when movable treasure is found and kept without the finder making a reasonable attempt to locate the rightful owner. However, most states make an exception for treasure trove, artifacts, and all other objects that have obviously been buried for a long time (generally those treasures not of this century).

Most states also set a waiting period during which the owner must appear to claim lost or mislaid property. Usually the owner is given a year to establish his or her rights. But in two states—Texas and Louisiana—the finder may have to wait ten years to gain ownership of his or her find. In these two states, too, with the exception of movable objects, anything found on land owned by the state becomes the property of the state.

What if you accidentally find a fortune while you are working for someone else? Much would depend on circumstances, as well as on the state in which the treasure was found, but in a dozen or so recent cases, the courts have shown a tendency to award at least part of the treasure to the employer.

In disputes between employer and employee, most courts use as their precedent a case that began in 1968. That year, while on patrol in Vietnam, a young soldier searching a cave came across $150,000 in American greenbacks and an equal amount of South Vietnamese currency. The Army laid claim to the treasure, and the soldier argued his case all the way to the Federal District Court in Washington, D.C.— where every dime of the find was awarded to the Army because the soldier had been in its employ when he entered that cave and made his fabulous discovery.

Since most legal disputes arise after a find has been reported and publicized, one faces the question of whether it is best to publicize the discovery of a treasure or simply pocket the money as quietly as possible. There are two schools of thought.

Aside from the laws requiring you to report found property and make every effort to establish its legal status, there are some very good reasons why many treasure hunters seek all the publicity they can get.

If, for example, it can be established that a potful of gold coins passed through the hands of Jesse James or another bandit of equal renown, the numismatic value of those coins will almost certainly go soaring. Publicity about such a discovery would also bring collectors to the finder of the coins, perhaps making it possible to auction them off at even higher prices.

Many treasure hunters find that publicity about one success brings in information that may lead to other successes. Millions of Americans have bits and pieces of information about long-lost treasures stashed away on the homestead; most have no real idea of how to go about locating it. Many of them, upon reading about a successful treasure hunter, will seek him out and offer to trade their information for a share of the loot. All too often the information is useless or the treasure nonexistent, but frequently it leads the treasure hunter from one strike to another.

Well-known treasure hunter Roy Volker finds that his publicity often causes him to receive such invitations. They don't always pan out, but sometimes they do. An instance of the latter occurred in the winter of 1978, when he finally agreed to join three casual acquaintances in searching for a cache they believed their grandfather had buried many years ago on his Illinois farm.

Later claiming that he had to be nearly dragged along, Volker joined the three on their expedition and set to work with his metal detector. The first few sweeps produced just a few coins. Then Volker got a strong reading around the roots of an old oak—and dug out a chest containing 14,000 coins, some of them quite valuable.

Many treasure hunters feel that no amount of money compensates for the trouble that can be caused by widespread publicity. There is, this group feels, something about the word "treasure" that causes the worms to come crawling out of the woodwork.

There is some justification for this belief. Bitter family feuds, some of them lasting for years, have erupted over the division of buried treasure. Defending the legal right to a treasure has often cost its finder more than the treasure was worth, and often the defense must be made against clearly fraudulent claims. Such claims probably reached a high point (or a low point, depending on your view) when a New York City man found a large sum of cash in a house he had purchased—then had to defend himself against nearly two dozen lawsuits, each filed by individuals claiming that he or she had stashed away the money and fully intended to retrieve it. Because of such incidents, a large and growing number of treasure hunters feel it is best to comply with the law while holding publicity to the absolute minimum.

Mining Claims

As with hunting all treasure, the first rule when prospecting for gold, gems, or any other mineral is to obtain permission in advance and always avoid trespassing. In some of the Western states especially, prospectors have found it very profitable to work the abandoned mines of yesteryear—but you must be absolutely certain the mine is not being worked, and you must obtain permission to dig from its owner.

"Many owners of land, especially owners of mining property, do not want others removing gemstones or mineral specimens," warns a spokesman for the Denver office of the Bureau of Land Management. "Serious disputes sometimes result when a person wanders onto private land and starts digging without permission." He fails to add that more than one of those "serious disputes" has ended with a fatal shooting.

Assuming, however, that you have obtained proper permission, have been doing a little prospecting, and have found an area rich in mineral deposits, you may want to stake a legal claim to the site. By staking such a claim, you obtain the exclusive right to develop and extract any minerals found on or under the land.

The first requirement in establishing a claim is the actual discovery of a valuable mineral. The mineral can be metallic or nonmetallic, and the amount found must be such that it produces, in accordance with federal law, ". . . evidence of such character that a person of ordinary prudence would be justified in further expenditure of his labor and means, with a reasonable prospect of success, in developing a valuable mine. . . ." This law prevents, as you can see, the random filing of purely speculative claims, a provision that greatly benefits the individual prospector.

How you begin the process of filing your claim depends on who holds title to the land on which you have discovered minerals or on who holds the mineral rights to the property. The title to the land may be held by one person, the mineral rights by another, and it is the latter in which you are interested.

If the mineral rights are owned by an individual or a company, your first step is to negotiate with that owner for the rights to work the claim you intend to file. If the land or the mineral rights are state-owned, you should contact the state land commission for information, and proceed according to state laws.

If you have made your strike on lands under the jurisdiction of the Forest Service, the Bureau of Land Management, or the Bureau of

Reclamation (all of which, under the multiple-use concept of public-land management, encourage prospecting and mining, within reasonable limits), or on other government lands, certain specific procedures have been established for filing a claim. In addition to following these procedures, you must also comply with state and local laws; pamphlets explaining these state laws are published by every state having a significant amount of public land.

In any instance where you intend to stake a claim on federal land, you must file a written notice with the district ranger or forest officer, or with the regional office of the land agency involved. This application must include the exact location of the claim, its boundaries, the mineral to be mined, and other pertinent information.

You must then mark off the boundaries of the claim. This usually means erecting posts or markers of some sort at the four corners of the claim-site, though some states may require slightly different markings. In the filing of placer claims, most states require no corner markers, but demand that you post a notice of your claim somewhere on the site, usually at the spot where the initial discovery was made.

Your claim must also be recorded. At the office of the county recorder for the county in which your claim is located, you must place on record the name of the finder of the mineral deposit, the date of the discovery, the type of mineral found, the name under which the mine will be operated, and a description of the site.

An individual may hold an unlimited number of claims, but each must result from a separate discovery of valuable minerals, must be properly recorded, and must be maintained by what is known as assessment work. Federal and state requirements regarding this assessment work are usually the same.

This means, simply, that once you have filed your claim, you must work it in order to keep it. The federal government requires that you do at least $100 worth of work, or add improvements with that much value, each year. Statements describing the work or improvements must be filed annually with the county recorder where the claim is filed.

Each step in filing a claim should be carried out to the letter of the law. It is quite possible that you could establish a valid claim, perform the annual assessment work, and be on your way to riches, then lose it all because of a single error you made in filing or maintaining the claim.

Filing a claim on public land does not give you ownership of that land. To acquire ownership of the land itself, you must secure it by patent, a somewhat more complicated process.

Such patents are issued after application to the Bureau of Land Management. Application for a patent means you will be required to pay the costs of an official survey, file proof of possessory rights, pay a filing fee, post and publish notices of filing, and, if the patent is granted, pay the purchase price. The purchase price for gold-bearing patents is $5 an acre and half as much for placer claims. But the cost of the land is usually only a small part of the total cost of securing a patent. The process is so lengthy and complicated that most applicants hire attorneys, and the other costs can run into thousands of dollars.

Although there are many good reasons why you may ultimately wish to own the land on which your mining claim is located, a patent is by no means necessary in order for you to continue to hold the rights established by your mining claim, and such rights can be sold, leased, or disposed of in your will.

More detailed information about filing a claim on public land can be obtained by writing any office of the Bureau of Land Management or Forest Service, or from forest supervisors. Publications of special interest include *Regulations Pertaining to Mining Claims; Staking a Mining Claim on Federal Lands; Patenting a Mining Claim on Federal Lands;* and *Mineral and Mining Claims in the National Forest Wilderness.*

Treasure Hunting and Taxes

If you decide not to publicize your find of a fortune in buried treasure, and if you remain absolutely quiet about your discovery of the mother lode and state your claim to it as if it were barely worthwhile, there is still one "person" who will have to know: Uncle Sam.

The laws are very specific in regard to the tax a person must pay on all of his or her income, even if that income is derived from a hobby and not an occupation. This includes any and all profits derived from the sale of treasure and artifacts. A treasure hunter can search for years before making a big strike and then end up paying most of it in taxes if he or she doesn't plan ahead, preferably with the help of a good tax accountant or attorney.

Without such help, there are still certain things you can do to hold your taxes in line. Start by keeping accurate records of all the money you spend in pursuit of your hobby: transportation, hotels, food, metal detectors and other equipment, and any legal fees that might be incurred. All of these are legal deductions, because your profits are taxable. Metal detectors and other equipment should be depreciated over a period of three years.

If you find artifacts and do not sell them, you need pay no taxes on their value. But many treasure hunters use these as a tax deduction while placing them in museums where they can be shared with the public and where they rightfully belong. To do this you must first have the item or items appraised by an independent and qualified appraiser. Then you must obtain verification from the museum that they have accepted the item or items at the appraised value. If you have many such items to donate, you might consider parceling them out one or a few at a time, thus spreading the tax deductions out over the years and taking them as needed.

As long as you can prove that treasure hunting is a hobby and not your profession, you pay taxes on your finds only in the year that you sell them for a profit, or, in the case of money, in the year that currency is placed back in circulation. This is a fact that every treasure hunter should know and use to advantage.

Many treasure hunters use their treasure to build a retirement fund. Because the value of most treasure increases at a rate that at least keeps pace with inflation, there often is no reason to rush out and sell it as soon as it is found. By waiting and selling it off in small parcels after your retirement, when, presumably, your other income and thus your tax bracket will be lower, you may be able to greatly ease, or even erase altogether, the pain of the tax bite. One couple in Arkansas has quietly amassed a fortune in diamonds from the famous diamond field in that state, stashing them away in a bank safe deposit box and saving them for just this purpose.

If you do decide to hold treasure aside until your golden years, a safe deposit box is advisable. If you hide it elsewhere, it may well become a part of the hidden billions that make treasure hunting such a rewarding, fascinating, and profitable sport. Let me know, care of my publisher, of your success. Again, good hunting!

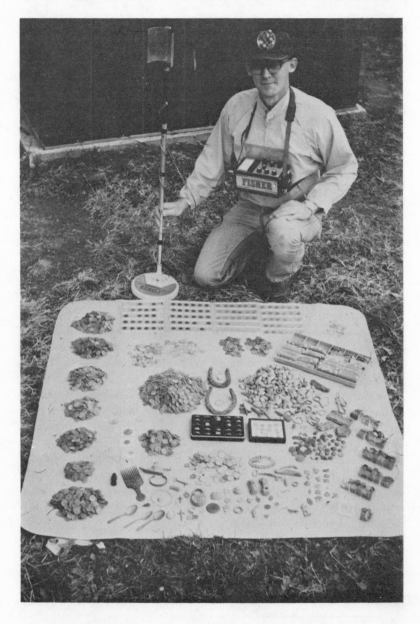

A treasure hunter proudly displays his finds. COURTESY OF FISHER RESEARCH LABORATORY LIBRARY, INC.

Appendix

Clues to Treasure Sites

Alabama • The ghost town of Arberchoochee in Cleburne County was abandoned around 1900. Prior to that, it had been a booming gold mining camp.

The ghost town of Demopolis in Marengo County was founded around 1810, abandoned in 1830. The ruins of many old plantation houses remain standing in the area.

In Limestone County, somewhere near the town of Athens and close to the crossing of a stream, Confederate troops dropped two metal strongboxes containing $100,000 in gold and silver into a bog as they were fleeing from Union soldiers in 1865.

Alaska • In the St. Elias Mountains near the Yellow River, three miners lost their lives during a blizzard in 1884. The diary of one said they had stashed 500 pounds of nuggets in a nearby cave which, as far as can be determined, has never been located.

Within a 10-mile radius of the town of Juneau, where major gold strikes were made in 1880, remnants of hundreds of miners' shacks can be found, many of them certainly worth searching through.

The beaches around Nome, which once yielded about $10 million in gold annually, are one of the world's greatest treasure hunting sites, not only for the precious metal that remains but also for the countless valuable bottles and other artifacts left behind by the sourdoughs of gold rush days.

Arizona • Coronado National Memorial in Cochise County is located somewhere close to the site where Coronado camped around 1540 with more than 1,000 fellow explorers. Prior to leaving the area, they buried a large quantity of bronze artillery and other weaponry that would be worth a fortune today.

The ghost town of Cerro Colorado lies a few miles north of Nogales, in the Quinlan Mountains. It once had 10,000 inhabitants and was a center of silver-mining activity. Today only several hundred abandoned buildings remain to tell of its former glory.

The ghost town of Pearce in Cochise County once produced more than $30 million worth of gold, as well as silver and other minerals, and served as headquarters for several outlaw groups. It has been abandoned since around the turn of the century.

The Lost Virgin de Guadalupe Silver Mine is believed to lie in the Tumacacori Mountains in Santa Cruz County. The Spaniards worked this mine until 1648. Mexican miners took silver from it early in the last century, then the mine was lost once more.

Arkansas • The ghost town of Old Washington in Hempstead County has many abandoned buildings dating back to 1820. It was in this town that the Bowie knife was invented, and hundreds of these, extremely valuable, have been found in recent years.

A lost diamond mine is said to lie somewhere east of Murfreesboro in Pike County.

The lost Fred Conley Gold Mine is believed to lie within 10 miles of Eureka Springs, in Carroll County.

Jesse James is said to have buried about $32,000 in gold, stolen from the Hot Springs stagecoach, in the mountains of Perry County.

California • Starting near the town of Sattley, northwest of Lake Tahoe in Sierra County, and stretching for about 175 miles, both sides of County Highway 49 are dotted with ghost towns. There are more than 10,000 abandoned buildings along this stretch of road, and the area was once a center of gold mining activity.

The famous Lost Gunsight Silver Mine is believed to be somewhere in the Panamint Mountains in Calaveras County.

In 1876 bandits stole $123,000 in gold from a stagecoach and, before their capture, hid it near the village of Myrtletowne, just east of Eureka in Humboldt County.

In 1894 a worker at the San Francisco mint made off with 290 pounds of gold bullion and buried it near Shelter Cove, in Humboldt County.

Colorado • A group of bandits known as the Reynolds Gang are said to have buried $100,000 in gold in Park County, near the tiny town of Hall Valley.

Jesse James and his gang supposedly stashed more than $50,000 in gold and silver coins near their hideout at Half Moon Gulch, which is in Lake County, near Leadville.

Treasure Mountain derives its name from the fact that in 1790 a party of French explorers buried about $3 million in gold bullion there. The mountain is near Summitville, in Mineral County.

Near the ghost town of Higbie, in Otero County, Spaniards of the sixteenth century are said to have concealed about $12 million in gold they had stolen from the Indians. Early Spanish armor has been found in the region.

Connecticut • New London, near the mouth of the Thames River, was settled in 1646, and several major treasures have been found in the region. The remains of numerous shipwrecks, some dating back to 1790 and possibly holding treasure, can actually be seen on nearby sandbars when conditions are just right.

The pirate Blackbeard is said to have cached a large treasure in the vicinity of Brooklyn, in Windham County.

Gold and silver coins of English origin have been found with some regularity on the beaches near Madison, in New Haven County. Minted in the late 1700s, the coins are believed to come from the wreck of an unknown sailing ship that was briefly exposed during a hurricane in the 1950s.

Colonial artifacts are frequently found along the waterfront around New Haven, which was founded in 1637.

Delaware • In 1699, according to legend, pirates from Madagascar hid two large treasures near New Castle, one in a well somewhere near the town jail, the other in the vicinity of Taylor's Bridge.

Captain Kidd and his band of pirates are said to have buried at least two treasure chests on Kelley Island, which lies in Delaware Bay off Bombay Hook National Wildlife Refuge. Coins from that era are frequently found on nearby beaches.

HMS *Pusey*, bound from Jamaica to Wilmington, with a fortune in Spanish coins, sank during a gale in 1757. She is believed to lie somewhere near Reedy Island in the Delaware River, which is the site of numerous wrecks and one of the best treasure hunting spots in the state.

Cape Henlopen, near Lewes, has been the scene of numerous shipwrecks, and gold and silver coins are frequently found on its beaches. Ships that have gone down in the region and are worth seeking include the English merchantman *Cornelia*, which sank in 1757 with more than $30,000 in gold and silver coins, and the British warship *DeBraak*, which sank in 1798 while carrying millions in gold bullion and gold and silver coins.

Florida • The Florida Keys are probably the most productive treasure hunting area in the western hemisphere. Several major discoveries are made there each year, many of them by accident. Probably the best of these is Indian Key, which served as a salvage camp for the Spaniards during the era when so many of their treasure ships were being lost.

In the early 1800s a pirate known as Billy Bowlegs supposedly buried $5 million in gold and silver coins in Franklin County and another $3 million in a cave near Pensacola.

Somewhere near Cross City, in Dixie County, eight barrels of money were hidden by two Bahamians just before Andrew Jackson had them hanged for selling arms and whiskey to the Seminoles.

In 1820 a United States naval vessel sank near the mouth of the Suwannee River, taking to the bottom its entire crew and exactly $5 million in gold that was to be paid to Spain in exchange for Florida.

The inlet leading to the port at St. Augustine holds at least 75 wrecks from the eighteenth century, many of them certainly holding worthwhile treasure. Coins from these wrecks are frequently found on nearby beaches.

Georgia • Tybee Island at the mouth of the Savannah River has served as a lair for dozens of pirates over the centuries. A number of treasures are said to be hidden there, and the island also yields coins and relics that wash ashore from several shipwrecks in nearby waters.

During the eighteenth century at least 50 large ships sank in the waters off Savannah Beach, and the shores along here yield numerous gold and silver coins.

In May 1865, as the Civil War drew to a close, Jefferson Davis met with his cabinet for the last time, at Washington, in Wilkes County. At this meeting Davis is said to have ordered the burial of the gold reserves of the Confederacy, which would be worth at least $500 million today. The Confederate gold has never been found. Many experts believe it was hidden in a number of locations throughout the surrounding area.

After the burning of Atlanta, seven Union soldiers were hanged for the theft of about $6 million in gold, silver, and jewelry. They died without revealing where the loot was hidden, but it is said to be somewhere near the town of Lithonia, which is about 12 miles east of Atlanta.

Hawaii • The Keakauailau Treasure, a vast hoard of gold, allegedly lies buried high in the Koolau Mountains above Honolulu.

A hoard of very old gold coins, minted by the vanished Hawaiian monarchy, is said to be hidden in a cave somewhere in the Koko Head State Park near Waikiki Beach on Oahu.

Ancient Chinese coins are sometimes found on Maili Beach on the western shores of Oahu. These almost certainly come from one or more ships sunk nearby.

Idaho • In 1865, members of a notorious gang of bandits, with a posse hot on their trail, were seen throwing $180,000 worth of gold bullion into Mud Lake, which is in Jefferson County, about 50 miles north of Pocatello. Only three of the 20-pound gold bars have been recovered, as far as is known.

The notorious Plummer Gang, which ravaged Idaho shortly after the Civil War, stole 300 pounds of raw gold in a robbery in 1869. The loot is said to be hidden near Sentinel Rocks, a few miles north of the town of Rigby in Bonneville County.

The Plummer Gang is said to have hidden another $500,000 in gold bullion in a cave behind a waterfall on the Snake River, somewhere in Power County.

Illinois • The ghost town of Bishop Hill is located 3 miles north of the present town of the same name, in Henry County. The old town was abandoned in 1862, and only a few ruins are visible.

After the high waters recede each spring, hundreds of silver dollars minted in the latter part of the last century are found along the west bank of the Ohio River near Galconda, in Pope County. These coins have been washing ashore for years, and local legend says they come from a riverboat that went to the bottom carrying millions in silver.

Near the village of Cave in Rock, in Pope County, $200,000 in gold and silver coins is supposedly hidden in a cave near the west bank of the Ohio River. Scattered gold and silver coins have been found in the region, giving some credence to the legend.

Indiana • In 1828, four bandits robbed a passenger train of $90,000 in gold bullion, plus a large amount of coins and currency. They were caught only four days later and went to the gallows without revealing where the loot was hidden. Because of their limited movement prior to their capture, most experts agree that this hoard has to be hidden in the vicinity of Marshfield, in Warren County, and most also feel certain that the treasure still awaits discovery.

Somewhere near the town of Seymour, in Jackson County, the infamous Reno brothers hid a safe containing $80,000 in cash, unable to hang on to it because a posse was hot on their trail. This is another well-documented treasure.

The hoodlum Jim Colosimo, who ruled the rackets in Chicago until he was murdered by Frankie Yale on orders from Al Capone, is said to have hidden diamonds worth several million dollars somewhere on the outskirts of Crown Point, in Lake County.

John Dillinger is known to have buried huge amounts of loot on a farm owned by his father. The farm is in Morgan County, near the town of Mooresville. According to FBI accounts at the time, at least $600,000, and possibly a great deal more, was buried there.

Iowa • Bonnie and Clyde Barrow reportedly buried a large amount of money in a wooded area on the bank of the Raccoon River not more than 3 miles from the town of Dexter, which is in Dallas County.

An eccentric miner named Tom Kelly, while on his deathbed in 1867, said that he had buried a fortune in gold and silver on the steep rise known as Kelly's Bluff, which is now in the very heart of the city of Dubuque. Several parts of the treasure have been found, confirming the story, but experts believe that at least $250,000 remains hidden.

During an Indian attack in 1865, an Army paymaster hid several thousand dollars in gold coins near Fort Atkinson, which was in what is now Winnesheik County. He died in the attack before he could tell anyone where the payroll was hidden.

Two wealthy brothers named Ives buried numerous caches of money on their farm near the town of Sunbury, in Cedar County, early in this century; $200,000 was recovered in 1935, but a great deal more waits to be found.

Kansas • The famed Santa Fe Trail, which was heavily traveled from 1820 to 1880, cuts across the southern portion of this state and is very productive of relics and artifacts. Campsites along the trail are frequently indicated by markers.

A steamboat, the *Francis X. Aubrey,* sank near Leavenworth on the Missouri River late in the last century. It held about $500,000 in bullion and coins. Coins from the wreck have been found on the river bank near Leavenworth

National Cemetery, in Leavenworth County.

On the Arkansas River, within 10 miles of Dodge City, Indians attacked a Mexican wagon train in 1815, along a branch of the Santa Fe Trail. The Mexicans buried $500,000 in gold that they had intended to use for buying weapons for use by Mexican insurgents. Before the survivors of the attack could return to claim the gold, a flood occurred, and all signs of the burial site were wiped away.

Kentucky • Somewhere in Logan County, near Russellville, Jesse James and his gang were forced to stash away gold coins that were worth $50,000 in 1868. They had stolen the money from the Russellville Bank, but with a posse only minutes behind, were forced to bury the loot on the outskirts of town.

On the south bank of the Ohio River near West Paducah silver coins from the latter half of the last century have been found by treasure hunters for many years. They are believed to come from the hulk of a steamboat that sank somewhere upstream.

Somewhere between Covington and Newport, on the Ohio River across from Cincinnati, in Kenton County, an associate of the notorious Dutch Schultz is said to have buried about $4 million in cash during the final days of Prohibition.

In what is now the Levi Jackson Wilderness State Park near London, in Laurel County, Indians attacked a group of travelers known as the McNitt Party in 1784. The pioneers buried all they owned during the battle, and the few survivors were later unable to locate the site. Numerous incidents of this kind occurred along this early westward route.

Louisiana • Remnants of many old shipwrecks can be seen during extremely low tides on the beaches near the ruins of Fort Livingston, at the southern end of Grand Terre Isle. Over the years, treasure hunters have reclaimed a large number of gold and silver coins along these beaches. The area around the fort, which was occupied by both Union and Confederate troops during the Civil War, has yielded a large number of valuable relics.

Probably the most eagerly sought treasure in this state lies on what was once the Parlange Plantation, near New Roads, in Pointe Coupee Parish. During a raid by Union troops, the Parlange family buried treasure worth $400,000 on their land. The entire family died in a riverboat accident, leaving their fortune unclaimed.

In 1871 two steamboats, the *Oregon* and the *John Adams,* sank in the Mississippi River below New Orleans. The two ships were know to be carrying gold bullion and coins worth $800,000 at the time, many times as much today. Both sank in the waters between Islands #82 and #83. Thousands of coins have washed ashore on these two islands over the years, and experts regard them as the two finest treasure hunting spots in Louisiana.

More than $30 million in treasure is allegedly buried in various spots along the Red River in the vicinity of Coushatta, in Red River Parish. Part was concealed by townspeople who hoped to keep it out of the hands of Union troops, then had their markers swept away in a flood, but a great deal was also hidden by a band of outlaws known as the Murrells.

Maine • Try Pond Island in Casco Bay, off Sagadahoc County. Many small caches of gold and silver Spanish coins have been found here over the years, and a pirate named Edward Lowe is said to have buried several treasure chests somewhere on the island.

Blackbeard is said to have buried a tremendous hoard on Smuttynose Island, in the waters off York County. Many old coins have turned up on the shores of this island.

After storms, very old and valuable coins are found with some regularity around Fort Williams, just south of Portland in Cumberland County. Numerous ships have sunk in these waters since colonial times, and they account for the coins and artifacts that are found on surrounding beaches.

Maryland • It is known that local tribes once had a highly productive silver mine somewhere near Silver Run, in Carroll County. An early settler found about 750 pounds of high-grade silver ore while digging a well, but the mine that provided the Indians with vast amounts of silver has yet to be found.

Before committing suicide in jail in 1828, a notorious murderess and slave trader named Patty Cannon left a will in which she mentioned several buried treasures, including a cache of coins worth $100,000 at the time. None is known to have been found. Patty Cannon owned a farm near Reliance, on the Sussex and Caroline county line, and a tavern, where she specialized in robbing and murdering her guests, on the Nanticoke River near the village of Riverton, in Wicomico County. It is thought that she buried her treasures on these premises.

"Ye treasure lies hidden in a clump of trees near 3 creeks lying 100 or more paces north of the second inlet above Chincoteague Island." So wrote the pirate Charles Wilson in a confession given shortly before he went to the gallows. The treasure, worth about $2 million in the eighteenth century, consists of a dozen chests plundered from a Spanish galleon. The directions given by the pirate would place the treasure on Assateague Island, in Maryland, but just above the Virginia line. Because this island has suffered such tremendous erosion over the years, and has been struck by so many hurricanes, it is possible that this well-documented treasure now lies underwater.

Legend says that Holland Island, in the northern Chesapeake, derives its name from the fact that a treasure-laden Dutch ship sank there in the 1700s. In any case, old Dutch gold and silver coins have a way of turning up on its shores.

Massachusetts • Martha's Vineyard, off the coast of Massachusetts, was settled in 1642 and is dotted by the ruins of many old buildings. Several hundred shipwrecks have occurred around its shores, and it is a treasure hunter's dream, especially in the area around Edgartown Pond, where large numbers of early English coins have been found.

The *Whidah,* a pirate ship captained by Black Sam Bellamy, was wrecked on the eastern shore of Cape Cod in 1717. Only one crew member survived. The ship was carrying $200,000 in plunder, most of it in Spanish coins. The wreck is thought to be somewhere near the town of Wellfleet.

The ghost town of Dogtown is a favorite treasure hunting spot in this state. It is located just west of Long Beach on Cape Ann, in Essex County. The old town was abandoned around 1830, and many valuable relics have been taken from the ruins of several hundred buildings that remain clearly visible.

Michigan • A lost gold mine is located somewhere in Porcupine Mountain State Park in Ontonagon County. Early settlers here found the native Americans wearing large gold nuggets as ornaments and using more gold to trade for goods. The mine has never been located.

Just before his death, the founder of the House of David religious sect said he had buried $11 million in currency on the grounds of a mansion used by the group. The mansion is in Berrien County, near the town of Benton Harbor.

In 1895 the steamship *Chicora* sank in Lake Michigan off the town of St. Joseph. Its cargo included silver ingots, gold coins, and a large amount of bottled whiskey. Coins from the wreck have been found on nearby beaches.

Minnesota • The west bank of the Red River in the northwestern extremity of the state is considered a hot spot by treasure hunters. Many riverboats were lost in these waters during the last century, and currents frequently carry gold and silver coins ashore on the west bank.

In Pipestone County, somewhere near Pipestone National Monument, Jesse James and his gang allegedly hid $55,000 in gold coins and bullion.

The most famous treasure in this state is supposedly buried in a metal box under a fencepost in a 10-mile stretch of State Route 52 in Olmsted County between the towns of Chatfield and Rochester. During the 1930s, the Ma Barker–Alvin Karpis Gang hid $100,000 in ransom money here, but were later unable to relocate the spot. Countless other searchers have had no better luck.

Mississippi • Natchez Trace, the 450-mile trail that once served as the main route between Natchez and Nashville, Tennessee, has been in use since prehistoric times. Much of the original road still survives, as do some very old buildings along its length, and the trail has been the source of many extremely valuable artifacts.

The steamboat *Ben Sheerod,* which sank in the Mississippi River near the town of Black Hawk, in Wilkinson County, in 1837, was carrying gold coins worth $75,000 at the time. Coins from the wreck are sometimes found along the eastern shore of the Mississippi in this area.

Somewhere within sight of the railroad station in the town of Holly Springs, in Marshall County, a Union Army paymaster buried $80,000 in gold coins to keep it out of the hands of Confederate troops. He was shot to death soon thereafter and the coins were never found.

Missouri • About 8 miles west of Mound City, where the Missouri River sweeps through Holt County, the partial hulk of a steamship can be seen when the river is at its lowest. Some experts believe this is the *Sultana,* which sank in 1865 carrying $65,000 in gold coins; but it might be the *Caruthers,* which went down a few years earlier with a cargo that included $30,000 in gold coins. Coins from the wreck sometimes wash ashore in the area.

During the Civil War a doctor named Talbot was murdered by robbers after he refused to tell them where he had buried a barrel filled with gold coins. This fabulous treasure is thought to be on the grounds of his mansion, which is on State Route 71, a few miles from the town of Barnard, in Nodaway County.

The famous Confederate raider Quantrill is known to have buried a vast amount of gold, worth at least $10 million at the time, close to the rock pinnacle known as Belle Starr's Needle, which is in the Clark National Forest, in Laclede County.

Montana • The ghost town of Nevada, a short distance west of Virginia City in Madison County, was once headquarters for several outlaw gangs and was the scene of numerous trials and hangings. Local legend says that outlaw caches are hidden there.

Somewhere just north of the junction of Cottonwood and Baggs Creeks, in Deer Lodge County, is a fabulous lost gold mine. Two miners took hundreds of pounds of gold from it in just a few weeks after its discovery, left for supplies, and were never again able to find the site.

Just west of Malta, in the hills of Phillips County, Butch Cassidy and the Sundance Kid are said to have buried $100,000 in gold and currency.

Kid Curry, who also rode with the Wild Bunch, stole $100,000 from a passenger train in 1901, and it, too, is said to be hidden in the vicinity of Malta.

Nebraska • Devil's Nest, a wooded area along the Missouri River about 10 miles north of Linky, in Knox County, is dotted by caves that served as outlaw hideouts for at least seventy years. Numerous bandit caches are supposedly hidden here.

Somewhere near Seneca, in Thomas County, a prospector returning from the California goldfields in 1853 was attacked and wounded by thieves. He escaped and buried a fortune in gold, but died before he could reclaim it or reveal its whereabouts. This treasure has been sought for years. It is thought to be within 2 miles of the present town limits.

In 1867 highwaymen stole at least 400 pounds of pure gold from a stagecoach, then were caught on the Lodgepole Creek, just east of the town of Sidney in Cheyenne County. Evidence strongly indicated they had buried the gold along the banks of the river, but they went to the gallows without telling where it was hidden.

Nevada • The town of Goldfield, on U.S. 95 in Nye County, once had a population of 40,000 and its mines produced over $100 million worth of gold. Today it is virtually deserted, but vast amounts of treasure are thought to be hidden in and around its deserted buildings.

During the 1880s, a successful gold miner hid gold then worth $250,000 near Tohakum Peak, about 2 miles from the northern end of Pyramid Lake in Washoe County. Returning for it the next spring, he was unable to locate it.

The Comstock Lode, about 10 miles north of Reno, once produced hundreds of millions of dollars in gold and silver. The entire area is heavily dotted with ghost towns, abandoned mines, and old mining camps. Major discoveries are made almost annually in this area, so it is regarded as the finest treasure hunting spot in the state of Nevada.

New Hampshire • Near Woodsville, where the Connecticut and Ammonoosuc rivers come together in Grafton County, a miser named Woods allegedly buried a fortune in gold around 1829, somewhere in the vicinity of a sawmill he owned.

A British merchantman, the *King Edward,* sank in 1685 near Star Island, about 10 miles southeast of Portsmouth. A large amount of gold and silver was among the cargo, and old coins from the wreck have been found on the shores of this island.

In 1775, during the early days of the American Revolution, Governor John Wentworth, fleeing from the approaching enemy, hid seven chests containing gold and silver coins, plus gold and silver tableware, somewhere in the vicinity of Smithtown, which is in Rockingham County.

New Jersey • Probably the favorite treasure hunting spot in the state is at Sandy Hook, a point of land thrusting out into Lower New York Bay, where hundreds of ships, carrying many millions in treasure, have been wrecked over the years. There are miles of beaches here, and hardly a year goes by that they do not yield worthwhile amounts of treasure.

During the 1930s a miserly farmer named Arthur Barry buried $100,000 in currency on his farm in Sussex County, on County Road 517 near the town of Andover. Dying, he told his family of the hoard, but they were unable to find it.

Retreating British soldiers during the Revolution paused long enough to bury two trunks filled with gold coins on Apple Pie Hill, about 3 miles south of Chadsworth in Burlington County.

New Mexico • During the Depression a Mexican millionaire, said to be an embezzler fleeing his government, flew into this country with $30 million worth of gold bullion he hoped to sell the U.S. government. Unsuccessful in this, he is said to have buried the gold near the base of a flat mesa a few miles from the town of Shiprock in San Juan County.

Somewhere on Powell Mountain, in McKinley County east of Gallup, Zuni Indians hid a vast fortune in gold, silver, and precious jewels, to keep it out of the hands of Spaniards. The Spaniards murdered hundreds of Zuni in their attempts to learn its location, but the treasure was never found.

In 1860, while under attack near the present town of Grants, a group of miners was forced to bury an entire wagon train load of silver bars. The treasure, never located, is said to consist of six tons of silver.

New York • The 360-mile long Erie Canal, stretching from Buffalo to Albany, once connected New York City with the Hudson Valley and the Great Lakes. Many of its locks and buildings still exist, and around them treasure hunters continue to find old coins, bottles, and relics.

Silver Creek, near the town of Dunkirk on Lake Erie, derives its name from the numerous silver coins that have been found on nearby beaches. The coins probably wash ashore from the wreck of the steamship *Atlantic,* which sank here in 1852 and took to the bottom a cargo of newly minted coins.

Numerous ships have gone down over the years near Montauk Point, at the eastern tip of Long Island, and gold and silver coins have been found in this region. The coins probably come from the wreck of the privateer *Marey* which went to the bottom in 1763, while loaded with coins and bullion.

North Carolina • Beaufort, which was settled early in the eighteenth century and is located in Carteret County, served as a base for pirates for nearly a century. At least a dozen major treasures are said to be buried in the vicinity.

Somewhere near Deep River in Randolph County, probably in a cave, a mass-murderer named David Fanning hid a huge amount of plunder just before fleeing to Nova Scotia in 1787.

Over the centuries more than 300 ships have gone down in the treacherous waters off Cape Lookout, off Carteret County. More than 3,000 have been lost around Cape Hatteras, which lies just to the north. Millions of dollars worth of treasure lie beneath these waters. Best beach areas for treasure hunting are in the areas of Duck, Kitty Hawk, Nags Head, Buxton, Avon, and Portsmouth Island.

Near a bridge over Caler Fork, close to the town of Franklin in Franklin County, lies a stash of 50 pounds of emeralds. The prospector who hid them there was struck by a car soon after, and described the location as he was dying, but relatives were unable to find the treasure.

North Dakota • Belmont, in Grand Forks County, is now a ghost town, the ruins barely visible, but until 1897 it was a thriving community. That year it was destroyed by a flood and the same flood swept several safes containing gold, silver, and currency into the Red River. The safes were never recovered.

Somewhere near Belfield in Stark County, a group of settlers led by one Dr. Dibbs found a vast network of abandoned gold mines in 1894. The veins were so rich that they extracted several hundred pounds of ore from a single shaft before leaving. They were later unable to find their way back to what is now known as "The Mountain of Gold."

A returning California gold miner hid $200,000 in gold nuggets along the banks of the Missouri River within the city limits of Stanton, which is in Mercer County. He was then struck ill and before he recovered, the flooding river swept away his markers, and his fortune was lost.

Ohio • On a farm then owned by the Pierpont family, John Dillinger is said to have buried more than $1 million in cash. The farm is on County Road

65, near the town of Leipsic in Putnam County.

In December 1876 a train plunged into a gorge near Ashtabula in Ashtabula County. One car held $2 million in gold bullion. The car split open, allowing the bullion to sink into the muddy depths of the river, and the gold was never recovered.

Near the town of Cheshire in Gallia County, along the west bank of the Ohio River, treasure hunters have long been able to find gold and silver coins that wash ashore from the wreck of an unknown riverboat.

Oklahoma • About 10 miles from Boise City, on a mountain known as Sugarloaf Peak, lies a well-documented treasure worth millions. It was buried there by a group of French miners who are known to have struck it rich in California. They hid it while going into Boise City for a night on the town, where all four members of the party were killed in a gunfight.

It is believed that the notorious Dalton Gang hid much of their booty in a cave or caves in the Grass Mountains of Major County, near the town of Orienta.

In 1879, during a Comanche raid, settlers supposedly hid about half a million dollars in gold coins near the banks of the Washita River in Custer County.

Oregon • The San Pedro Gold Mine was worked by Native Americans and Mexicans long before European settlers reached this area, and was reportedly one of the richest mines in the world. It is thought that the lost mine is located along Big Inlet Creek on the southern slope of Diamond Peak, which places it in Lane County.

Several major pirate treasures are thought to be buried in the stretch of beach between Cascade Head and the port of Newport, a distance of about 20 miles. Near the port, where the Elk River enters the bay, robbers are said to have buried stolen diamonds worth $1 million in the 1930s.

In Curry County, on the beach at the mouth of the Rogue River, survivors of the wreck of a Spanish galleon are said to have buried chests holding millions in treasure. Gold and silver coins have been found in the area, so the old legends may be true.

Pennsylvania • The ghost town of Old Economy is in Beaver County, a few miles northeast of Ambridge. The town was founded in 1825 and abandoned shortly after the start of this century. Many of its original buildings remain, and some valuable artifacts have been found in the region.

During the Civil War, with Union troops in close pursuit, Confederate raiders hid 15 tons of silver bullion in a cave about 3 miles north of Uniontown, in Fayette County. The silver had been stolen while on its way to the mint in Philadelphia.

During the Revolution, a small band of Tories, under the command of one Captain Doane, secreted gold, silver, and other treasure then worth about $100,000 in an abandoned well in the vicinity of Wernersville in Berks County.

Rhode Island • Legend says that British General Richard Prescott buried his personal fortune somewhere on his farm shortly before he was captured by patriots during the Revolution. The farm is located on State Route 114 near the outskirts of Portland.

The pirate William Kidd is said to have buried a substantial treasure on Block Island, in the waters off Newport County, and another at Brenton Point in Rhode Island Sound.

The pirate Charles Harris, who was hanged in Newport, admitted burying a large treasure at the base of Newport Cliffs, which is just south of the present city of Newport.

South Carolina • On North Island in Winyah Bay, off Georgetown County, a band of Tories buried a vast hoard of gold and silver in 1781. They were killed before they could reclaim this well-documented treasure, which has been the subject of many unsuccessful searches.

Somewhere near the Mulberry Plantation on the Cooper River in Berkeley County a band of thieves, hanged in 1716, allegedly hid a vast treasure of gold, coins, and jewelry.

On December 12, 1864, Union soldiers ambushed a fleet of Confederate boats on the Congaree River, about 2 miles north of Sandy Run in Calhoun County. One boat sank, carrying to the muddy bottom gold coins worth more than $150,000 at the time.

South Dakota • Several worthwhile treasures are thought to be hidden in and around the ghost town of Bloomington, which is 4 miles north of Vermillion in Clay County. Once a thriving community, Bloomington was obliterated by a band of outlaws in 1877.

Dozens of major treasures are thought to be hidden in the vicinity of Deadwood, which was once one of the wildest mining towns and is in Meade County. Among the well-documented treasures is $85,000 in gold coins robbed from the Deadwood Stage in the 1870s and thought to be hidden somewhere on Deadwood Mountain.

In 1879, outlaws ambushed a stage en route to Cheyenne, Wyoming, from Deadwood. They stole 450 pounds of gold bars and buried these just north of Sturgis, in Meade County, probably along the banks of Lame Johnny Creek. A posse killed all the outlaws the day following the robbery, but the gold was never recovered.

Tennessee • An outlaw named John Murrell allegedly hid gold worth more than $1 million near his stone house on County Road 76, about 3 miles south of Dancyville in Fayette County.

A miser named Cefe Winton is known to have buried a fortune in gold coins on or around his farm on State Route 41 near Hillsboro in Coffee County. He and his wife were tortured to death by robbers, but refused to reveal their hiding place. Several thousand dollars in gold was found on the farm more than fifty years ago, but a great deal more almost certainly remains.

Rampaging Cherokees are thought to have buried about $1 million in stolen gold in a burial mound somewhere near Log Mountain, just north of the town of Luttrell in Grainger County.

Texas • The ghost town of St. Mary's may be well worth exploring. Founded in 1840, and a haven for pirates and privateers for many years, the town is abandoned and in near ruins, but it is said to hold several caches of pirate treasure. The site is in Refugio County, near the town of Bayside on Capona Bay.

The most famous treasure in this state, without a doubt, is the Lost Bowie Silver Mine, believed to be somewhere in San Saba County. In 1759, while under attack by Indians, Spaniards stored $33 million in silver bullion in the mine shaft, then blasted it shut. Most of the Spaniards died in the attack. It was a year before the survivors could return and by then a landslide had concealed the location of the mine shaft.

There is some evidence to indicate that early Spanish conquistadors buried a vast treasure in an abandoned mine shaft in the vicinity of the Stillhouse Hollow Reservoir, near Belton in Bell County. This long-sought treasure is said to be worth no less than $20 million.

Utah • About 10 miles southeast of the town of Castle Dale in Emery County, in a place then known as Buckhorn Wash, Butch Cassidy and his gang paused long enough, near the start of this century, to bury $72,000 in gold and silver coins.

Probably the most eagerly sought treasure in this state is the Montezuma Hoard, thought to be worth $10–$100 million. The Aztecs spirited it out of Mexico to keep it out of the hands of Cortez. Consisting of gold, silver, and precious jewels, it is, according to legend, hidden somewhere in the mazelike canyons around White Mountain in Kane County.

Another famous hoard, the Treasure of the Golden Jesus, said to consist of more than three dozen burro loads of pure gold, including an enormous crucifix made of solid gold, has been sought since 1810, when it was supposedly hidden in a cave close to the Escalante River in Garfield County.

Vermont • Late in the Civil War, Confederate raiders stole more than $110,000 in gold coins from three banks in St. Albans. It is known that they buried the loot somewhere in the vicinity of Highgate Springs, in Franklin County. Caught, they refused to reveal the treasure's location before they were hanged.

Somewhere near Newport, in Orleans County, British troops fleeing the patriots during the Revolution buried gold and silver coins then valued at 75,000 pounds sterling. This famous hoard, now commonly known as the Hell's Half Acre Treasure, is believed to be somewhere on the southern shore of Lake Mephremagog.

Virginia • As the Civil War drew to a close, a Confederate general, with the help of his slaves, hid more than $4 million in gold coins and bars on a farm about 1 mile south of the town of Forest, in Roanoke County. The slaves were killed to protect the secret.

Cape Henry, located between Norfolk and Virginia Beach, offers some of the finest treasure hunting in this state. More than 100 ships, many carrying treasure, have been lost in this area, so it steadily produces coins and relics. In addition, numerous pirate caches are thought to be hidden along the shores of the Cape.

Washington • In 1852, according to many accounts, a sea captain named James Scarborough buried a barrel containing a fortune in gold bars and coins along the banks of the Columbia River. The site is thought to be in Willipa Hills, in Pacific County, just across the river from the town of Astoria, Oregon.

Near Cape Flattery at the northwestern tip of the state, where the Spaniards once had a settlement, many coins and relics have been turning up in recent years. Also thought to be hidden in this part of Clallam County is thousands of dollars worth of gold that was stolen in 1861 by a treasury agent named Victor Smith. Gold coins from an unknown shipwreck also wash up on beaches in this county.

West Virginia • About $350,000 in gold bullion, hidden by Confederate raiders during the Civil War, is thought to be buried on the banks of a fork of the Buckhannon River, near its confluence with Bear Fork Creek in Gilmer County.

In the early part of this century a miser named Dennis Atkins is said to have buried $200,000 in gold coins on the banks of the Tug Fork River. The treasure is thought to be just north of the town of Kermit in Mingo County.

Wisconsin • Numerous gold coins have been found along the shores of Lake Superior in and around the town of Superior, which is in Polk County. The coins almost certainly wash ashore from the wreck of the *Benjamin Noble,* which sank near here while carrying a fortune in gold.

John Dillinger reportedly buried $750,000 in bank loot in the dense woods behind the Little Bohemia Lodge, which he sometimes used as a hideout. The lodge is on State Route 51, a few miles south of Mercer in Iron County.

Wyoming • The area around Independence Rock, a landmark on the old Oregon Trail, offers some of the best relic hunting in the United States. The rock, rising more than 200 feet above the plains and the nearby Sweetwater River, is about 50 miles southwest of Casper, in Natrona County, and is reached by State Route 220.

Cache Creek, which winds through Teton County near Jackson Hole, derives its name from the fact that two separate treasures, worth at least $150,000 each at the time, were definitely hidden somewhere along its banks in the last century. Both treasures were outlaws' loot.

The following list of Treasure Hunting Clubs is reprinted by permission of the International Treasure Hunting Society, P.O. Box 3007, Garland, TX 75041. The Historical Societies are the last listing under each state.

Treasure Hunting Clubs and Historical Societies

ALABAMA

Montgomery Gem & Mineral Society
  P.O. Box 3273
  Montgomery, AL 36109

Regar Memorial Museum of
Natural History
  1411 Gurne Avenue
  Anniston, AL 36201

Warrior's Basin Treasure
Hunters Association
  440 Merrywood Drive
  Birmingham, AL 35214

Alabama Historical Association
  3121 Carlisle Road
  Birmingham, AL 35213

ALASKA

Alaska Historical Library
  State Capitol
  Juneau, AK 99801

ARIZONA

Arizona Treasure Hunters
  2190 East Apache Boulevard
  Tempe, AZ 85281

Grand Canyon Winnies
Arizona State Club
  615 West Vista
  Bisbee, AZ 85603

Lake Havasu Treasure Club
  Box 37005
  Lake Havasu City, AZ 86403

Old Pueblo Lapidary Club
  Box 2163
  Tucson, AZ 85702

Arizona Pioneers Historical Society
  949 East Second Street
  Tucson, AZ 85719

ARKANSAS

El Dorado Treasure Seekers
  P.O. Box 1095
  El Dorado, AR 71730

Mr. B. Doug Rice
  P.O. Box 1358, HSRC
  Hot Springs, AR 71901

Treasure Cover's
  1125 North "S" Street
  Fort Smith, AR 72901

Arkansas Historical Association
  University of Arkansas
  Fayetteville, AR 72701

CALIFORNIA

American River Gem & Mineral Club
  Box 374
  Rancho Cordova, CA 95670

American Society of Dowsers
  1520 Idlewood Road
  Glendale, CA 91220

Big "D" Detector Club
  8851 East Linsford Street
  Rosemead, CA 91770

The California Searchers
  P.O. Box 3343
  San Leandro, CA 94578

Campbell Gem & Mineral Guild
  3448 Cecil Avenue
  San Jose, CA 95117

Mr. Charles Carfrae
  8420 East Devenir Street
  Downey, CA 90242

Centinela Valley Gem
  1515½ South Fairfax Avenue
  Los Angeles, CA 90019

Chino Valley Prospectors
  5443 "B" Street
  Chino, CA 91710

Coachella Valley Mineral Society
  P.O. Box 512
  Indio, CA 92201

Conejo Rock & Mineral Club
  Box 723
  Newbury Park, CA 91320

East Bay Mineral Society
  53 McCartney Road
  Alameda, CA 94501

Fluorescent Mineral Society
  9111 Morehart Avenue
  Pacoima, CA 91331

Foothill Gem & Mineral Club
  10933 Woodward Avenue
  Sunland, CA 91040

Gem & Treasure Hunting Association
  2493 San Diego Avenue
  San Diego, CA 92110

Gold Prospectors
  P.O. Box 507
  Bonsall, CA 92003

Golden State Treasure Hounds
  1501 Kelly Street
  Bakersfield, CA 93304

House of Treasure Hunters
  5714 El Cajon Boulevard
  San Diego, CA 92115

Indian Wells Valley Gem
  Box 1481
  Ridgecrest, CA 93555

International Treasure Club Digest
  Box 7030
  Compton, CA 90224

L.E.R.C. Treasure Hunting Club
  2814 Empire Avenue
  Burbank, CA 91504

Living West
  7513 Sausalito Avenue
  Canoga Park, CA 91304

LA Historical Bottle Club
  Box 60762, Terminal Annex
  Los Angeles, CA 90060

Mining & Prospecting Club
  2314 Empire Avenue
  Burbank, CA 19504

Montebello Mineral & Lapidary Club
  Box 582
  Montebello, CA 90640

Monterey Bay Mineral Society
  Box 12
  Salinas, CA 93901

Mother Lode Mountain Searchers
    Route 3, Box 630
    Sonora, CA 90507

Nevada County Gem & Mineral Club
    Box 565
    Nevada City, CA 95959

Palomar Gem & Mineral Club
    2210 South Escondido Boulevard
    Escondido, CA 92025

Prospector's Club of
Southern California
    ATTN: Mr. Bill Smillie
    10502 Illona
    Los Angeles, CA 90064

Redwood Empire Treasure
Hunters of Northern California
    5201 Lavell Road
    Santa Rosa, CA 95401

Riverside Gem & Mineral Society
    24950 Cottonwood Avenue
    Sunnymead, CA 92388

Riverside TH'ers Club
    c/o Mr. Rudy Iporsh
    6484 Midever Avenue
    Riverside, CA 92504

Roseville Rock Rollers
    Box 212
    Roseville, CA 95678

Sacramento Mineral Society
    Box 1451
    Sacramento, CA 95807

San Diego Treasure Hunting
    3784 Thirtieth Street
    San Diego, CA 92104

San Fernando Valley Young Historians
    10940 Sepulveda Boulevard
    Mission Hills, CA 91340

San Gabriel Valley Lapidary
    Box 44
    San Gabriel, CA 91778

San Pablo Bay Gem & Mineral Club
    Box 636
    San Pablo, CA 94806

Santa Barbara Mineral & Gem Club
    Box 815
    Santa Barbara, CA 93102

Santa Cruz Mineral & Gem Society
    Box 343
    Santa Cruz, CA 95060

Santa Rosa Mineral & Gem Society
    Box 7036
    Santa Rosa, CA 95401

Southgate Mineral & Lapidary Club
    Box 212
    South Gate, CA 90280

The Treasure Hunter
    Box 188
    Midway City, CA 92655

Treasure Hunter Society
of Santa Clara Valley
    1366 Mary Lee Way
    San Jose, CA 95118

Tri-City Lapidary Society
    Box 279
    San Clemente, CA 92672

United Prospectors Club
    31217 Tower Road
    Visalia, CA 93277

California Historical Society
   2029 Jackson Street
   San Francisco, CA 94109

COLORADO

Eureka (Colorado Treasure Club)
   6195 West Thirty-eighth Avenue
   Wheatridge, CO 80033

High Plains Rock & Art Society
   Box 513
   Akron, CO 80720

Mile High Gem Guild
c/o Mr. Ed Draper
   2604 South Williams Street
   Denver, CO 80210

Pikes Peak Chapter GPAA
   P.O. Box 7821
   Colorado Springs, CO 80933

Prospectors & TH'ers Guild
   c/o Examino Establishment
   Segundo, CO 81070

Sangre De Christo Adventure League
   P.O. Box 6755
   Colorado Springs, CO 80934

Colorado State Historical Society
   200 Fourteenth Avenue
   Denver, CO 80203

CONNECTICUT

Yankee Territory Coinshooter
   Box 3021
   Enfield, CT 06082

Connecticut Historical Society
   1 Elizabeth Street
   Hartford, CT 06105

DELAWARE

First State Treasure Hunters Club
   23 Sandalwood Drive, Apt. #2
   Sandalwood, DE 19713

Delaware Historical Society
   Sixth and Market Streets
   Wilmington, DE 19801

FLORIDA

Century Village Lapidary
   Chatham K-230
   West Palm Beach, FL 33409

Darwin's Treasure Finders
   Florida Artifacts TH'ers
   4478 Park Boulevard
   Pinellas Park, FL 33565

Florida Artifact Recovery
   Box N
   Fort McCoy, FL 32637

Florida Marine Historical &
Archaeological Society
   Box 991
   Maitland, FL 32751

Florida Treasure Hunters
   907 Twenty-third Avenue
   Tampa, FL 33605

Gem & Mineral Society of Palm Beach
   Box 3041
   West Palm Beach, FL 33402

Peninsular Archaeological
   1412 Sixth Avenue
   Tarpon Springs, FL 33589

Florida Historical Society,
   University of South Florida Library
   Tampa, FL 33620

GEORGIA

Georgia Historical Commission
116 Mitchell Street SW
Atlanta, GA 30303

HAWAII

Hawaiian Coin Diggers
91-193 EWA Beach Road
EWA Beach, Oahu, HI 96706

Hawaiian Historical Society
560 Kawaiahoa Street
Honolulu, HI 96803

IDAHO

Eagle Rock Numismatic Society
272 West Twenty-first Street
Idaho Falls, ID 83401

Gem Coinshooters Detectors Club
209 East Thirty-sixth Street
Boise, ID 83704

Magic Valley Gem Club
Box 967
Twin Falls, ID 83301

Idaho State Historical Society
610 North Julia Davis
Boise, ID 83706

ILLINOIS

Mr. Paul Ackerman
3641 North Marshfield Avenue
Chicago, IL 60613

AH Electronics
2131 Hammond Drive
Schaumburg, IL 60195

Black Hawk Rock Club
6150 South Meridian
Rockford, IL 61102

Gem City Rock Club
Box 1034
Quincy, IL 62301

Illinois-Iowa Treasure Hunting Club
ATTN: Mr. Earl Strupp
1521 Nineteenth Avenue
Rock Island, IL 61201

Jolly Roger Club
Wood Road
Ashton, IL 61006

Land of Lincoln Coinshooters
Association
921 North Ninth Street
Springfield, IL 62702

Mr. Bill Langford
314 Westwood Drive
Wheaton, IL 60187

Lemont Coin Shooter Association
1501 Harrison
La Grange Park, IL 60525

Midwest Historical Research Society
4113 North Kenneth Avenue
Chicago, IL 60641

Northern Illinois Prairie Prowlers
2110 North Richmond Road
McHenry, IL 60050

Orland Treasure Finders
14231 South Union Avenue
Orland Park, IL 60462

Park Forest Earth Science
    Box 235
    Park Forest, IL 60466

Prairie Pirates Treasure Hunter Club
    1009 South Tonti Circle
    Peoria, IL 61605

Rene's Treasure Trove
    214 East Front Street
    Bloomington, IL 61701

Tri-State Treasure Hunters
    505 South Eighth Street
    Quincy, IL 62301

Trove Hunters of America
    P.O. Box 911
    Pekin, IL 61554

Illinois Historical Society
    Centennial Building
    Springfield, IL 62706

INDIANA

Elkhart Mineral Society
    59020 Pepper Mint Drive
    Elkhart, IN 46514

Hoosier Hiets Treasure Hunters Club
    RR #5
    Seymour, IN 47274

Mid-America Prospectors
    P.O. Box 1231
    Elkhart, IN 46514

Prospectors Club International
    P.O. Box 1057
    Anderson, IN 46015

Vigo Rock & Gem Club
    Indiana State University
    Terre Haute, IN 47801

Wabash Valley Gem & Mineral Club
    c/o Rev. Eugene E. Parker
    RR #2
    Brookton, IN 47923

Indiana Historical Society
    140 North Senate Avenue
    Indianapolis, IN 46202

IOWA

Central Iowa Treasure Hunters Club
    110 Fifth Street NW
    Mitchellville, IA 50169

Feathers & Old Lace Treasure Club
    U.S. 71
    Storm Lake, IA 50588

Indian Bluffs Treasure Hunting Club
    323 North Chestnut Street
    Monticello, IA 52310

Iowa Metal Go-K-tors Club
    1047 Evergreen
    Waterloo, IA 50603
    (Dorothy Morgan, Secretary)

Erma L. Martindale
    1818 East Elm Street
    Des Moines, IA 50317

Treasure Hunting & Rock
Club of Monticello
    120 North Chestnut Street
    Monticello, IA 52310

Iowa State Historical Society
    Iowa City, IA 52240

KANSAS

Mr. Jim Berryman
520 West Seventh Street
Hutchinson, KS 67501

Chanute Gem & Mineral Society
934 South Lincoln
Chanute, KS 66720

Hutchinson Gem & Mineral Society
Box 252
Hutchinson, KS 67501

Mid-America Treasure Hunters Club
1508 East Thirty-fifth Street
Hutchinson, KS 67501

Mid Western Artifact Society
8175 Monrovia
Lenexa, KS 66215

Mr. Larry E. Swank
c/o YMCA of Hutchinson & Reno
716 East Thirteenth Street
Hutchinson, KS 67501

Topeka Treasure Hunters
P.O. Box 1021
Topeka, KS 66601

Kansas State Historical Society
120 West Tenth Street
Topeka, KS 66612

KENTUCKY

Mr. Bill Harrod
R #4 Pryor Valley Road
Shepherdsville, KY 40165

Kentucky TH'ers Association
Benton, KY 42025

Kyana Geological Society, Inc.
Louisville Zoo Gardens
1100 Trevilian Way
Louisville, KY 40213

N.O.S.L. Treasure Hunters
13030 Dixie Highway Lot 50
Louisville, KY 40272

Old Prospectors Metal Club
2919 Alford
Louisville, KY 40212

Ollie & Co.
12217 Blossom Road
Louisville, KY 40229

Kentucky Historical Society
Old State House
Frankfort, KY 40601

LOUISIANA

Mr. Thomas D. Brown
809 Jefferson Heights Avenue
Jefferson, LA 70121

The Gem & Mineral Society of Louisiana
P.O. Box 50633
New Orleans, LA 70150

Louisiana Coin Hunters & Relic Club
2019 Clover Lane
Alexandria, LA 71301

Louisiana Historical Association
Box 44222, Capitol Station
Baton Rouge, LA 70804

MAINE

Maine Historical Society
485 Congress Street
Portland, ME 04111

MARYLAND

B & L Metal Detectors
    4121 Old North Point Road
    Baltimore, MD 21222

Heritage Hunters of Maryland
    9764 Matzon Road
    Middle River, MD 21220

Maryland Historical Society
    201 West Monument Street
    Annapolis, MD 21201

MASSACHUSETTS

Bay State Coinshooters
    44 Old Mansion Lane
    Whitman, MA 02382

Colonial Treasure Seekers
    37 Spring Street
    West Springfield, MA 01089

Merrimack Valley TH'er Club
    57 Woodmont Avenue
    Haverhill, MA 01830

New England Treasure
Finders Association
    P.O. Box 523
    West Springfield, MA 01089

Northern Berkshire Mineral Club
    320 Federal Street
    Greenfield, MA 01301

Massachusetts Historical Society
    1154 Boylston Street
    Boston, MA 02115

MICHIGAN

Ishpeming Rock & Mineral Club
    405 South Rose Street
    Ishpeming, MI 49849

Kalamazoo Geological & Mineral
Society
    7637 V. Avenue East
    Vicksburg, MI 49097

Michigan Prospector's Club
    7007 Cooley Lake Road
    Union Lake, MI 48085

Michigan Treasure Seekers
    601 Glenwood Avenue
    Owosso, MI 48867

Michigan Historical Society
    2117 Washtenaw Avenue
    Ann Arbor, MI 48104

MINNESOTA

Bloomington Mineral Club
    5929 Upton Avenue South
    Minneapolis, MN 55410

Little Crow Lapidary & Mineral Club
    c/o Mrs. Lee Payne
    Route 4
    Willmar, MN 56201

The Maplewood Mineral Club
    79 Grove Street
    Mahtomedi, MN

Minnetonke Gem & Mineral Club
    134 Inglewood Street
    Long Lake, MN 55356

Minnesota Historical Society
    690 Cedar Street
    St. Paul, MN 55101

MISSISSIPPI

Mississippi State Department of
Archives and History
  Box 571
  Jackson, MS 39205

MISSOURI

Mid Missouri Coin & Relic Hunters
  107 Rice Boulevard
  California, MO 65018

Mo-Kan Packrats
  P.O. Box 10661
  Kansas City, MO 64118

Ozark Mountain Gem & Mineral
Society
  526 South Forest Court
  Springfield, MO 65806

Pike County Mineral & Gem Society
  RR #3
  Middletown, MO 63359

Missouri Historical Society
  Jefferson Memorial Building
  St. Louis, MO 63112

MONTANA

Montana Historical Society
  225 North Roberts Street
  Helena, MT 59601

NEBRASKA

Fremont Treasure Hunters
  335 North Williams
  Fremont, NE 68025

Midwest Historical Detector Club
  Box 55066 Station B
  Omaha, NE 68155

Midwest Historical Research &
Detector Club in Springfield
  850 N. Second Avenue
  Springfield, NE 68059

Nebraskaland Treasure Hunters
  Box 2402, Station B
  Lincoln, NE 68502

Nebraska Mineral & Gem Club
  3510 North Fifty-eighth Street
  Omaha, NE 68104

Nebraska State Historical Society
  1500 R Street
  Lincoln, NB 68508

NEVADA

The Clark County Gem
Collectors, Inc.
  Box 5846
  Las Vegas, NV 89102

50 States Treasure Hunters
Association, Inc.
  Box 715
  Virginia City, NV 89440

Nevada State Historical Society
  Box 1129
  Reno, NV 89504

NEW HAMPSHIRE

New Hampshire-Yankee
Treasure Hunters & Prospectors
  265 Washington Street
  Keene, NH 03431

New Hampshire Historical Society
30 Park Street
Concord, NH 03301

NEW JERSEY

Down To Earth Lapidary Club
RD 2926 Burd Road
Pennington, NJ 08534

South Jersey Treasure Hunter's Club
P.O. Box 176
Haddonfield, NJ 08033

New Jersey Historical Society
230 Broadway
Newark, NJ 07104

NEW MEXICO

Treasure Hunting Unlimited
406 Broadway
Truth or Consequences, NM
87901

New Mexico Historical Society
Palace of the Governors
Santa Fe, NM 87501

NEW YORK

Atlantic Treasure Club
c/o Charles Citti
136 Hempstead Avenue
Rockville Centre, NY 11571

Atlantic Treasure Hunters
c/o Mr. Fred Padovan
220-28 Sixth Avenue
Bayside, NY 11364

Mr. Richard W. Chase
Horseheads Hid. Hoard
1891-7 Acres Road
Millport, NY 14864

Chemung Valley Gem Society
c/o Ms. Evelyn Haskins
Box 205-Haskins Road
Erin, NY 14838

The Empire State Treasure Seekers
15 Rustyville Road
Loudonville, NY 12211

Granite State Treasure Hunters Club
93 South State Street
Concord, NH 03301

New York Aces
2 River Street
Richfield Springs, NY 13439

Niagara Frontier Relic Hunters
c/o Mr. Daniel P. Bell
Box 204
Lancaster, NY 14086

Treasure Pleasure Seekers
NY State Metal Detectors Club
366 Brookview Drive
Rochester, NY 14617

New York Historical Society
170 Central Park West
New York, NY 10024

NORTH CAROLINA

SE Association of Relic Hunters
123 East Davis Street
Burlington, NC 27215

The Senclad Searchers
    17 Partridge Road
    Wilmington, NC 28401

Stanley's Metal Detector Sales
    5 North Front Street
    Wilmington, NC 28401

North Carolina Department of
Archives and History
    Box 1881
    Raleigh, NC 27602

NORTH DAKOTA

The Central Dakota Gem &
Mineral Society
    1527 North Nineteenth Street
    Bismarck, ND 58501

North Dakota Historical Society
    Bismarck, ND 58501

OHIO

Buckeye Treasure Hunters Club
    218 North Market Street
    Minerva, OH 44657

Canton Wagon Train
    c/o Richard Bruder
    6033 Knob NE
    Louisville, OH 44641

Greater Miami Valley Treas.
    109 First Street
    Tipp City, OH 45371

Licking Co. Rock & Mineral
    295 South Twenty-first Street
    Newark, OH 43055

Low-K-Ters
    7237 Parma Park Boulevard
    Cleveland, OH 44130

Mid-Ohio TH-ers
    c/o Ms. Paulette E. Gaston
    6419 Montford Road W
    Westerville, OH 43081

PA-Ohio Treasure Hunters Club
    638 Chestnut Ridge Road
    Hubbard, OH 44425

The Penny Place
    3163 North Street
    Millersport, OH 43046

Y-City Treasure Hunters Club
    3730 Sunrise Circle
    Zanesville, OH 43701

Ohio Historical Society
    Fifteenth Avenue at North High
    Street
    Columbus, OH 43210

OKLAHOMA

Central Oklahoma Treasure Club
    Route 1, Box 62
    Ukon, OK 73099
    ATTN: Mr. Larry L. Biehler

Green County Treasure Club
    1588 Colorado
    Bartlesville, OK 74003

Indian Territory Treasure
Hunting Club
    P.O. Box 15061
    Tulsa, OK 74115

World Championship Treasure
Hunters
    Mr. DeWayne Holland
    1901 Seran Drive
    Wewoka, OK 74884

Oklahoma Historical Society
    Historical Building
    Oklahoma City, OK 74105

OREGON

The Eugene Mineral Club
    2020 Hayes Street
    Eugene, OR 97405

FRL
    2130 Arthur Street
    Klamath Falls, OR 97601

Oregon Treasure Hunters League
    P.O. Box 14052
    Portland, OR 97214

Seekers Unlimited
    c/o Mr. K. Menolascina
    13709 SE Stark Street
    Portland, OR 97233

Springfield Rock Club
    440 North Twenty-first Street
    Springfield, OR 97477

Oregon Historical Society
    1230 SW Park Avenue
    Portland, OR 97205

PENNSYLVANIA

Beaver Co. Rock & Mineral Society
    1902 Fifth Avenue
    Beaver Falls, PA 15010

Central Pennsylvania Rock Club
    P.O. Box 654
    Camp Hill, PA 17011

Hatboro Metal Detector Club
    c/o Mr. Al Duffield
    12 Belmar Road
    Hatboro, PA 19040

Moraine Rockbusters Inc.
    4642 Hampton Valley Drive
    Allison Park, PA 15101

Northwestern Lehigh Jaycees
    Route 1
    New Tripoli, PA 18066

Research Treasure Hunters
    1310 Beulah Road
    Churchillboro
    Pittsburgh, PA 15235

The Tuscarora Lapidary Society
    121 County Line Road
    Bryn Mawr, PA 10910

Pennsylvania Historical Society
    1300 Locust Street
    Philadelphia, PA 19107

RHODE ISLAND

Good Samaritan Club
    65 Baldwin Street
    Pawtucket, RI 02860

Ocean State Coachmen
    c/o Douglas T. Olney
    7 Gail Court
    Coventry, RI 02816

Rhode Island Historical Society
    52 Powell Street
    Providence, RI 02906

SOUTH CAROLINA

South Carolina Historical Society
    University of South Carolina
    Columbia, SC 29208

SOUTH DAKOTA

South Dakota Historical Society
    Memorial Building
    Pierre, SD 57501

TENNESSEE

Tennessee Valley Rock
and Mineral Club
    c/o Ms. Janet Dinsmore
    4310 Tee Pee Drive
    Chattanooga, TN 37406

Tennessee Historical Society
    State Library and Archives
    Building
    Nashville, TN 37219

TEXAS

Austin Gem & Mineral Society
    P.O. Box 4327
    Austin, TX 78765

Austin Relics Club
    P.O. Box 992
    Austin, TX 78767

Cowtown Treasure H'ers
    P.O. Box 10195 Oaks Branch
    Fort Worth, TX 76114

Cross Timbers Gem & Mineral
Society
    620 Highland Avenue
    Dublin, TX 76446

Exploration Society of
Corpus Christi
    603 Ninth Street
    Corpus Christi, TX 78419

Fireball Electronics
    1807 East Eighth
    Odessa, TX 79760

Fredericksburg Rockhounds
    c/o Mr. Jack Smith
    Box 42
    Center Point, TX 78010

Golden Crescent
Historical Association
    2601 Bon Aire
    Victoria, TX 77901

Golden Triangle Explorers Society
    P.O. Box 443
    Wylie, TX 75098

The Golden Triangle
Treasure Hunters Club
    Box 1562
    Orange, TX 77502

International Treasure
Hunting Society
    P.O. Box 3007
    Garland, TX 75041

Lone Star Treasure Hunters
    c/o Mr. Ben Hines
    2328 McAdams Avenue
    Dallas, TX 75224

Lubbock Gem & Mineral Society
    P.O. Box 6371
    Lubbock, TX 79413

Metal Detecting & Hobby
Club of Victoria
    Route 2 Box 225-C
    Victoria, TX 77901

North Texas Relic Hunters Club
    P.O. Box 443
    Wichita Falls, TX 76307

Pioneer Heritage Preservation
Society
    616 Arkansas
    South Houston, TX 77587

Research & Recovery Club
    1213 Preston Road
    Pasadena, TX 77503

Mr. Larry Sandridge
    5409 Camden Lane
    Pearland, TX 77581

Texhoma Rockhounds Inc.
    Tioga, TX 76271

The Tri-City Gem & Mineral Society
    3201 Rosewood
    Temple, TX 76501

Victoria Gem & Mineral Society
    Box 3078
    Victoria, TX 77901

West Texas Gem & Mineral Society
    1316 North Golder
    Odessa, TX 79763

Texas State Historical Association
    Box 8059, University Station
    Austin, TX 78712

UTAH

Gold Bug Club
    4231 West 3150 South
    Granger, UT 84120

International Society of
Treasure Hunters & Rockhounds
    2111 Wyoming Street
    Salt Lake City, UT 84109

Utah State Historical Society
    603 East South Temple
    Salt Lake City, UT 84102

VERMONT

Vermont Historical Society
    State Administration Building
    Montpelier, VT 05602

VIRGINIA

Eastern Virginia Relic Club
    c/o W. C. Turpin
    9285 Warwick Boulevard
    Huntin Pk
    Newport News, VA 23607

N. Virginia Relic Hunters
    Box 49
    RR#1 Ball Mill
    Midland, VA 22728

Shenandoah Valley Relic
    c/o J. Bracken
    807 Berryville Avenue
    Winchester, VA 22601

Tidewater Treasure Hunters
    H & S Detector Center
    2106 Thoroughgood Road
    Virginia Beach, VA 23455

Virginia Historical Society
    428 North Boulevard
    Richmond, VA 23221

WASHINGTON

Cascade Treasure Club
    17925 SE 313th
    Auburn, WA 98002

Magnolia Gem & Mineral Society
    2840 Thirtieth Avenue West
    Seattle, WA 98199

Northwest Treasure Hunters
    1024 East Fifteenth Avenue
    Spokane, WA 99203

Okanogan Treasure Hunters
    Box 1106
    Okanogan, WA 98840

Puget Sound Treasure Hunters Club
    c/o Ms. Rose Reed
    6105 Twentieth Street E
    Tacoma, WA 98424

Sunny O. Kanagan Treasure Club
    Pateros, WA 98846

Washington State Historical Society
    315 North Stadium Way
    Tacoma, WA 98403

WEST VIRGINIA

West Virginia Historical Society
    E-400 State Capitol Building
    Charleston, WV 25305

WISCONSIN

Driftless Area Gem Club
    P.O. Box 65
    Oakdale, WI 54649

Valley Rock & Mineral Club
    P.O. Box 1081
    Appleton, WI 54911

West Allis Bowmen, Inc.
    Mr. Eddie Tiarks
    10826 West Grant Street #3
    West Allis, WI 53227

Wisconsin Association of Treasure
Hunters
    P.O. Box 47
    Milwaukee, WI 53201

Wisconsin Association of Treasure
Hunting
    Box 177
    Menomonee, WI 53051

Wisconsin State Historical Society
    816 State Street
    Madison, WI 53706

WYOMING

Casper Seekers
    P.O. Box 3615
    Casper, WY 82602

Wyoming State Historical Society
    State Office Building
    Cheyenne, WY 82001

Gold-Bearing Regions in the U.S.

The following is a list, state by state and county by county, of known gold-bearing regions in the United States. You have at least some chance of finding gold if you prospect in one of these counties. States not listed contain no known deposits.

Alabama • Chilton, Clay, Cleburne, Coosa, Elmore, Randolph, Talladega, Tallapoosa.

Alaska • (No counties. Gold exists in the following regions.) Afognak, Ambler River, Anchorage, Baird Mtns., Bendeleben, Bering Glacier, Bethel, Bettles, Big Delta, Candle, Chandalar, Charley River, Circle, Cordova, Dillingham, Eagle, Fairbanks, Goodnews, Gulkana, Healy, Holy Cross, Hughes, Juneau, Kodiak, Kotzebue, Lake Clark, Livingood, Medfra, Melozitna, Middleton Is., Mt. Fairweather, Mt. Hayes, Mt. McKinley, Nabesna, Naknek, Nome, Norton Bay, Nulato, Ophir, Port Moller, Ruby, Russian Mission, Seldovia, Seward, Shungnak, Sitka, Skagway, Sleetmute, Solomon, Sumdum, Survey Pass, Talkeetna, Talkeetna Mts., Tanana, Taylor Mts., Teller, Tyonek, Valdez, Wiseman, Yakutat.

Arizona • Cochise, Gila, Graham, Greenlee, Maricopa, Mohave, Pima, Pinal, Santa Cruz, Yavapai, Yuma.

Arkansas • Garland.

California • Amador, Butte, Calaveras, Del Norte, El Dorado, Fresno, Humboldt, Imperial, Inyo, Kern, Lassen, Los Angeles, Madera, Mariposa, Merced, Mono, Napa, Nevada, Placer, Plumas, Riverside, Sacramento, San Bernardino, San Diego, San Joaquin, Shasta, Sierra, Siskiyou, Stanislaus, Trinity, Tulare, Toulumne, Yuma.

Colorado • Adams, Arapahoe, Baca, Boulder, Chaffee, Clear Creek, Conejos, Costilla, Custer, Dolores, Douglas, Eagle, Fremont, Gilpin, Gunnison, Hinsdale, Huerfano, Jefferson, Lake, La Plata, Mineral, Moffat, Montezuma, Ouray, Park, Pitkin, Rio Grande, Routt, Saguache, San Juan, San Miguel, Summit, Teller.

Georgia • Bartow, Carroll, Cherokee, Cobb, Dawson, Douglas, Fannin, Forsyth, Gilmer, Gwinnett, Habersham, Hall, Haralson, Lumpkin, Madison, McDuffie, Murray, Paulding, Rabun, Towns, Union, White.

Idaho • Ada, Bingham, Blaine, Boise, Bonneville, Camas, Cassia, Clearwater, Custer, Elmore, Idaho, Jerome, Latah, Lemhi, Minidoka, Owyhee, Shoshone, Valley.

Illinois • Cumberland, Jackson, Lake, Peoria, Stephenson, Will, Winnebago.

Indiana • Brown, Cass, Clark, Dearborn, Franklin, Gibson, Greene, Jackson, Jefferson, Jennings, Monroe, Montgomery, Morgan, Ohio, Pike, Putnam, Sullivan, Vanderburgh, Warren.

Iowa • Hardin, Lyon, Marion, Woodbury.

Kansas • Atchison, Brown, Doniphan, Ellis, Jackson, Jefferson, Leavenworth, Marshall, Nemaha, Pottawatomie, Shawnee, Trego, Wyandotte.

Maine • Cumberland, Franklin, Hancock, Knox, Oxford, Penobscot, Somerset, Waldo, Washington.

Maryland • Baltimore, Carroll, Frederick, Howard, Montgomery.

Michigan • Charlevoix, Emmet, Kalkaska, Manistee, Marquette, Montcalm, Newaygo, Ottawa, St. Joseph, Wexford.

Minnesota • Cook, Fillmore, Koochiching, Olmsted, Scott, St. Louis.

Missouri • Adair, Linn, Livingston, Macon, Putnam.

Montana • Beaverhead, Broadwater, Carbon, Cascade, Chouteau, Deer Lodge, Fergus, Flathead, Gallatin, Granite, Jefferson, Judith Basin, Lewis and Clark, Lincoln, Madison, Meagher, Mineral, Missoula, Park, Phillips, Powell, Ravalli, Sanders, Silver Bow, Sweet Grass, Toole.

Nebraska • Franklin, Harlan, Seward, Stanton.

Nevada • Churchill, Clark, Douglas, Elko, Esmeralda, Eureka, Humboldt, Lander, Lincoln, Lyon, Mineral, Nye, Ormsby, Pershing, Storey, Washoe, White Pine.

New Hampshire • Coos, Grafton.

New Mexico • Bernalillo, Catron, Chaves, Colfax, Dona Ana, Grant, Harding, Hidalgo, Lincoln, Mora, Otero, Rio Arriba, Sandoval, San Miguel, Santa Fe, Sierra, Socorro, Taos, Union, Valencia.

New York • Westchester.

North Carolina • Alamance, Ashe, Buncombe, Burke, Cabarrus, Caldwell, Catawba, Cherokee, Clay, Davidson, Davie, Franklin, Gaston, Granville, Guilford, Halifax, Henderson, Jackson, Macon, McDowell, Mecklenburg, Moore, Nash, Orange, Person, Polk, Randolph, Rowan, Rutherford, Stanly, Swain, Transylvania, Union, Vance, Warren, Watauga, Wilkes, Yadkin.

North Dakota • Bottineau, McHenry, Pierce, Ransom, Ward.

Ohio • Clermont, Richland.

Oregon • Baker, Clackamas, Coos, Crook, Curry, Douglas, Grant, Jackson, Jefferson, Josephine, Lake, Lane, Linn, Malheur, Marion, Union, Wallowa, Wheeler.

Pennsylvania • Lebanon.

Rhode Island • Kent, Providence.

South Carolina • Abbeville, Anderson, Cherokee, Chesterfield, Edgefield, Greenville, Greenwood, Kershaw, Lancaster, Laurens, McCormick, Newberry, Oconee, Pickens, Saluda, Spartanburg, Union, York.

South Dakota • Custer, Lawrence, Pennington.

Tennessee • Blount, Hamilton, Monroe, Polk, Roane, Sevier.

Texas • El Paso, Howard, Llano, Uvalde, Williamson.

Utah • Beaver, Emery, Garfield, Grand, Iron, Juab, Kane, Millard, Morgan, Piute, Rich, Salt Lake, San Juan, Sevier, Summit, Tooele, Uintah, Utah, Wasatch, Washington, Wayne, Weber.

Vermont • Lamoille, Orleans, Washington, Windham, Windsor.

Virginia • Amherst, Buckingham, Carroll, Culpeper, Cumberland, Fairfax, Fauquier, Floyd, Fluvanna, Goochland, Halifax, Louisa, Montgomery, Orange, Patrick, Prince William, Spotsylvania, Stafford.

Washington • Asotin, Benton, Chelan, Clallam, Clark, Cowlitz, Douglas, Ferry, Garfield, Grant, Grays Harbor, Jefferson, King, Kittitas, Lincoln, Okanogan, Pacific, Pend Oreille, Pierce, Skagit, Skamania, Snohomish, Stevens, Whatcom, Whitman, Yakima.

West Virginia • Tucker.

Wyoming • Albany, Big Horn, Carbon, Converse, Crook, Fremont, Goshen, Hot Springs, Johnson, Laramie, Lincoln, Natrona, Park, Platte, Sheridan, Sweetwater, Teton, Weston.

Gem and Mineral Regions in the U.S.

ALABAMA

Clay Co. • Azurite, garnet, malachite, marcasite.
Cleburne Co. • Beryl, garnet, kyanite, malachite, marcasite.
Coosa Co. • Beryl, tourmaline.
Limestone Co. • Geodes.
Tuscaloosa Co. • Agate, chert, jasper, onyx.

ALASKA (by region)

Northwestern Alaska • Jade.
Southeastern Alaska • Agate, garnet, jade.

ARIZONA

Apache Co. • Agate, obsidian, peridot, petrified wood.
Cochise Co. • Agate, amethyst, azurite, malachite, shattuckite.
Coconino Co. • Agate, obsidian, petrified wood.
Gila Co. • Agate, amethyst, azurite, bloodstone, carnelian, chalcedony, chrysocolla, epidote, garnet, hypersthene, obsidian, opal, peridot, petrified wood, serpentine, turquoise.
Graham Co. • Agate, azurite, banded agate, chalcedony, malachite, obsidian, onyx, opal, petrified wood, turquoise.
Greenlee Co. • Agate, amethyst, azurite, chalcedony, chrysocolla, garnet, jasper, malachite, obsidian, onyx, opal, petrified wood, rose quartz, shattuckite, turquoise, variscite.
Maricopa Co. • Agate, amethyst, chalcedony, fire agate, jasper, marble, onyx, opal, petrified wood, plume agate.
Mohave Co. • Agate, chalcedony, chalk turquoise, jasper, petrified wood.

Navajo Co. • Garnet, petrified wood.
Pima Co. • Azurite, chalcedony, malachite, obsidian, shattuckite.
Pinal Co. • Chalcedony, chrysocolla, obsidian, peridot.
Yavapai Co. • Agate, carnelian, chalcedony, chrysocolla, chrysoprase, jade, jasper, moonstone, obsidian, onyx, petrified wood, quartz crystal.
Yuma Co. • Agate, chalcedony, garnet, jasper, obsidian, petrified wood, quartz crystal, rhyolite, turquoise.

ARKANSAS

Garland Co. • Novaculite, quartz crystal.
Hot Springs Co. • Quartz crystal, smoky quartz.
Montgomery Co. • Quartz crystal.
Pike Co. • Diamond.
Scott Co. • Diamond.

CALIFORNIA

Alameda Co. • Agate.
Amador Co. • Diamond, rhodonite.
Calaveras Co. • Agate, chalcedony, chrysoprase, petrified wood, quartz crystal.
Colusa Co. • Travertine.
Contra Costa Co. • Agate, chalcedony.
Del Norte Co. • Agate, jasper, petrified wood.
El Dorado Co. • Agate, garnet, idocrase, jasper, nephrite, petrified wood, vesuvianite.
Fresno Co. • Chert, jasper, petrified wood, smoky quartz.
Humboldt Co. • Agate, jade, jasper, petrified wood.
Imperial Co. • Agate, andalusite, chalcedony, dumortierite, garnet, jasper, kyanite, opal, petrified palm root, petrified wood.
Inyo Co. • Agate, amethyst, bloodstone, epidote, garnet, geode, jasper, obsidian, onyx, opal, quartz crystal, turquoise.
Kern Co. • Actinolite, agate, colemanite crystal, jade, jasper, morrisonite, petrified wood, quartz crystal, rhodonite, rose quartz.
Lake Co. • Jasper, onyx, quartz crystal.
Los Angeles Co. • Agate, chalcedony, jasper, rhodonite.
Madera Co. • Chiastolites, garnet.
Marin Co. • Agate, jade, petrified whalebone.
Mariposa Co. • Quartz crystal.
Mendocino Co. • Agate, jade, jasper, opal, quartz.
Modoc Co. • Agate, jasper, obsidian.
Mono Co. • Geode, obsidian.
Monterey Co. • Agate, jadeite, jasper, nephrite, rhodonite, serpentine.

Napa Co. • Cinnabar, jasper, onyx, quartz crystal.

Nevada Co. • Opal, petrified wood.

Placer Co. • Garnet, jade.

Riverside Co. • Actinolite, agate, amazonite, aquamarine, beryl, calcite, chalcedony, corundum, diopside, epidote, fire agate, garnet, geode, idocrase, jasper, petrified wood, quartz crystal, rhodonite, rose quartz, rubellite, spinel, topaz, tourmaline.

Sacramento Co. • Agate, jade, opal.

San Benito Co. • Benitoite, diopside, garnet, jade, jadeite, natrolite, serpentine.

San Bernardino Co. • Actinolite, agate, amethyst, aragonite, bloodstone, chalcedony, crawfordite, epidote, geode, jasper, moss agate, onyx, opalite, petrified wood, rhodonite, travertine, verde antique.

San Diego Co. • Beryl, garnet, kunzite, quartz crystal, rhodonite, topaz, tourmaline.

San Francisco Co. • Jasper, nephrite.

San Luis Obispo Co. • Agate, jade, jasper, marcasite, onyx, quartz, sagenite.

San Mateo Co. • Petrified whalebone.

Santa Barbara Co. • Agate.

Santa Clara Co. • Agate, jasper.

Santa Cruz Co. • Agate, petrified whalebone.

Siskiyou Co. • Agate, californite, idocrase, jade, quartz crystal, rhodonite.

Solano Co. • Onyx, travertine.

Sonoma Co. • Actinolite, jasper.

Trinity Co. • Agate, jade, jasper, rhodonite.

Tulare Co. • Agate, chrysoprase, jade, quartz crystal, smoky quartz, thulite, topaz.

Tuolumne Co. • Agate, gold quartz, jasper, marble, petrified wood, pyrite.

Ventura Co. • Agate, azurite.

COLORADO

Baca Co. • Azurite.

Chaffee Co. • Agate, aquamarine, beryl, jasper, onyx, petrified wood, phenacite.

Clear Creek Co. • Amazonite, garnet.

Custer Co. • Petrified wood.

Delta Co. • Jasper.

Douglas Co. • Amazonite, petrified wood, smoky quartz, topaz.

Elbert Co. • Agate, jasper, petrified wood.

El Paso Co. • Agate, amazonite, garnet, phenacite, topaz, tourmaline, zircon.

Fremont Co. • Agate, coprolite, onyx, petrified wood, rose quartz, satin spar.

Garfield Co. • Oil shale, petrified wood.

Jefferson Co. • Amazonite, barite crystal, beryl, topaz, tourmaline.

Kiowa Co. • Agate, jasper.

Las Animas Co. • Rose agate.

Mesa Co. • Agate, amethyst, flint, petrified wood.

Mineral Co. • Agate, amethyst, jasper, petrified wood.

Moffat Co. • Agate, chalcedony, jasper, opal.

Montrose Co. • Amazonite, coprolite, covellite, jasper, phenacite, smoky quartz, topaz.

Ouray Co. • Quartz crystal, rhodonite.

Park Co. • Agate, beryl, fluorite, jade, moss opal, petrified wood, topaz.

Rio Grande Co. • Agate, petrified wood.

Saguache Co. • Agate, amethyst, jade, turquoise.

San Juan Co. • Feldspar, mica, quartz crystal, rhodonite.

San Miguel Co. • Jasper, petrified bone.

Sedgwick Co. • Agate, petrified wood.

Teller Co. • Agate, amazonite, amethyst, jade, petrified wood, phenacite, quartz, crystalsiderite, smoky quartz, topaz, zircon.

Weld Co. • Agate, barite, petrified wood.

CONNECTICUT

Fairfield Co. • Albite, beryl, epidote, fluorite, mica, quartz crystal, scheelite, siderite, spodumene, topaz, tremolite, wolframite.

Hartford Co. • Amethyst, azurite, datolite, malachite, prehnite, quartz, smoky quartz.

Litchfield Co. • Calcite, fluorite, galena, garnet, graphite, kyanite, magnetite, opal, prehnite, pyrite, quartz, siderite, sphalerite, tourmaline, tremolite.

Middlesex Co. • Actinolite, amblygonite, apatite, austinite, bertrandite, beryl, columbite, chrysoberyl, feldspar, fluorite, garnet, hiddenite, kunzite, lepidolite, mica, pollucite, rose quartz, spodumene, topaz, tourmaline.

New Haven Co. • Garnet, kyanite, pyrite, quartz crystal, rose quartz.

FLORIDA

Hillsborough Co. • Agatized coral.

Pinellas Co. • Agatized shark bone.

Polk Co. • Chalcedony.

GEORGIA

Barrow Co. • Beryl, tourmaline.

Brooks Co. • Agate.

Cobb Co. • Agate, jasper, topaz.

Elbert Co. • Aquamarine, garnet, smoky quartz.
Forsyth Co. • Moonstone, ruby.
Habersham Co. • Kyanite, ruby.
Hall Co. • Diamond.
Jones Co. • Agate, jasper.
Lincoln Co. • Lazulite, rutile.
Lumpkin Co. • Garnet.
Meriwether Co. • Beryl, jasper, opal.
Morgan Co. • Amethyst, beryl.
Paulding Co. • Garnet.
Rabun Co. • Amethyst, garnet, quartz, rose quartz, ruby.
Towns Co. • Ruby, sapphire.
Troup Co. • Amethyst, aquamarine, rose quartz.
Washington Co. • Opal.
Wilkes Co. • Kyanite, lazulite, rutile.

IDAHO

Benewah Co. • Garnet.
Blaine Co. • Agate, petrified wood.
Butte Co. • Agate, petrified wood.
Canyon Co. • Agate, petrified wood, white plum agate.
Lemhi Co. • Petrified wood.
Nez Perce Co. • Agate, garnet, jasper, opal, petrified wood, sapphire.
Owyhee Co. • Agate, jasper, opal, petrified wood.

ILLINOIS

Hancock Co. • Geode.
Jefferson Co. • Diamond.
McDonough Co. • Diamond.

INDIANA

Allen Co. • Agate, coral, jasper.
Brown Co. • Diamond, topaz.
Miami Co. • Diamond.
Morgan Co. • Diamond, garnet, ruby, sapphire, topaz.

IOWA

Clayton Co. • Agate, jasper, onyx.
Des Moines Co. • Geode.
Dubuque Co. • Agate, diamond, jasper.

Henry Co. • Agate, jasper, petrified wood.
Lee Co. • Amethyst, chalcedony, geode, jasper.
Muscatine Co. • Agate, corals, jasper, petrified wood.
Page Co. • Agate.

KANSAS

Cherokee Co. • Marcasite, sphalerite.
Franklin Co. • Petrified wood.
Wallace Co. • Opal.
Woodson Co. • Amethyst.
Wyandotte Co. • Agate.

KENTUCKY

Fayette Co. • Onyx.
Graves Co. • Agate, chalcedony, jasper.
Hart Co. • Onyx, petrified wood.
Lyon Co. • Agate, chalcedony, jasper.
Rockcastle Co. • Jasper.

LOUISIANA

Ouachita Pa. • Agate, jasper, petrified wood.
Vernon Pa. • Petrified wood.

MAINE

Androscoggin Co. • Amblygonite, apatite, beryl, garnet, lepidolite, spodumene, pollucite, tourmaline.
Cumberland Co. • Actinolite, beryl, columbite, garnet.
Franklin Co. • Columbite, spodumene.
Hancock Co. • Beryl.
Kennebec Co. • Cancrinite, nephelite, sodalite, zircon.
Knox Co. • Spodumene.
Oxford Co. • Agate, amblygonite, amethyst, apatite, aquamarine, beryl, chrysoberyl, esophorite, herderite, lepidolite, pollucite, quartz crystal, rose quartz, smoky quartz, spodumene, tourmaline.
Sagadahoc Co. • Beryl, lepidolite, tourmaline.
Washington Co. • Agate, jasper.

MARYLAND

Allegany Co. • Barite crystal, quartz crystal, siderite.

Baltimore Co. • Antigorite, calcite crystal, garnet, jasper, quartz, serpentine, smoky quartz, tourmaline.

Calvert Co. • Jasper.

Carrol Co. • Azurite, garnet, malachite.

Cecil Co. • Onyx, serpentine, williamsite.

Frederick Co. • Onyx, malachite.

Garrett Co. • Picrolite, serpentine, williamsite.

Hartford Co. • Jasper, serpentine.

Montgomery Co. • Beryl, opal, serpentine.

Washington Co. • Cuprite, onyx.

MASSACHUSETTS

Franklin Co. • Agate, amethyst, beryl, garnet.

Hampden Co. • Amethyst, beryl, datolite, marcasite, prehnite.

Hampshire Co. • Amethyst, beryl, datolite, galena, prehnite, pollucite, spodumene.

Middlesex Co. • Scheelite.

Worcester Co. • Beryl, chiastolite, spodumene.

MICHIGAN

Dickinson Co. • Actinolite, beryl.

Emmet Co. • Agate, petoskey stone.

Houghton Co. • Agate, garnet.

Keweenaw Co. • Agate, chlorastrolite, domeykite, thomsonite.

Marquette Co. • Jasper, jaspilite, tourmaline.

Ontonagon Co. • Agate, datolite, malachite, tenorite.

MINNESOTA

Carlton Co. • Agate, garnet, jasper.

Cook Co. • Agate, heulandite.

Lake Co. • Agate, thomsonite.

Morrison Co. • Garnet, staurolite.

Pipestone Co. • Catlinite.

St. Louis Co. • Agate, jasper.

Winona Co. • Agate.

MISSISSIPPI

Harrison Co. • Jasper.

Wayne Co. • Petrified wood.

Tallahatchie Co. • Amber.

MISSOURI

Bollinger Co. • Agate, jasper.
Cape Girardeau Co. • Agate, jasper.
Crawford Co. • Amethyst.
Franklin Co. • Amethyst.
Jackson Co. • Amethyst.
Lewis Co. • Agate.
Madison Co. • Agate, jasper.
St. Louis Co. • Agate, barite, galena, geode.
Wayne Co. • Agate, jasper.

MONTANA

Beaverhead Co. • Corundum, quartz.
Cascade Co. • Beryl.
Custer Co. • Agate, sapphire.
Dawson Co. • Agate.
Deer Lodge Co. • Azurite, sapphire.
Fergus Co. • Sapphire.
Gallatin Co. • Agate, corundum, petrified wood, rose quartz.
Granite Co. • Sapphire.
Jefferson Co. • Amethyst, barite, tourmaline.
Judith Basin Co. • Sapphire.
Lewis and Clark Co. • Garnet, ruby, sapphire, spinel, topaz.
Madison Co. • Garnet, jasper, onyx, quartz crystal, serpentine, tourmaline.
Meagher Co. • Agate.
Missoula Co. • Quartz.
Park Co. • Amethyst, arsenopyrite, garnet, iceland spar, petrified wood, travertine.
Powell Co. • Agate, amazonite, sapphire.
Prairie Co. • Agate, petrified wood.
Ravalli Co. • Beryl, fluorite.
Rosebud Co. • Agate.
Silver Bow Co. • Amethyst, epidote, fluorite, garnet, sapphire.
Yellowstone Co. • Agate, jasper.

NEBRASKA

Cass Co. • Horn coral, petrified wood.
Dawes Co. • Chalcedony.
Gage Co. • Geode.
Jefferson Co. • Agate, jasper, petrified wood.
Lincoln Co. • Agate, jasper.

Morrill Co. • Agate, opal.
Nance Co. • Agate, jasper, petrified wood.
Saunders Co. • Agate, petrified wood.
Sioux Co. • Agate, chalcedony, petrified wood.

NEVADA

Clark Co. • Amethyst, jasper, onyx.
Douglas Co. • Topaz.
Elko Co. • Agate, azurite, chalcedony, petrified wood.
Esmeralda Co. • Agate, chalcedony, petrified wood, turquoise.
Eureka Co. • Azurite, sulfur crystal.
Humboldt Co. • Agate, fire opal, jasper, petrified wood, rhodonite.
Lander Co. • Chert, jasper, turquoise.
Lincoln Co. • Agate, chalcedony, chrysocolla, jasper, malachite, petrified wood, quartz.
Lyon Co. • Agate, jasper, opal.
Nye Co. • Onyx, petrified wood.
Pershing Co. • Opal, petrified wood.
Washoe Co. • Agate, garnet, idocrase, jasper, obsidian, petrified wood, piedmontite.
White Pine Co. • Garnet.

NEW HAMPSHIRE

Carroll Co. • Amethyst, danalite, helvite, phenacite, quartz crystal, smoky quartz, topaz.
Cheshire Co. • Amethyst, apatite, aquamarine, beryl, fluorite, garnet, quartz crystal, rose quartz, tourmaline, spodumene.
Coos Co. • Amethyst, quartz crystal, topaz.
Grafton Co. • Apatite, beryl, columbite.
Merrimack Co. • Beryl, garnet.
Rockingham Co. • Spodumene.
Sullivan Co. • Aquamarine, beryl, rose quartz.

NEW JERSEY

Bergen Co. • Amethyst, natrolite, opal.
Cape May Co. • Jasper, quartz crystal.
Mercer Co. • Albite, calcite, chabazite, datolite, natrolite, stilbite, tourmaline.
Middlesex Co. • Marcasite, petrified wood, pyrite.
Morris Co. • Carnelian, serpentine.

Passaic Co. • Agate, amethyst, carnelian, chabazite, datolite, heulandite, pectolite, prehnite.

Sussex Co. • Aragonite, corundum, garnet, pyrrhotite, rhodonite, spinel, tourmaline, willemite.

Union Co. • Calcite, chalcedony, prehnite, sphalerite, stilbite.

Warren Co. • Calcite, chalcedony, garnet, molybdenite, prehnite, serpentine, sphalerite.

NEW MEXICO

Bernalillo Co. • Agate, chalcedony, jasper, opal.

Catron Co. • Agate, amethyst, jasper, topaz.

Chaves Co. • Agate.

Eddy Co. • Agate, diamond, quartz crystal, onyx.

Grant Co. • Agate, onyx.

Hidalgo Co. • Agate, chalcedony, serpentine.

Luna Co. • Agate, carnelian, onyx, travertine.

Otero Co. • Garnet, onyx, turquoise.

Rio Arriba Co. • Agate, beryl, dumortierite, feldspar, petrified wood.

San Juan Co. • Agate, petrified wood, ricolite.

Sante Fe Co. • Beryl, jasper, turquoise.

Sierra Co. • Agate, carnelian, fluorite, petrified wood.

Socorro Co. • Agate, chalcedony.

Valencia Co. • Agate, jasper, obsidian, petrified wood.

NEW YORK

Dutchess Co. • Quartz crystal.

Erie Co. • Satin spar.

Essex Co. • Garnet, rose quartz, wollastonite.

Herkimer Co. • Quartz crystal.

Jefferson Co. • Hematite, serpentine.

Madison Co. • Celestite.

Niagara Co. • Calcite.

Orange Co. • Jasper, quartz crystal, sunstone, tourmaline.

Putnam Co. • Magnetite, opal, serpentine.

Rockland Co. • Pink garnet, spene.

St. Lawrence Co. • Calcite, hexagonite, pyrite, serpentine, sphalerite, talc, tremolite.

Saratoga Co. • Beryl.

Ulster Co. • Quartz crystal.

Warren Co. • Garnet.

Westchester Co. • Beryl, garnet, quartz, rose quartz.

NORTH CAROLINA

Alexander Co. • Aquamarine, hiddenite, quartz, rutile, sapphire.
Ashe Co. • Aquamarine, beryl, garnet, moonstone, rutile.
Avery Co. • Epidote, garnet, unakite.
Buncombe Co. • Kyanite, moonstone.
Burke Co. • Amethyst, diamond, garnet.
Clay Co. • Garnet, opal, ruby, sapphire.
Granville Co. • Agate, jasper.
Haywood Co. • Emerald, sapphire, tourmaline.
Iredell Co. • Actinolite, beryl, rose quartz, sapphire, tourmaline.
Macon Co. • Garnet, rhodonite, ruby, sapphire.
Mitchell Co. • Actinolite, beryl, biotite, emerald, epidote, feldspar, garnet, rhodonite, unakite.
Orange Co. • Agate, serpentine.
Rutherford Co. • Diamond, emerald, garnet.
Warren Co. • Amethyst.
Wilkes Co. • Agate, beryl, jasper.
Yancey Co. • Emerald, feldspar.

NORTH DAKOTA

Adams Co. • Petrified wood.
Billings Co. • Agate, petrified wood.
Kidder Co. • Agate, jasper.
McLean Co. • Petrified wood.
Morton Co. • Petrified wood.
Stark Co. • Chalcedony, jasper, quartz crystal.
Ward Co. • Quartz, gemstones.

OHIO

Coshocton Co. • Flint, selenite crystal.
Franklin Co. • Petrified wood.
Licking Co. • Amethyst, chalcedony, flint, jasper.
Montgomery Co. • Agate, gem granite.
Muskingum Co. • Jasper.
Ottawa Co. • Celestite, fluorite.
Wood Co. • Barite, calcite.

OKLAHOMA

Canadian Co. • Agate, jasper, petrified wood.

Comanche Co. • Zircon.
Dewey Co. • Agate, chalcedony, jadeite, jasper, petrified wood.
Greer Co. • Alabaster.
Jackson Co. • Quartz.
Major Co. • Agate, jasper, petrified wood.
Ottawa Co. • Sphalerite.
Pushmataha Co. • Green quartz.

OREGON

Baker Co. • Agate, jasper, petrified wood.
Benton Co. • Agate, jasper.
Crook Co. • Agate, carnelian, geode, moss agate.
Curry Co. • Jade, serpentine.
Deschutes Co. • Agate, carnelian, geode, jasper, moss agate.
Grant Co. • Agate, petrified wood.
Harney Co. • Agate, obsidian, opal.
Jackson Co. • Agate, bloodstone, jasper, petrified wood, rhodonite.
Jefferson Co. • Agate, amethyst, geode, opal.
Lake Co. • Geode, obsidian, opal.
Lane Co. • Agate, petrified wood.
Lincoln Co. • Agate, agatized coral, bloodstone, jasper, petrified wood, sagenite, sardonyx.
Linn Co. • Agate.
Malheur Co. • Agate, geode, jasper, petrified wood.
Morrow Co. • Agate, geode, opal.
Polk Co. • Agate, jasper, petrified wood.
Union Co. • Agate, jasper.
Wallowa Co. • Agate.
Wasco Co. • Agate, amethyst, bloodstone, chalcedony, geode, jade, jasper, opal, quartz, sagenite.
Wheeler Co. • Agate, jasper.

PENNSYLVANIA

Adams Co. • Azurite, cuprite, garnet.
Bedford Co. • Calcite, quartz, spar.
Berks Co. • Calcite, epidote, feldspar, garnet, hematite, kyanite, magnetite, quartz crystal, unakite, zeolite.
Bucks Co. • Galena, sphalerite.
Carbon Co. • Autunite, carnotite.
Chester Co. • Anglesite, azurite, feldspar, garnet, geothite, hornblende, kyanite, magnetite, malachite, martite, phlogopite, pyrite, pyromorphite, pyrrhotite, quartz, quartz crystal, sphalerite, stibnite, sulfur, wulfenite.

Cumberland Co. • Phosphorite.

Delaware Co. • Actinolite, apatite crystal, deweylite, feldspar, garnet.

Lancaster Co. • Actinolite, aragonite, calcite, chalcedony, chromite, dolomite, hematite, malachite, marcasite, quartz crystal, pyrite, serpentine.

Lebanon Co. • Anthophyllite, biotite, garnet, hematite, magnetite, serpentine.

Lehigh Co. • Calamine, corundum, geothite, greenockite, jasper, quartz crystal, sphalerite.

Monroe Co. • Quartz crystal.

Montgomery Co. • Calcite, copper and lead minerals, galena, natrolite, quartz crystal, sphalerite, stibnite, zeolite.

Northampton Co. • Calcite, graphite, limonite, serpentine, talc, uraninite.

Perry Co. • Travertine.

Schuylkill Co. • Chlorite, galena, pyrite, quartz crystal, siderite, sphalerite.

Somerset Co. • Quartz.

Westmoreland Co. • Limonite, pyrite.

York Co. • Agate, azurite, limonite, pyrite.

RHODE ISLAND

Bristol Co. • Jasper.

Providence Co. • Amethyst, beryl, fluorite, quartz crystal.

SOUTH CAROLINA

Abbeville Co. • Beryl, jasper.

Aikens Co. • Amethyst, chalcedony, zircon.

Anderson Co. • Aquamarine, beryl, garnet, tourmaline.

Cherokee Co. • Amethyst, emerald, garnet, tourmaline.

Chesterfield Co. • Emerald, topaz.

Greenville Co. • Beryl, garnet, tourmaline.

Spartanburg Co. • Diamond, garnet, tourmaline, zircon.

York Co. • Tourmaline.

SOUTH DAKOTA

Custer Co. • Agate, amblygonite, beryl, chalcedony, feldspar, garnet, jade, jasper, lepidolite, mica, petrified wood, quartz crystal, rose crystal, sillimanite, tourmaline.

Fall River Co. • Agate, chalcedony, jasper, petrified wood, vanadite.

Harding Co. • Agate, petrified wood.

Lawrence Co. • Garnet, rose quartz.

Meade Co. • Aquamarine, beryl, gastrolith, geode, petrified wood, selenite.

Pennington Co. • Agate, apatite, beryl, chalcedony, feldspar, galena, garnet, jasper, lepidolite, petrified wood, rose quartz, staurolite, tourmaline.

Shannon Co. • Agate, jasper, petrified wood.

TENNESSEE

Bedford Co. • Agate, opal.

Carter Co. • Unakite.

Coffee Co. • Agate.

Marion Co. • Jasper, onyx.

TEXAS

Brewster Co. • Agate, amethyst, carnelian, chalcedony, citrine, fire opal, jasper, labradorite, moonstone, novaculite, petrified wood, quartz.

Burnet Co. • Garnet, topaz.

Culberson Co. • Agate.

De Witt Co. • Agate, jasper, petrified wood.

Duval Co. • Agate, jasper, petrified wood.

El Paso Co. • Agate.

Fayette Co. • Petrified wood.

Gillespie Co. • Amethyst, garnet, petrified wood, topaz.

Gonzales Co. • Petrified wood.

Hidalgo Co. • Agate.

Hudspeth Co. • Agate, amethyst, jasper.

Jeff Davis Co. • Adularia, agate, amethyst, carnelian, chalcedony, citrine, jasper, moonstone, opal, petrified wood, quartz crystal.

Lee Co. • Petrified wood.

Live Oak Co. • Agate, petrified wood.

Llano Co. • Amethyst, garnet, quartz crystal, topaz, tourmaline.

McMullen Co. • Petrified wood.

Mason Co. • Amazonite, cassiterite, fluorite, quartz, topaz.

Pecos Co. • Agate.

Potter Co. • Petrified wood.

Presidio Co. • Agate, amethyst, carnelian, chalcedony, citrine, jasper, moonstone, opal, petrified wood, quartz crystal.

Reeves Co. • Agate, amethyst, carnelian, chalcedony, citrine, jasper, moonstone, opal, petrified wood, quartz crystal.

Taylor Co. • Smoky quartz, topaz.

Terrell Co. • Agate.

Travis Co. • Topaz.

Trinity Co. • Petrified wood.

Walker Co. • Petrified wood.

Webb Co. • Agate, jasper.

Zapata Co. • Agate, jasper.

UTAH

Beaver Co. • Agate, garnet, obsidian, quartz crystal.
garnet, obsidian, quartz crystal.
Box Elder Co. • Obsidian, variscite.
Carbon Co. • Agate.
Emery Co. • Agate, azurite, chalcedony, obsidian, petrified wood.
Garfield Co. • Agate, barite, jasper, onyx, petrified wood.
Grand Co. • Agate, jasper, petrified wood.
Iron Co. • Agate, geode, jasper.
Juab Co. • Agate, geode, jasper, topaz.
Kane Co. • Agate, petrified wood.
Millard Co. • Jasper, obsidian.
Salt Lake Co. • Agate, onyx.
Sevier Co. • Agate, azurite.
Tooele Co. • Agate, geode, obsidian.
Utah Co. • Onyx, variscite.
Washington Co. • Agate, alabaster, azurite, garnet, jasper.
Wayne Co. • Agate, barite, jasper, petrified wood.
Weber Co. • Azurite, garnet.

VERMONT

Windsor Co. • Actinolite, magnetite, pyrite, talc.

VIRGINIA

Albemarle Co. • Amethyst, jasper.
Amelia Co. • Albite, amazonite, cleavelandite, garnet, topaz, zircon.
Bedford Co. • Beryl, garnet, tourmaline.
Madison Co. • Blue quartz, epidote, unakite.
Page Co. • Epidote, jasper, onyx.
Prince Edward Co. • Amazonite, amethyst, kyanite.
Rockbridge Co. • Beryl, unakite.

WASHINGTON

Benton Co. • Petrified wood.
Chelan Co. • Onyx, thulite.
Cowlitz Co. • Carnelian, sardonyx
Douglas Co. • Jadeite, thulite.
Kittitas Co. • Agate, chalcedony, jasper, petrified wood.

Klickitat Co. • Agate, jasper, petrified wood.
Lewis Co. • Carnelian, sardonyx.
Snohomish Co. • Azurite, garnet, petrified wood.
Yakima Co. • Carnelian, sardonyx.

WEST VIRGINIA

Hampshire Co. • Jasper.
Hardy Co. • Aragonite, stilbite.
Mineral Co. • Geode.

WISCONSIN

Ashland Co. • Agate, jasper.
Bayfield Co. • Agate, jasper.
Clark Co. • Agate, jasper.
Dane Co. • Diamond.
Douglas Co. • Agate.
Iron Co. • Agate.
La Crosse Co. • Diamond, jasper.
Ozaukee Co. • Diamond.

WYOMING

Albany Co. • Agate, jasper, petrified wood.
Big Horn Co. • Agate.
Carbon Co. • Agate, jade, jasper, petrified wood.
Fremont Co. • Actinolite, agate, aventurine, garnet, jade, jasper, petrified wood, rhodonite, ruby, sapphire, serpentine.
Goshen Co. • Beryl, jasper.
Johnson Co. • Petrified wood.
Lincoln Co. • Agate, petrified wood.
Natrona Co. • Agate, amazonite, jade, petrified wood.
Platte Co. • Agate, azurite, garnet.
Sweetwater Co. • Agate, chalcedony, corundum, eden wood, jade, jasper, moss agate, petrified wood.
Uinta Co. • Petrified wood.

Books and Magazines for Treasure Hunters

BOOKS

BANCROFT, CAROLINE. *Lost Gold Mines and Buried Treasures.* Johnson, 1964. $1.25.
COFFMAN, FERRIS L. *Atlas of Treasure Maps.* Nelson, 1957. $10.00

EBERHART, PERRY. *Treasure Tales of the Rockies.* Swallow, 1968. $7.00.

EVANS, A. T. *Treasure Hunter's Yearbook.* Annual. Eureka Press. $4.00.

GARRETT, CHARLES. *Successful Coin Hunting.* Ram Publishing, 1974. $4.95.

HORNER, DAVID L. *Treasure Galleons: Clues to Millions in Sunken Gold and Treasure.* Dodd, Mead, 1971. $10.00

MITCHELL, JOHN D. *Lost Mines & Hidden Treasures of the Old Frontier.* Rio Grande. $7.50.

RIESEBERG, HARRY E. *Complete Guide to Buried Treasure Land & Sea.* Fell, 1969. $5.95.

MAGAZINES

Canadian Treasure (P.O. Box 2071, Vancouver 3, B.C.). One year, 4 issues, $3.50.

Research & Recovery (P.O. Box 70025, Houston, TX 77007). One year, 4 issues, $3.50.

Treasure (Jess Publishing Co., Inc., 7950 Deering Avenue, Canoga Park, CA 91304). One year, 12 issues, $12.

Treasure Hunter (Box 188, Midway City, CA 92655). One year, 4 issues, $3.

Treasure Hunter's Newsletter (Eight State Associates, Box 1438, 1918 Pearl Street, Boulder, CO 80302). One year, 4 issues, $5.

Treasure Hunting Unlimited (422 Broadway, Truth or Consequences, NM 87901). One year, 4 issues, $5.

Treasure News (P.O. Box 907, Bellflower, CA 90706). One year, 12 issues, $3.

Treasure Search (Jess Publishing Co., Inc., 7950 Deering Avenue, Canoga Park CA 91304). One year, 6 issues, $6.

Treasure World (Drawer L, Conroe, TX 77301). One year, 6 issues, $3.50.

True Treasure (Drawer L, Conroe, TX 77301). One year, 6 issues, $3.50.

Additional Sources for Treasure Hunting

GEMS AND MINERALS

Most states offer a large number of informative booklets on gem and mineral prospecting. These frequently give precise descriptions of the sites of known deposits, as well as information about the local laws on prospecting and mining. After you have decided where you are going to search, you will want to contact these agencies. Here are the names and addresses of offices to contact:

Geological Survey of Alabama
    P.O. Drawer O
    University, AL 35486

State of Alaska
    Department of Natural Resources
    Division of Mines and Geology
    Box 5-300
    College, AK 99701

Arizona Bureau of Mines
    University of Arizona
    Tucson, AZ 85721

Arkansas Geological Commission
    Little Rock, AR 72204

California Division of Mines and
Geology
    P.O. Box 2980
    Sacramento, CA 95812

Colorado Bureau of Mines
    215 Columbine Building
    1845 Sherman Street
    Denver, CO 80203

State of Connecticut
    Connecticut State Library
    231 Capitol Avenue
    Hartford, CT 06115

State of Delaware
    Division of Economic
    Development
    45 The Green
    Dover, DE 19901

Georgia Department of Mines
    State Division of Conservation
    19 Hunter Street SW
    Atlanta, GA 30303

Idaho Department of Commerce and
Development
    State of Idaho
    Capitol Building, Room 108
    Boise, ID 83707

State of Indiana
    Department of Natural Resources
    Geological Survey
    611 North Walnut Grove
    Bloomington, IN 47401

Iowa Conservation Commission
    300 Fourth Street
    Des Moines, IA 50319

Kansas Geological Survey
    University of Kansas
    1930 Avenue A
    Campus West
    Lawrence, KS 66044

Kentucky Geological Survey
    307 Mineral Industries Building
    University of Kentucky
    Lexington, KY 40506

State of Maine
    Department of Conservation
    State Office Building
    Augusta, ME 04330

Massachusetts Museum of Science
    236 State Street
    Springfield, MA 01103

State of Michigan Tourist Council
    Department of Natural
    Resources
    Commerce Center Building
    300 South Capitol Avenue
    Lansing, MI 48926

State of Minnesota
    Department of Economic
    Development
    51 East Eighth Street
    St. Paul, MN 48926

Mississippi Geological Economic and
Topographical Survey
    2525 North West Street
    P.O. Box 4915
    Jackson, MS 39216

Missouri Geological Survey and
Water Resources
    Buehler Park
    Rolla, MO 65401

Montana Department of Highways
    Advertising Unit
    Helena, MT 59601

Nevada Department of Economic
Development
    Capitol Building
    Carson City, NV 89701

State of New Hampshire
    Division of Economic
    Development
    Concord, NH 03301

New Jersey Map and Publication
Sales Office
    Bureau of Geology and
    Topography
    Trenton, NJ 08625

New Mexico Bureau of Land
Management
    Albuquerque District Office
    3550 Pan American
    Freeway, NE
    Albuquerque, NM 87107

University of the State of New York
    State Education Department
    New York State Museum and
    Science Service
    Albany, NY 12224

State of North Carolina
    Department of Natural
    Resources
    Box 27687
    Raleigh, NC 27611

North Dakota Highway Department
    Capitol Grounds
    Bismarck, ND 58501

Ohio Department of Natural Resources
    Division of Geological Survey
    Fountain Square
    Columbus, OH 43224

Oklahoma American Association of
Petroleum Geologists
    P.O. Box 979
    Tulsa, OK 74101

State of Oregon
    Department of Geology and
    Mineral Industries
    1069 State Office Building
    Portland, OR 97201

Commonwealth of Pennsylvania
    Department of Environmental
    Resources
    Topographic and Geologic
    Survey
    Harrisburg, PA 17120

Rhode Island Development Council
    Roger Williams Building
    Hayes Street
    Providence, RI 02908

State of South Carolina
    State Development Board
    Division of Geology
    P.O. Box 927
    Columbia, SC 29202

South Dakota Department of Natural
Resource Development
    South Dakota Geological Survey
    Science Center
    University of South Dakota
    Vermillion, SD 57069

Tennessee Department of Conservation
Division of Geology
G-5 State Office Building
Nashville, TN 37219

Texas American Association of
Petroleum Geologists
P.O. Box 979
Tulsa, OK 74101

State of Utah
Utah Geological and Mineral
Survey
103 UGS Building
University of Utah
Salt Lake City, UT 84112

State of Vermont
Department of Libraries
Montpelier, VT 05602

Commonwealth of Virginia
Department of Conservation and
Economic Development
Division of Mineral Resources
Box 3667
Charlottesville, VA 22903

State of Washington
Division of Geology and Earth
Resources
Department of Natural
Resources
Olympia, WA 98504

University of Wisconsin Extension
Geological and Natural History
Survey
1815 University Avenue
Madison, WI 53706

The Geological Survey of Wyoming
Box 3008
University of Wyoming
University Station
Laramie, WY 82071

Index